A volume in the series

*Anthropology of Contemporary Issues*
EDITED BY ROGER SANJEK

A full list of titles in the series appears at the end of the book.

# The Varieties of Ethnic Experience

KINSHIP, CLASS, AND GENDER AMONG
CALIFORNIA ITALIAN-AMERICANS

## Micaela di Leonardo

*Cornell University Press*

Ithaca and London

First published 1984 by Cornell University Press.
First printing, Cornell Paperbacks, 1984.
Second printing 1992.

Printed in the United States of America

**Library of Congress Cataloging in Publication Data**

di Leonardo, Micaela, 1949–
    The varieties of ethnic experience.

    (Anthropology of contemporary issues)
    Includes index.
    1. Italian American families—California—San Francisco Bay
Area.   2. Italian Americans—California—San Francisco Bay Area—Ethnic
identity.   3. Kinship—California—San Francisco Bay Area.   4. San
Francisco Bay Area (Calif.)—Social conditions.   I. Title.   II. Series.
F868.S156D48   1984        305.8′51′079461        83-45929
ISBN 0-8014-1632-9 (alk. paper)
ISBN 0-8014-9270-X (pbk.: alk. paper)

Dedicated with equal indebtedness
to the *paesani* who shared their
time, memories, and friendship
with me, and to John Willoughby

# Contents

# Diagrams and Tables

[9]

# Preface

The issue of racial and ethnic difference in American life has been of concern since the eighteenth century, when Benjamin Franklin worried about undue German influence in the new republic. When we include Native Americans, Blacks, and Mexicans in our vision of the total polity—as their white contemporaries did not—it becomes clear that interethnic contact and conflict have been central to North American history since the era of white arrival.

Influenced perhaps by this central importance, studies of racial and especially of ethnic groups have tended to consider them in isolation from the institutions and populations of the broader society, and consequently to focus inward on "ethnic culture" rather than outward on social and economic environment. This inward focus has often allowed a climate of imprecision to obtain, so that, for example, "ethnic behavior" refers only to ethnic men, "the Black family" really means impoverished Black families, and "the Italian family" encompasses only working-class Italians. This imprecision extends to the actual study of ethnic and racial families, which—in abstraction from the actual web of kinship—tend to be considered only as sites of parent-child interaction.

In this book I approach ethnicity differently. Rather than assuming a homogeneous ethnic culture and thus reporting on the Italian Family, the Italian Mobility Experience, and the Italian Woman, I assume ethnic variety and attempt to understand it. Central to this effort are three methodological innovations.

First, instead of considering only working-class white ethnics, I study members of Italian-American households whose economic

[11]

statuses range widely. Second, in order to bypass implicit judgments about normative ethnic behavior, I explicitly consider the meaning and reality of kinship, economy, and gender for my informants. Third, this study attempts to bridge the gap between the present and the past through seeing individuals in terms of their life histories, and through placing those histories in the contexts of broader regional, national, and global economic-historical change.

These new approaches allow me to consider the interrelations among ethnicity, economy, kinship, and gender—and to assess their changing relationships over time. In doing so, I reconsider the construction of individual and collective ethnic identity, dispute current models of ethnic mobility, offer new perspectives on ethnic family and kinship, and reevaluate ethnic gender.

This last clause needs elaboration. Recent feminist research has done much to bring American women's history and contemporary reality into visibility. But as we begin to see the varying lives and perceptions of white women, often we do not consider minority and ethnic women, or see them only as stereotypes. Commenting on Black women's relative invisibility, the authors of *Black Women's Studies* say: "All the women are white, all the Blacks are men" (Hull et al. 1982). One might well add: "And all the white ethnic women are traditional working-class mothers." I reach beyond this stereotype here to consider the varying experiences and the complex perceptions of a group of Italian-American women, and to set them in the larger context of ethnic gender in the United States.

This study breaks from tradition in another way. American race and ethnicity have heretofore been studied largely as phenomena of the urban Eastern Seaboard and industrial Midwest. In looking at Italian-American life in California, I depart from that model and contribute to a growing scholarship on the social history and contemporary reality of the Western states. Too often the West has been seen as a region of Hollywood myth rather than history, an area in which ethnic and racial life—really most social life—is somehow less authentic, less historically meaningful, than that which obtains farther East.

In fact, our conceptions of race and ethnicity inescapably involve perceptions of regional difference, of the meaning of kinship and family, of economic functioning, and of sex and gender. Disentangling these complex webs of meaning and demonstrating their current functions in American popular culture is one of the tasks of this study.

This book, then, can be read on a number of levels. It is an anthropological case study; it is also a work in history. It is meant to be a theoretical contribution, but it speaks as well to Italian-Americans and others as general readers. While it is concerned only with members of one group in one area, it has implications for our understanding of family, economy, culture, and gender in American life—and of their complex links to the larger global economy.

I thank all those who have helped me with this book, in all its stages. As these stages span seven years of work, and as my analysis draws on a number of disciplines, my debts are many.

My original interest in the relations among class, kinship, ethnicity, and gender was spurred by my work with Carol Stack, who also helped with the first conception of the research. The basis for this interest was laid through my work with Gerald D. Berreman on ethnomethodology and on the theories of power and stratification, and with Nelson H. H. Graburn on kinship and network theory. Graburn as well has been the source of unflagging assistance, excellent teaching, and editorial advice for more than a decade. Naomi Quinn's incisive criticism helped me to clarify my perspective at the beginning stages of the work. Ann R. Markusen's concern with regional analysis was part of the inspiration of Chapter 3, and her comments helped me to improve its exposition. Arlie Russell Hochschild's work on the sociology of emotion had a major influence on my analysis of ethnic identity; she also read and commented on several chapters of the first draft. Susan Gal provided both encouragement and advice throughout the research and writing process. My treatment of theories of ethnicity in particular owes much to our mutual discussions. Patricia Zavella and I shared field sites and experience. I have benefited from her help and encouragement throughout. I am grateful to Alan Derickson for introducing me to the new social history. A major acknowledgment is due to Heidi I. Hartmann. Her work on gender and economics has been a continuing source of inspiration, and she read with care and editorial expertise the entire first draft of the manuscript.

Many scholars helped me during the revision process. Roger Sanjek, my editor, and Louise Lamphere and Peter Schneider offered excellent and detailed readings of the entire manuscript. Louise Tilly, who had inspired its analysis, commented very helpfully on Chapter 2. I also thank Walter Lippincott, director of Cornell University Press, and Peter Agree for their interest in and help with the book. Patricia Cooper, Sherry Gorelick, and Brett Williams offered the unstinting praise that is the best encouragement to further work.

Many others, throughout the process, have supported me in ways too numerous to list. I wish to acknowledge the help of Susan Allen-Mills, J. G. Bell, Brian J. Bertino, Eileen Boris, Susan Cobble, Laura Cover, Marvin Feuerberg, Frank Kucera, Susan Sperling Landes, Nelson Lichtenstein, Paola Sensi-Isolani Nagarvaia, Bonnie Anna Nardi, the late Jo Dorothy Reed, Gail Schroeger, Roberta Spalter-Roth, Beverly Stone, Carolyn Tipton, Norman Waitzman, and Robin Wells. I am also grateful to Joanne L. Delaplaine for her imaginative graphic work.

John Willoughby provided crucial and unwavering support, advice, and encouragement throughout the research and writing process. His own research stimulated me to develop a genuinely political-economic perspective on the interactions of ethnicity, kinship, class, and gender. He actively participated in some of the research, and also, with great unselfishness, and an acute sense of my clerical skills, typed the entire first draft of the manuscript.

I am also grateful to The Mabelle McLeod Lewis Memorial Fund for financial support, which allowed me to finish the field research, and to the Department of Anthropology of the University of California at Berkeley for financial support and the loan of equipment. My tenure at the Collegiate Seminar Program (Strawberry Creek College) of the University of California was important in two ways: the lively intellectual atmosphere provided both by my teaching colleagues and by students stimulated my work; and my teaching salary allowed me to support myself during the bulk of the research and writing period.

Finally, I am grateful to my informants, who must retain their pseudonyms and their privacy. But to them, and to John Willoughby, I dedicate this book.

MICAELA DI LEONARDO

*Washington, D.C.*

# The Varieties of
# Ethnic Experience

Nel mezzo del cammin di nostra vita
Mi ritornai per una selva oscura,
Che la diritta via era smarrita.
Ah quanto a dir qual era è cosa dura
Questa selva selvaggia ed aspra e forte,
Che nel pensier rinnuova la paura!
Tanto è amara, che poco è più morte:
Ma per trattar del ben ch'i' vi trovai,
Dirò dell'altre cose ch'io v'ho scorte.
                              Dante, *Inferno*

# [1]

# "When a Person Speaks Sincere": The Setting and the Study

This book is the result of more than two years of field research among Italian-American families in Northern California. As I am also Italian-American, and grew up in Northern California, the usual ethnographic encounter was in a sense reversed: instead of learning to understand members of a different culture, I learned that I had not understood members of my own. Confronting my own misleading sense of expertise, I became more aware of others' misperceptions; the lack of fit between my field data and the findings of others induced me to question and review theory. The following chapters echo this back-and-forth process of testing and altering theory to fit data, and of reinterpreting data through the use of new theory and method.

I had always known that there were a considerable number of Italian-Americans in California. Even to casual visitors, the San Francisco Bay Area bears an Italian imprint. Italian-owned businesses, especially those dealing with food, are clustered in the cities and scattered across towns and suburbs. California-produced Italian breads, cheeses, sausages, and wines are widely available in supermarkets. Italian names are prominent in local governments and in telephone directories.

The tourist areas of San Francisco, except for Chinatown, are in the regions originally settled most heavily by Italians—North Beach and Fisherman's Wharf. North Beach, even though most residents are now Chinese, still has many Italian restaurants, cafes, delicatessens, bakeries, and travel and insurance agencies—a sufficient scaffolding for the evocation of the romantic East Coast "Little Italies" of ethnic novels and films.[1] Fisherman's Wharf is now a seafood restaurant and shopping area. But its restaurants were established in conjunction with an Italian fishing industry now in decline, and its shopping centers, such as Ghirardelli Square and the Cannery, are converted Italian food-processing factories.

Here, and in part in the winemaking regions north of San Francisco, ethnicity is a commodity, a kind of local color or atmosphere, like cable cars or fog, to be consumed by tourists.[2] A popular guidebook described "Little Italy" as "the most colorful foreign colony in the city, Chinatown not excepted. Its Italian flavor is as real as the garlic that hangs in clouds along the streets where the hamburgers are thick on slices of French bread and the waiters drown their salads in wine vinegar and the pots of spaghetti are filled and refilled a dozen times a day" (Caen 1949:168).

But Italians in fact settled heavily throughout California during the peak years of their immigration to the state. Nearby Oakland and San Jose, neither of them featured as centers of ethnic charm in the guidebooks, had, after San Francisco, the second and fourth largest populations of Italians in the state in 1930. By 1970, Italians remained the most populous of all European groups in each of the three cities, but were the largest proportion of the population in San Jose, not San Francisco.[3] Italians were, and are, dairy and truck farmers and orchardists throughout the state's agricultural regions. In the towns, cities, and suburbs, successive generations have fanned out to fill the changing occupational niches as the regional economy has evolved over this century.

The Italian pattern of emigration to and settlement in California, and in the Western states generally, is distinct from that of the Midwest and Eastern Seaboard. There, Italians arrived in increasingly large numbers in the early decades of the century, emi-

1. See Scherini 1976:29.

2. The effects of tourism on "natives," particularly the commoditization of culture, are increasingly subject to study. See, for example, McCannell 1976; V. Smith 1977; and Graburn 1980.

3. By 1950 the growth of Los Angeles had upset these percentage rankings. See Palmer 1965:125–26. In 1970, first- and second-generation Italian-Americans represented 16 percent of all European foreign stock in Oakland, 20 percent in San Francisco, and 28 percent in San Jose (calculated from the 1970 Census, vol. 1, pt. 6 [California], sec 2).

grating mostly from southern Italy and Sicily. They worked upon arrival largely in urban factories, or at jobs directly related to a highly industrialized urban economy.[4] In contrast, Italians began arriving in California in significant numbers a half century earlier, at the time of the 1849 Gold Rush. By the 1860s and 1870s, when the state had only 1 percent of the total national population, well over a quarter of all Italians in the United States were living in California.[5] They worked in mining and lumber, and participated in developing fishing, agriculture, and food processing in the state—all prior to California's rather late industrial development (Palmer 1976:101). And these immigrants were almost all from the northern Italian provinces. Southern Italians did not represent even half of the total until 1918 (Palmer 1965:365). This is in part a function of their early emigration: Italians from the northern provinces were the first to emigrate in numbers. It is also probably due to chain migration: later northern emigrants were drawn to areas of the United States heavily settled by relatives and friends from their home regions.

Despite these unusual features, California's Italian-Americans have been little studied until very recently. The rich, if patronizing, social work-oriented literature of the 1920s through the 1940s (such as P. Williams 1938 and Covello 1944) has few West Coast counterparts. Paul Radin's single 1935 study is small, and concerned mainly with the question of allegiance to Mussolini and thus of fascist sympathies among San Francisco's Italian-Americans. Community and neighborhood studies involving participant-observation or historical research focus on the Eastern Seaboard or the Midwest.[6] And general works on Italian-Americans give little or no information on those who settled in California.[7]

A vision of Italian-American social life has arisen from the Midwest and Eastern studies, with the help of a few very popular works on Southern Italian peasants: Edward Banfield's *Moral Basis of a*

4. See Lopreato 1970: chap. 3; Nelli 1970; Rolle 1972: chap. 8; and Yans-McLaughlin 1977.

5. Calculated from Palmer 1965:360.

6. Examples are Whyte 1943; Gans 1962; Nelli 1970; Barton 1975; Yans-McLaughlin 1977; Briggs 1978; M. Cohen 1978; E. Ewen 1979; and J. Smith 1981.

7. See Tomasi and Engel 1970; Lopreato 1970; Rolle 1972; Gambino 1974; and Mindel and Habenstein 1976.

*Backward Society* (1958), Carlo Levi's *Christ Stopped at Eboli* (1947), and Ann Cornelisen's *Torregreca* (1969) and *Women of the Shadows* (1976). Southern Italians originally, and thus Italian-Americans, in this composite picture, are impoverished or working-class; immersed in family concerns and uncaring for the general welfare (Banfield's "amoral familism"); and remain in their poor economic position because they (especially mothers) hold down their children and are present-oriented (Gans), unable to cooperate (Banfield), fatalistic and at one with their impoverished region (Levi, Cornelisen), and patriarchal (Gans).[8] Because of these characteristics, Italian-Americans do not assimilate to United States society as well as other immigrant groups and thus remain working-class (Yans-McLaughlin).

Aside from the signal error of inferring Italian family life of the early years of this century from studies done at mid-century,[9] this vision is strikingly like that which informs the concept of the Culture of Poverty applied to Third World poor and impoverished American racial minorities, especially Black Americans. Although Lewis (1966), the originator of the concept, intended it to mean only that the impoverished, once thrust into their economic position, reacted to it by adopting some self-destructive behavioral patterns, the concept has been widely used as if it meant that the "disorganized" or improper family life of the poor is the direct

8. Muraskin (1974) in fact traces Banfield's influence on Gans (1962); Nelli (1970); and Suttles (1968). He goes on to argue that Banfield's own data, rather than supporting the amoral familism hypothesis, are much more elegantly interpreted as realistic adaptations to poverty and oppression.

While their general effect has been similar to that of Banfield, the intents of Levi's and Cornelisen's works were very different. Levi's is a poetic narrative of his incarceration in a Lucanian village by the Mussolini government, and of his understanding of the tragedy of the villagers' lives. Recently the *New York Times Book Review*, after the disastrous Italian earthquake of December 1980, quoted Levi to the effect that Southern Italians are fated to be victims: "After this year's earthquake, Dr. Levi's words are prescient: "In a world apart, I am glad to travel in my memory to that other world, hedged in by custom and sorrow, cut off from history and the state, eternally patient, to that land without comfort or solace, where the peasant lives out his motionless civilization on barren ground in remote poverty, and in the presence of death" (December 21, 1980:27). Cornelisen, writing much later, echoes the air of hopelessness in Levi's work. Her focus is on women, and she is extremely sympathetic to their lives and struggles; nevertheless, she sees self-destructive behavior on an individual level, but not the larger political-economic forces that set the stage.

9. Briggs 1978 discusses this ahistorical tendency at length.

cause of their condition.[10] This position has been thoroughly criticized (Leacock 1971; Stack 1974; B. Williams 1975). These critiques point out that intrinsic to the functioning of the American economy are sets of low-paying occupations that determine poverty for those who fill them. Stack's study of a poor Black community in the Midwest, in particular, presents clear evidence that the so-called disorganized, pathological patterns of impoverished Blacks are in fact highly structured, functional strategic adaptations to life in poverty. She brings to this critical analysis, as well (with Piven and Cloward, 1971), the understanding that the welfare system benefits employers in that it perpetuates a "reserve army of labor." Members of the reserve army are manipulated by the cutoff or reinstatement of benefits to accept employment in or termination from unpleasant, poorly paid jobs, the numbers of which multiply or contract with fluctuations in the overall economy (1974:124–129).

This vision of Italian-American social and economic behavior, and often of white ethnic behavior in general, is like that which informs the Culture of Poverty concept in that it focuses on family life as the cause of economic failure or success. It divorces individuals' economic statuses from the larger economy and its evolutions, and from its entire ethnic/racial infrastructure of institutional racism; ethnic/racial migration; job, capital, housing, and educational networks; societal ethnic/racial economic stereotypes; and union seniority systems. Like the Culture of Poverty concept, it blames the victim.

The 1960s and 1970s witnessed the rise of the white ethnic renaissance, a movement paralleling, borrowing from, and partially reacting against the Civil Rights and Black Power movements. Dormant ethnic associations revived, new ones formed, festivals began or were renewed, press coverage expanded dramatically, and popular and scholarly books on particular groups poured from the publishers.[11]

This new ethnic pride influenced Italian-Americans as much as others. It was certainly one of the mobilizing forces in my choice, as an anthropologist, to study my own coethnics. But as I read new

10. The classic statement of this perspective is Moynihan 1965.

11. See Glazer and Moynihan 1970, 1975; Greeley 1971; Novak 1971; Bennett 1973; and Stein and Hill 1977.

work on Italian-Americans done by Italian-Americans themselves, I began to realize the force of the popular but deficient model of Italian and Italian-American social life. Writers either accepted this model, writing defensively of possessive mothers, *campanilismo*, peasant fatalism, and political apathy—or they "protested too much," scouring historical sources and contemporary statistics for evidence of Italian-American economic and educational achievement, of civic responsibility and cultural superiority.[12] Whether accepting or protesting, these writers were in bondage to the model, a model whose analogue for Black Americans had been discredited.

Italian-American writings on Italian-Americans in California add a further twist to this picture: they convey the impression that Californian or Western Italians were uniquely prosperous and civil, "a distinction from which the Italians who settled on the East Coast fell short" (Gumina 1978:x). This perception incorporates the folk notion that northern Italians, who predominate in California, were racially superior to Southerners.[13] In addition, popular novels of the "family saga" genre have extended the currency of the impression that only San Francisco Italians have amassed wealth (Fast 1978; Gambino 1981).

This perspective on Italian-Americans, including the presumption of innate racial hierarchies, of better or worse families, and of the responsibility of "family culture" for group mobility, is in fact the major approach to European-American ethnicity in the United States.[14] It is due both to confusion concerning the definition of ethnicity and to certain particularities of United States history.

### Ethnicity—Theory and Reality

Ethnicity is a phenomenon of state societies (those with organized governments), involving the labeling, from within or without,

12. See Gambino 1974; Tomasi 1973:75; and Vecoli 1973:119 for acceptance of the model, and Lopreato 1970; and Rolle 1972:59–63 for protesting too much.

13. See also Rolle 1972:73–74. Giovinco 1973; chap. 6 traces the evolution of this image in both American and Italian-language periodicals.

14. This, however, is by no means the case for work on racial groups in America, or on regional or entrepreneurial ethnic groups in Europe or the Third World. Examples of such work in the United States are Nee and Nee 1972; Genovese 1972; Gutman 1976; and Camarillo 1979. Examples for Europe and the Third World are Barth 1969; Nagata 1974; A. Cohen 1974; Despres 1975; Hechter 1975; Wolf and Cole 1974; Warren 1978; Aguilar 1979; and Gal 1979.

of particular populations as somehow different from the majority, and of their members as genealogically related to one another. The members may not necessarily *be* related to one another, nor do they necessarily behave differently from the majority: it is the labeling itself, the cultural process, that is crucial to the construction of ethnicity.

This labeling, the mutual process of identity-construction, happens at ethnic boundaries, and both affects and is affected by the economic and political positions of groups. Ethnic groups, however, may either coincide with or crosscut class divisions. Ethnicity is thus always both cognitive and economic, and as economies alter, so do ethnic boundaries and ideologies.

Ethnic groups are then intermediate phenomena between kinship groups and nations, and the three entities have structural similarities. Kinship, ethnic, and state ideologies may all involve the use of religious symbolism; and ethnic groups and states exploit kinship imagery, including the imagery of proper or improper gender behavior—depending on whether one is inside or outside the boundary. And like those of families and of nation-states, ethnic processes alter with changing historical periods and vary according to their characteristic economies.

Much work on ethnicity, however, defines it solely as normative behavior, ignoring boundaries, economy, and history. Ironically, because this perspective ignores changing material realities, it also misses much of the cognitive element of ethnic processes: ethnic boundaries and thus ideologies alter with changing economies. An emphasis on normative behavior also prevents researchers from attending to age, generational, class, and gender divisions within populations.[15]

This theoretical tendency sets the stage for the vision of unchanging, homogeneous American ethnic groups with no particular connection to the larger economy. Ethnic cultures are merely mental tracks, transmitted through families (women), over which ethnics travel—rather than cognitive resources that they strategically choose and alter over time. This perspective's emphasis on family derives both from the prevalent use of kinship imagery in popular ethnic ideologies and from the necessity of relying on family in the

15. This theory of ethnicity builds on Weber 1978; Barth 1969; and Marx 1975, incorporating as well a model of ethnic ideology inspired by Marxist studies of ideology and cognitive anthropology's mentalist definition of culture.

[23]

absence of other explanatory factors. Focusing on ethnic boundaries rooted in economic and historical processes allows us instead
to see that all of daily life, not just family life, is part of the construction and reconstruction of ethnic identities.

## Ethnicity in the United States

Particularities of American history have also encouraged this fam-
ily-based perspective. Viewed cross-culturally, the United States
has an unusual ethnic history in that a large number of in-migrating
and native groups were incorporated over a relatively short period
of time, and in widely varying ways: through colonization, annexa-
tion, enslavement, contractual servitude, and independent migration in response to varying political-economic factors. These
groups, unlike many European and Third World ethnics, have
lived largely dispersed throughout the general population. Thus
the United States is unlike many other capitalist states in that its
labor force was, from the 1600s, heterogeneous. Because of historical accident, lighter-skinned northwestern Europeans largely arrived earlier than darker-skinned southeastern Europeans. Because
of racist oppression, Native Americans, Blacks, Asians, and Latinos
have been relegated to the periphery of the expanding economy.
Both by design and by accident, the American class system has had
the appearance of organization by color.[16]

While European working classes were developing self-conscious-
ness and organized political life, their counterparts in the United
States were also aware of racial and ethnic divisions, the possibility
of geographic mobility within the country, and the pervasive ideology promising economic and social mobility in return for effort.
This ideology was not a chimera, as the rapidly expanding econo-

16. Distinctions between racial and ethnic groups vary by historical period,
region, and speaker. In the United States at present, racial groups are those of
African, Asian, or Latin American descent, ethnics of European descent. "Ethnic
studies," however, usually refers only to racial groups. Some writers define racial
groups as genuinely oppressed in distinguishing them from ethnics (Berreman
1981:16; Vincent 1974), but this typology prevents us from understanding the
economic-historical process through which the dichotomy has emerged. Thus both
the histories of free Northern Blacks and those of the racist oppression of Irish,
Jews, Italians, etc. are lost, and our understanding of the malleability and changing
symbolic legitimation of systems of oppression is narrowed.

my, recurrent labor and protest movements, and the proliferation of technological improvements did secure limited mobility for a few, and rising standards of living for most. In this way the questions of the oppression of the working classes and the need to organize for economic democracy in Europe were partially transposed, in the U.S. context, to questions of the economic mobility and worth of racial and ethnic groups vis-à-vis the Wasp middle and upper classes and one another.[17]

Because racial and ethnic divisions coincided so strongly with occupational segregation and economic stratification, racial and ethnic labels became fused with class labels. Thus studies of race and ethnicity in the United States have tended to link these phenomena inextricably to the issue of mobility, and to use the notion of differing—better or worse—families, rather than the larger political economy, as the explanatory chain between class and culture.

This presumption that "class equals culture" has meant that those Blacks, Latinos, and Asians who were not impoverished, and those white ethnics who were not working-class, have been ignored as atypical, or else defined as assimilated and therefore no longer ethnic. There is also the related notion that only urban residents are ethnic, which denies authenticity to rural, suburban, and small-town dwellers. Because of these presumptions, we in fact know very little about the mutual connections among locality, class, ethnicity, and kinship over the course of American history. Research on ethnicity in the United States tends to be disguised research on ethnically based class divisions; instead of guiding research, the ethnic family model has replaced it.[18]

## The Study Design

It took the field experience itself, however, for me to understand that ethnicity, kinship, and gender profoundly interpenetrate with

17. See M. Davis 1980 for an analysis of the unique evolution of the U.S. working class; and Gutman 1977: chap. 1 for capital's use of work force diversity to assert control.

18. Anthropologists have tended to study racial/ethnic kinship that is coincidentally working- or lower-class (Stack 1974; Chock 1974; B. Williams 1975). Sociologists have tended to study working- or middle-class kinship that is coincidentally nonethnic, or in which ethnicity is ignored (Sussman 1953; Litwak 1960; Komarovsky 1962; Rubin 1976).

the evolving political economy. I suspected at the start, though, that class did *not* equal culture, and that ethnic and racial identity flourished in the suburbs and small towns of California. And of all the Italian-American women in my personal network, most worked outside the home, few were unremittingly nurturant, and many disliked cooking and housework. I determined to study Italian-American families in a range of economic situations, in city, suburb, and town, and with an emphasis on women's lives and perceptions. I knew, as well, that I wanted to set families in the contexts of their own and the state's economic history—to follow the antecedents of each family backward, if possible, to the point of immigration in order to chart both kinship patterns and economic behavior in different economic eras. I felt the focus on California Italian-Americans was warranted for two reasons: I would be contributing vital information on ethnicity in a neglected regional context; and the fact that I am myself Italian-American and from the area would help me to gain access to the families, usually a difficult task. My background, my theoretical orientation, and my willingness to see anew would enable me to provide a study of Italian-Americans that was a work neither of advocacy nor of detraction.

In carrying out this study, I decided to depart from the two designs most commonly used in research on families and race/ethnicity: random sampling and the community or neighborhood study. Random sampling—identifying a population through election registers, wedding announcements, or telephone directories and randomly selecting a portion of it—was inappropriate for my purposes. I wanted to study families formed through intermarriage as well as endogamous marriages. More important, I was certain that I would need sponsors in order to enter my informants' family networks. The information I was seeking was so personal and context-determined that it could be collected only as part of the process of casual and intimate relationships created by many sociable visits over time.

A community or neighborhood study, in which everyone living in one particular area becomes a research subject, was inappropriate for other reasons: I wished to study Italian-American families of different class statuses (neighborhoods tend to be class-homogeneous); and I wished to look at ethnicity in the suburbs, where most of the California population actually lives, as well as in towns and cities. Italian-Americans in Northern California live widely dispersed throughout the general population and maintain contacts with one another across large distances. To have studied them as a "community" would have been to falsify their social reality.

The random sampling and community study approaches were also problematic for me on the ground of access. I was concerned that the manner in which I contacted people might bias my results. On the one hand, contacting people through random sampling might result in an emphasis on individual psychology to the exclusion of the material and social surround, as is the case in much literature on ethnicity with this research design. On the other hand, undertaking a community study brings up another dilemma: How does the researcher analyze and portray differences in perceptions within the group when the group itself has been the unit of analysis? Too often the solution is to ignore interinformant variations—to dissolve individuals into a group perspective. I thus decided to use social networks in order to gain access to informants as well as to study those networks themselves. In this way I felt I could get at the connections of individuals and families to one another as naturally as possible. I would find connections where they existed but would not infer them where they did not. I would interview all members of every family with whom I had contact, and try to interview other members of their personal networks as well. In that way I would, I hoped, be able to observe connections whether of kinship or of friendship that crossed class divisions, as well as to accomplish my larger goal of seeing individuals in their social context.

I decided, then, to seek both Catholics and non-Catholics; individuals and families who were the result both of in- and out-marriage; people whose antecedents originated from all regions of Italy (I knew that those from the north would inevitably predominate); and families that bore some connection to the three Northern California metropolitan areas of heaviest early settlement—San Francisco, San Jose, and Oakland. In each case I wished to avoid parochialism: I knew that Northern California's Italian-Americans spanned these divisions, and I wanted the families and networks I was to study to be broadly representative. For the same reason I avoided focusing on cultural or ethnic brokers—individuals who were very active in ethnic voluntary associations. They were likely to have fixed views on topics related to their political work, and tended to be overstudied since they were most easily contacted. They were, in any event, unrepresentative of the larger population precisely because of their activism.

### Beginning: Lasciate Ogni Speranza Voi Ch'Entrate
### (Abandon Hope All Who Enter Here)
### Dante, *Inferno*

I began to try to meet Italian-Americans through those I already knew. A wealthy professional contact thought that I should first interview Paolo Bevilacqua:[19] "You want an Italian? *He's* the one you want to see. The guy's a *professional* Italian-American. Do you know what I mean? He makes it his business to know *everyone*. He deals in people. He makes money off it, and it's a personal crusade. Every little appointment, every little rung of the ladder—he takes it seriously, like his own family. Me, he treats like royalty; he's all over me like a dirty shirt. Know why? I've *made* it for *our people*. I can't look at it that way."

Bevilacqua answered his own telephone and made an appointment readily. His office was in a shabby building in a transitional area of the city in which he lived. I arrived on time; he burst out of an inner room and, apologizing profusely, asked me to come back in an hour. When I arrived at the office for the second time, I noted evidences of Italian-American clientele: Italian calendars, books, advertisements for Italian-run businesses. Bevilacqua again came trotting out of the inner office and ushered me in. For the next two hours he ran on excitedly about Dante, Michelangelo, little-known Italians in the Colonial United States, and how we must all learn about our heritage and transmit it to our children. He punctuated these monologues with frenzied searches through the books and papers piled over every available surface of the room. He gave me travel agency brochures on Italy and citations for obscure pieces of

19. In order to ensure my informants' privacy, I have altered all names, although I have retained the ethnic or American character of all given names and surnames. I have also slightly changed residence and occupation and obscured kin relations across families in cases where it would help to hide identity without marring the presentation of analysis.

scholarship on illustrious former immigrants. He perceived my "school paper" as a summary of historical research on great immigrants, and clung to this perception in the face of my considerable effort at explanation. He patted one of the many books he had dug out with an air of finality. "Read this—it's all in here for your paper."

As we were standing in the outer office saying goodbye, he began to talk about his experience as an ethnic in California. He drew his differences from the white nonethnic population with a starkness I was not accustomed to: he was not hostile, but they were definitely Other. Imperceptibly, he moved on to his lobbying efforts for a variety of ethnic and nonethnic causes. I had been standing, holding a coat, a heavy purse, and a pile of books, for forty-five minutes. I was thinking mainly about my feet. Later I realized that Bevilacqua's causes lined up on both the left and right of the political spectrum. He moved on to the "crime" of the film *The Godfather*. How terrible and unjust it was! And one of our own had written it, and another directed it! What a slander on the Italian people—we had little to do with such things. I forgot my feet as Bevilacqua, reminded by the late hour and his long-put-off departure, started talking about his family. Skating past my questions—questions leading up to a request for a family interview and thus contacts with others—he described his children's ingratitude. Ten minutes, and innumerable complaints, later, he suddenly remembered the time, cordially took leave of me, and hurried to his car.

My second interview took place through the kindness of a friend who arranged for a couple to be invited over for an afternoon so I could meet Joe Longhinotti: "You'll love him, he's *really* Italian, he knows everyone, he's always singing. He's a baker, he gives everyone *panettone*." The afternoon was lovely and wine-soaked. Our hosts, a wealthy couple who had moved to California after World War II, had a house with a beautiful view. They were wearing jeans. The Longhinottis arrived in Sunday visiting clothes. They were charming and very kind to me. They encouraged me to speak Italian, and I astonished myself with my abilities. Most of us around the table were Italian-American: we told stories, we joked, we asserted our superiority. But the afternoon really belonged to Joe. His were the best, the most beautifully paced anecdotes: "He's a real Toncini! You don't know Toncini, eh? He's the man that squeezed the dollar dry!" Joe evoked a cast of characters for us; we had never known any of them, but they took on substance, there at the table, and represented Italian-American community to us.

Joe would pause in his stories, cock an eye at us, and burst triumphantly into song. His wife Cetta would fidget nervously. She participated very little in the talk. I had not been told much about her—not even whether she was Italian. I moved beside her and asked her. Yes, she was; but her parents were from a different region of Italy than Joe's, and she had grown up in a different part of California. She summarized her family's immigration and settlement history in a few concise statements. It was like gold dropping into my lap. In halting Italian I asked her if I might interview her. She looked surprised but answered graciously in fluent Tuscan that she would love to help me but how would *she* know anything important enough for my book? I did my best to assure her that she would. When could we? Well, some evening, because she worked all day. Worked? I had assumed that she was a housewife.

As we were all leaving, our hosts told Joe and Cetta about their proposed trip to Italy. Wouldn't they come along too? No, they didn't think so. It was not until months later, when I had become familiar with the Longhinottis' economic situation, that I realized that they could no more have gone to Italy that year than on a luxury cruise.

These two occasions carried within themselves, although I did not yet know it, the themes of my fieldwork experience. I was sent to men, and then discovered women. I was sent to "authentic" Italian-Americans by others who vouched for their authenticity. This translated to affluent contacts sending me to the less well-off. People had strong ideas about ethnicity and about ethnic families, but they differed widely from person to person, from men to women; and it was women who had knowledge (as opposed to opinions) about families, and who were willing and articulate in sharing that knowledge. Many talked about community; but I instead discovered networks of different sorts, often disconnected to one another, and voluntary organizations either embedded in ideas of past or intent on creating future communities. And these ideas about ethnic families and communities were political ideas. They contained implicit value judgments about other ethnic and racial groups and about the economic-historical change that has pushed and pulled immigrants from abroad and from within the U.S. borders over the past century. They especially contained implicit evaluations of the quality of various groups' responses to that change.

Finally, these two visits introduced me to the fact that people would have their own ideas about who I was, why I was studying Italian-Americans, and what exactly I needed—or deserved—to know. I had expected eager or reluctant responses to my questions; I received also a great many prepared speeches, and some questions in turn. I learned, slowly, to listen to everything that my informants wanted to express, and to articulate explicitly the connections among topics that they drew implicitly. And I learned the primary ethnomethodological lesson: that I was not "collecting data," but engaging in complex emotional interactions with other human beings; it was necessary to understand their perceptions of me and of our interactions in order to interpret the information that they offered. Those perceptions and the structure of those interactions were in themselves important information. This does not mean that I have assumed the novelist's omniscience in the following pages, but rather that I offer the reader my interpretations of people's varying reactions to me and my questions, my reasons for those interpretations, and the effects I believe those reactions had on what people, in the end, said to me.

## Continuing Research: Mutual Perceptions

Aside from the regional origin and the religious and social variation I sought in the sample, I also looked for families representative of the staggered settlement history of California's Italians (including the post World War II influx) and of the variety of early family economic strategies—cooperative farming, individual orchard, dairy, and truck farming, fishing, small business, skilled labor, and service work, especially scavenging. I interviewed families whose present economic statuses spanned as widely as possible an income and occupational range. I also interviewed some women and men who were separated or divorced.

My sample, then, is a spectrum of families representing a broad

[31]

cross-section of the general Italian-American population in both a historical and a contemporary sense. It is not a random sample, although the fact that my informants are members of five unconnected cross-class social networks gives some assurance of lack of skewing. I have sacrificed numbers of informants for data quality and depth. I will not make claims about overall patterns among California's Italian-Americans, but instead will discuss the presence and linkages among various characteristics, investigate their historical evolution, and suggest hypotheses based on these findings. I will also show how life-history data led me to question historians' assertions and to check them with primary sources.

I met individuals originally through a friend's husband, a student of mine, some acquaintances of a relative, and members of a local college class on Italian-Americans. Many of these people in turn put me in touch with their relatives and friends. In this way I was both using individuals' personal networks in order to gain informants and studying the networks themselves in the process of being passed along them.

In the end, I had spent time formally and informally with most members of fifteen core families (see chart, Core family members). My assumptions about the need for sponsorship in order to do family research were borne out repeatedly over the course of my fieldwork. I attempted many times to contact individuals through others with whom I was barely acquainted: each time it was a dismal failure. One woman made a firm appointment and never showed up; others would set a date and then call back to cancel. Several times people became upset about the personal character of my questions ("Do you have brothers or sisters?") at the beginning of an interview. I let them turn these interactions into impersonal monologues about "old times," and continued my search for families elsewhere.

I tried at first to take notes during and after interviews, but soon realized that I was failing to record important information, and that individuals wanted and deserved my full attention. I borrowed a tape recorder; almost immediately its battery-run system broke down and, unable to afford the time or money necessary to repair it, I was reduced to asking permission to plug it into an electrical outlet before each interview. People were unfailingly good-natured about this. More than a few expressed justified amusement at my technical incompetence.

[32]

Core family members

| Name | Age | Present occupation | Regional origin | Generation |
|---|---|---|---|---|
| [ Gino Angeluzzi | 60s | retired doctor | Sicily | second |
| ⌊ Teresa Angeluzzi | 50s | nursing supervisor | — | — |
| Mary Angeluzzi | 30s | clerical | Sicily | third |
| Joe Angeluzzi | 30s | civil service | Sicily | third |
| Nick Angeluzzi | 20s | salesman | Sicily | third |
| Ann Angeluzzi | 20s | clerical | Sicily | third |
| Lucille Angeluzzi | 20s | student | Sicily | third |
| Edith Angeluzzi | teens | student | Sicily | third |
| Al Bertini | 50s | businessman | Latium | second |
| [ Jim Bertini | 30s | professional | Latium | third |
| ⌊ Jane Bateman | 30s | professional | — | — |
| [ Charles Brandis | 70s | retired professional | Piedmont | second |
| ⌊ Irma Brandis | 60s | housewife | Piedmont | second |
| Gus Brandis | 30s | professional | Piedmont | third |
| [ Maria Caputo | 80s | retired service | Piedmont | first |
| ⌊ Renato Caputo | d. 1930s | craftsman | Piedmont | first |
| Caterina Caputo | 60s | businesswoman | Piedmont | second |
| Lina Caputo | 60s | housewife | Piedmont | second |
| Angela Caputo | 50s | clerical | Piedmont | second |
| [ Dom Cipolla | 60s | professional-technical | Liguria | second |
| ⌊ Clelia Cipolla | 50s | low professional | Liguria/Milan | second |
| Jeannie Cipolla | 20s | student | Liguria/Milan | third |
| Louise Cipolla | 20s | student | Liguria/Milan | third |
| [ Sally Cruciano | 50s | clerical | — | — |
| ⌊ Joe Cruciano | 50s | professional | Basilicata | second |
| Rick Cruciano | 20s | student | Basilicata | third |
| Jim Cruciano | 20s | student | Basilicata | third |
| Clare Cruciano | 20s | student | Basilicata | third |
| [ Jarus DiVincenzo | 60s | retired businessman | Sicily | fourth |
| ⌊ Dorothy DiVincenzo | 50s | clerical | Switzerland | third |
| Ruth DiVincenzo | 30s | housewife | Sicily/Switzerland | fourth/fifth |
| Judy DiVincenzo | 30s | service | Sicily/Switzerland | fourth/fifth |
| David DiVincenzo | 20s | student | Sicily/Switzerland | fourth/fifth |
| Brian DiVincenzo | teens | student | Sicily/Switzerland | fourth/fifth |
| [ Nick Fante | 60s | professional | Genoa | second |
| ⌊ Maria Fante | 50s | saleswoman | Tuscany | second |
| Frank Fante | 20s | skilled craft | Genoa/Tuscany | third |
| Delores Fante | 20s | saleswoman | Genoa/Tuscany | third |

Note: [ = married to.                                        *(continued)*

[33]

Core family members (*continued*)

| Name | Age | Present occupation | Regional origin | Generation |
|---|---|---|---|---|
| ⌈ Nancy Ferrucci | 40s | professional | mixed northern | third |
| ⌊ Mike Borman | 40s | professional | — | — |
| David Borman | under 10 | student | mixed northern | fourth |
| Lisa Borman | under 10 | student | mixed northern | fourth |
| ⌈ Michael Giovan- nino | 60s | professional | Sicily | second |
| ⌊ Roberta Giovan- nino | 50s | clerical | — | — |
| ⌈ James Giovannino | 30s | professional | Sicily | third |
| ⌊ Mary Giovannino | 30s | professional | — | — |
| Cathy Giovannino | 20s | student | Sicily | third |
| Ruth Giovannino | teens | student | Sicily | third |
| ⌈ Hugh Colpo | 60s | skilled craft | Calabria | second |
| ⌊ Marilyn Colpo | 50s | housewife | Calabria | second |
| ⌈ Candy Lombardo | 30s | student | Calabria | third |
| ⌊ Sam Lombardo | 30s | professional | Naples | third |
| ⌈ Joe Longhinotti | 50s | baker | Lucca | second/third |
| ⌊ Cetta Longhinotti | 50s | clerical | Friuli | second |
| Mike Longhinotti | 30s | skilled craft | Lucca/Friuli | third |
| Tom Longhinotti | 30s | skilled craft | Lucca/Friuli | third |
| Greg Longhinotti | 20s | supervisorial | Lucca/Friuli | third |
| ⌈ Nick Meraviglia | 50s | professional | Umbria | second |
| ⌊ Pina Meraviglia | 40s | housewife | Veneto | second |
| Tony Meraviglia | 30s | skilled craft | Umbria/Veneto | third |
| Ron Meraviglia | 20s | skilled craft | Umbria/Veneto | third |
| John Meraviglia | 20s | student | Umbria/Veneto | third |
| ⌈ Lucia Mornese | 60s | retired clerical | Tuscany/ Piedmont | second |
| ⌊ Salvatore Mor- nese | 60s | clerical | Rome | first |
| Linda Mornese | 30s | clerical | mixed northern/central | second/third |
| ⌈ Richard Mornese | 20s | service | mixed northern/central | second/third |
| ⌊ Bobbie Rushov | 20s | professional | — | — |
| ⌈ Tony Ripetto | 60s | retired civil service | Liguria | second |
| ⌊ Agnes Ripetto | 60s | clerical | — | — |
| Frank Ripetto | 40s | clerical | — | — |

Note: [ = married to.

Core family members (*continued*)

| Name | Age | Present occupation | Regional origin | Generation |
|------|-----|--------------------|-----------------|------------|
| *Others Mentioned* | | | | |
| Louis Baca | 60s | small business | Piedmont | second |
| Paolo Bevilacqua | 60s | small business | Rome | first |
| Carl Motto | 50s | civil service | Milan | third |
| Maria Gennaro | 60s | housewife/Cetta Longhinotti's sister | Friuli | second |
| Anna Molinari | 50s | housewife/Cetta Longhinotti's sister | Friuli | second |
| Clara Agnesi | 40s | housewife/Joe Longhinotti's sister | Lucca | second/third |
| Sam Trento | 50s | professional | Basilicata | second |
| Edith Trento | 50s | housewife | — | — |
| Mike Sacco | 50s | skilled craft/Maria Fante's brother | Tuscany | second |

Note: [ = married to.

I attempted to remain neutral about the question of Catholicism. When I was asked about my religious affiliation, I was open but noncommittal about my lack of Catholic background. Devout Catholics varied in their reactions to this statement: most (like the Longhinottis and DiVincenzos) remained warm; a few (like Clelia Cipolla) made me aware of their disapproval. Most interesting, though, were the number of narratives my nonaffiliation inspired from recently lapsed Catholics and bitter ex-parochial school students. Most of the lapsed Catholics were middle-aged women; perhaps this was because few of the men had continued attending Mass after adolescence in the first place. Abramson points out that Italians have the lowest church attendance record of any American ethnic group; and Scherini calculates that San Francisco Italians have an unusually low level of affiliation with ethnoreligious groups (Abramson 1975; Scherini 1976:174). So again it appears that my sample was not of atypical Italian-Americans.

The middle-aged members of these fifteen families were surprisingly bilingual: out of thirty, twenty could communicate at least minimally in some dialect of Italian. Of the remaining ten, six were non-Italian in-marrying spouses, three were third generation, and one was a second-generation man who had grown up on the East Coast. At least twelve of the Italian speakers were actually fluent in their native dialect, and most of these could speak Tuscan, the standard national dialect, as well. (There were a few, of course, whose native dialect *was* Tuscan.) Some could speak several dialects.

None of these bilingual speakers expressed any interest in holding lengthy conversations with me in Italian, although I bravely indicated my willingness. I believe that this preference for English in the interview situation fit into an overall communication pattern. Almost all of these bilingual speakers used Italian only with aged relatives or during trips to Italy. Gal (1979) has shown that urban bilingual speakers in linguistically stratified communities tend to rank speech events by levels of intimacy and formality, and use the dominant language in all but the most informal situations. My familiarity with Italian, though, did encourage women and men to report past conversations in Italian to me, and to use Italian words and phrases liberally in their narratives.

Formally, I took individual and family life histories for all adults, focusing on kinship, economic, ethnic, and residential information. I obtained as much immigration and early settlement information as possible from adults whose parents were dead or unavailable. I constructed genealogies including all known relatives for middle-aged and older women and men, which we then went over together. Slowly, over the course of many visits, these Italian-Americans gave me detailed information on their own and more than fifty other related families. I also asked specific questions about ethnic identity, ethnic discrimination, gender, child rearing, social networks, relationships among relatives, and holidays. Informally, I phoned and visited, joked and talked about food and gardens, work and leisure, and general social issues. I attended local voluntary organization events, and receptions and talks held by academically oriented Italian-American groups.

Because I could visit people only intermittently in their homes, and usually could not follow them into their workplaces, and because there was little public life (cafe, street corner, village square) to observe, I could not approach the anthropological participant-observation ideal of total cultural immersion. But I quickly learned the enormous value of lengthy, repeated visits, phone conversations, and "idle chat": it was at the end of my second visit with Pina Meraviglia that she confessed to me she had not spoken to her brother in five years. During my third talk with Cetta Longhinotti, she began to explain about her difficulties with her daughter-in-law. And universally, individuals would casually mention relatives in the context of a discussion of jobs or holidays—relatives to whom they had never even alluded during my "exhaustive" genealogy interview.

Participant-observation is possible only if people will allow you to participate in activities with them. This is least likely to happen when the activities on hand are defined as private, and when you are perceived as a member of the same culture—why should you need to observe what everyone knows already? I could not use the timeworn anthropologists' approach of ignorance requiring teaching, since the only reason people were willing to talk with me in the first place was that I was a fellow *paesan;* and family behavior was universally seen as the most private realm of all. I relied, then, on the generosity and liking for me which some people displayed. This happened most often in situations where I fit into an already established role. A researcher's age always influences the character of her interactions with informants. My easiest rapport was with the middle-aged, who treated me almost invariably as a privileged, successful adult daughter. Some of them could not hear enough about how I was working my way through graduate school by teaching—how wonderful it was to be getting a Ph.D.—how well I spoke Italian (I did not). I could not hear enough about it either.

But there were obvious difficulties with a daughter role. Clelia Cipolla, at the beginning of our second interview, asked about my Thanksgiving. I explained that some friends and I had made dinner together. She recoiled: "You mean Mommy and Daddy *allowed* you to have Thanksgiving away from home?" The humor of the situation escaped me for the moment; the neon sign DATA lit up only some hours later.

Another approach to understanding the mutual perceptions of researcher and informants is the sociolinguistic concept of speech event: a culturally recognized social interaction with understood roles and structure.[20] Phone calls, court hearings, seminars, and

20. See Hymes 1962.

job interviews are all speech events. Most of my interviews were afternoon or evening visits to homes. Women invariably offered me coffee or tea (sometimes wine) and put out plates of cookies, cake, or fruit. Even when I was interviewing a husband alone, if the wife were home she would unobtrusively bring in a tray.

Because of this ritualized offering, and other indications—cleaned rooms, formal clothing, living room rather than kitchen as interview site—I concluded that, for most individuals my research visits were absorbed into a "coffee with friends" speech event model, where the friends are not so intimate that one does not have to make an effort in front of them. This was a contradiction to the daughter role and seemed to be one source of tension in my relationships with people. Some women showed an obvious enjoyment of the formal visit aspect: Pina Meraviglia's paper doilies between cup and saucer, Cetta Longhinotti's carefully arranged tray of cookies, and Angela Caputo's beautifully appointed living room were sources of pleasant, ritualized praise on my part, and gratified deprecation on theirs. The "coffee with friends" model suggests that Clelia Cipolla was disputing with me what speech event was to prevail, using our age differential to claim her right to discipline a disobedient daughter.

Other individuals had other models: Paolo Bevilacqua's was the ethnic broker's press conference or after-dinner speech; Carl Motto's was the public official's interview with a hostile press. I was also, at times, used as a safe listener: I sympathized over problems with children and in-laws. I was outside the network: information given to me would not return and further complicate matters. In these cases, interaction veered toward a "peer counseling" speech event. I found myself comfortable in this role, as it paralleled the rape crisis counseling that filled so much of my nonresearch life. A few women took advantage of my feminist perspective: when Dorothy DiVincenzo asked me if I thought she was returning to work in order to move away from her husband, she knew that, in contrast to her sister and daughters, I was unlikely to be shocked and disapproving.

Some saw me as an ethnic resource, and asked me to supply statistics and citations, or organizational connections, or names of local "successful" Italian-Americans. Many expressed the idea that they were helping me to speak for Italian-Americans. I was increasingly uncomfortable with this role as the fieldwork progressed, as it so often seemed to be tied to racist denigration of other groups.

For women in general, an important point seemed to be that I was a good person, "moral." Catholic women tended to perceive my rape crisis center work as analogous to religious "good works," and I was not behindhand in encouraging that perception, as I labored under a genuine handicap with some of them in not being a practicing Catholic. Non-Catholic women tended to see this work as feminist. All women were positive about it, and many took the opportunity to ask me for factual or self-defense information, or to voice their fears of attack. Listening, talking about empowerment through information and awareness, and inspecting door and window locks, I reciprocated their generosity—gave back something of value for all the information that was so willingly given to me.

But my major gift to individuals was a natural by-product of the life history interview: the return of memory. Nick Meraviglia said: "You know what it is—after talking to you, it brings out things I hadn't thought about in quite a while. . . . I feel good about it. . . . You gave me a charge having me relate the games we played in my childhood." And Salvatore Mornese exclaimed: "I think I talked more tonight than I talked in the last two years!"

For both women and men, and across the full age range, my status as a university-affiliated intellectual was always an issue. Despite the growth of community colleges and the high proportion, relative to Europe, of college-educated Americans, there is still a social gulf between those who feel at home with the baggage of higher education and those who do not. Some working-class individuals openly expressed their sense of intimidation. Pina Meraviglia, a high school graduate married to a professional man with a higher degree, confessed to me that she was certain she was "much too stupid" to go to college. Both Greg Longhinotti and Frank Fante told me that they regretted not having gone to college. David DiVincenzo asked me for advice about his academic future. Angela Caputo, Candy Lombardo, James and Mary Giovannino, Nancy Ferrucci, and Linda Mornese all expressed a sense of identity with me and engaged in extended academic shop talk.

I believe that people spoke to me freely about this issue because I took pains to make clear how much I felt I was in their debt: that their lives, their experiences, their perceptions were vitally important to me. Joe Longhinotti reacted poignantly to this explanation by reflecting that "when a person speaks sincere, I imagine it comes out as good as a professor."

I also realized, after some months, that few of these Italian-Americans were aware of the nationwide academic financial crisis, the facts of which I knew only too well. I then deliberately explained my restricted opportunity structure—worsening job markets, plummeting real wages, discrimination against women and universities' revolving-door tactics to reduce total faculty salaries—and gave the details of my annual income in graduate school. This exercise in demystification was cathartic for me and fascinating for them, and had some unexpected results: increased rapport through pity, a new willingness to share financial information, and a number of open-ended conversations about life goals and success. I discovered that many people had been ashamed to admit that they had made life choices that would not result in financial success. The fact that I had done so as well encouraged them to discuss with me their experiences with and ideas about social mobility.

Nevertheless, for some people my intellectual life remained exotic and remote. One day when we were relaxing out on her patio, Cetta Longhinotti plucked up her courage to ask me how many books I would read in a month. As I was blundering out something about how it depended on which month and what sorts of books one was considering, I mentioned detective mysteries. Cetta was openly shocked. Mysteries! How could I waste the time! It slowly dawned on me that Cetta had expected that I read only academic material. I learned from that encounter not only how little mutual knowledge I should assume, but also how very difficult it is to quantify the fluctuating behavior of daily life. My humbling experience in trying to count books stood me in good stead when I later asked women and men to quantify their contact with members of their social networks.

Because we all lived in large cities and suburbs, not villages, my fieldwork experience was discontinuous. I would see members of families at widely spaced intervals, whenever they could fit my visits into their schedules. This, oddly, mirrored the patterns of individuals' social lives. Their visits, parties, and phone calls fluctuated due to moves, crises, work schedules, feuds. I could not see in their historical descriptions the neat, synchronic diagrams in some of the literature on social networks. They could not, as I have stated, quantify their social lives—not without giving me important caveats: "It's been like this since Mother's been so ill." This was especially true of women: many who had ample time for interviews would suddenly have no time at all: a daughter's sudden decision to marry and to have a large wedding swallowed up a prospective two months' space during which her mother had thought I could interview her; a parent's or in-law's illness would delay an interview for months. Women, because they are expected to serve as unpaid nurses, baby-sitters, servants, have erratic rhythms of leisure and busyness. Even those women who worked outside the home were at the mercy of kin in a way that men were not. I learned to ask women especially about the historical evolution and fluctuation of family relationships and friendships in order to understand fully their patterns in the present.

Because of the time involved in giving life history and other information, my primary informants tended to be members of families, women and men, who had been temporarily "sidelined"—by illness, retirement, divorce, job transition, or children leaving home—those who for whatever reason had both the time for lengthy interviews and the motivation to make a stanger into a sort of friend. This, however, is almost always true for the fieldworker. It is important to make it explicit and to attempt to assess its effect on research results. In my case, I tended to have longer and more frequent interviews with the sidelined family members, and shorter, sometimes only one, interview with busier members. Gaining most information from "marginal" informants can be a serious problem in a village study; in this case, since I almost always interviewed many members of a family, I believe its effect was minimal.

It proved much harder to study "up"—to interview the wealthy—than "across" or "down." This is partially so because the affluent, especially affluent men, often have rigidly scheduled lives, but it is also the case that wealthy people are less pleased than others by scholarly interest in their personal lives. They receive such attention elsewhere, and it can seem dangerously close to society journalism; family secrets, once public, could bring financial harm.

I also found it more difficult to study the affluent because of an aspect of class—class determines a great deal about the comfort and privacy of one's workplace, and about whether or not one can receive visitors there. Some of my wealthier professional informants, men and women, insisted on confining interviews to their workplaces, thus preventing the establishment of an atmosphere in which they were likely to give me informal, lengthy responses to questions about kinship and ethnic identity.[21]

At home or at work, men in general were more difficult to interview. This was partly because of my age and sex, and partly, I think, because they had less well-developed models of the "coffee with friends" speech event.

Al Bertini, in his home, told me about his mother with tears in his eyes. When I later interviewed him in his office, he made the encounter into an elaborate exercise in stonewalling:

> Al: You know, you don't know what you're getting into.
> I: What do you mean I don't know what I'm getting into?
> Al: I mean you don't know your subject. You think you may have something but you may have nothing. You may have an empty chapter.
> I: Because?
> Al: Because there's nothing there.
> I: In your life?
> Al: Mmhmm.
>
> Al: [Discussing grade school.] I was trying to avoid being laughed at. Is that bad?
> I: It sounds like what happened to a lot of immigrant children.
> Al: Oh, I got a label! I just wondered how I was gonna fit into your study.

21. In the following chapters some narrators appear more often than others, primarily because of the great difference in response styles: some individuals tended toward monosyllables, while others spoke at length and gave examples. Short ellipses ( . . . ) indicate pauses and longer ones ( . . . . ) deleted material. Spacing indicates a lapse of time or separate conversation. I attempt in these transcriptions to give an accurate rendering of my informants' speech. I use colloquial forms to indicate intended informality, not to condescend. The reader will notice that the well-educated and affluent make considerable use of contractions and slang, and that many individuals move between colloquial and formal speech even within single utterances. I conducted some interviews without a tape recorder; even during recorded interviews individuals often waited until we had moved to a different room to give a considered reply or piece of information. In most of these cases I indicate the nature of the statement without attempting a precise quotation.

Al: We played kick the can and other games that are not played today. People today write books and do the sort of stuff that you're doing instead of enjoying life . . . You don't think that I'm going to let you off easy?

I: *Ho capito* [I understand].

Al: I think I understand that. You think I know Italian?

I: Yes.

Al: That shows me how much credibility your book is gonna have.

This exchange reminded me inescapably of Evans-Pritchard's report of his encounters with Nuer men:

I: What is the name of your lineage?

Cuol: Do you want to know the name of my lineage?

I: Yes.

Cuol: What will you do with it if I tell you? Will you take it to your country?

I: I don't want to do anything with it. I just want to know it since I am living in your camp.

Cuol: Oh well, we are Lou.

I: I did not ask you the name of your tribe. I know that. I am asking you the name of your lineage.

Cuol: Why do you want to know the name of my lineage?

I: I don't want to know it.

Cuol: Then why do you ask me for it? Give me some tobacco. (1940:x)

These scenes with men, so funny to the reader, so appalling to Evans-Pritchard ("One is just driven crazy by it") and to me, repeated themselves throughout my fieldwork. Perhaps they represent a universal male game.

James Giovannino, younger than Al Bertini and more familiar with social science research, displayed further refinements of the technique:

James: [To wife, Mary.] You know what she's really doing is studying arguments and she's looking at the pattern to see if I'm the dominant one because I'm Italian.

Mary: [Discussing relatives moving to California.] It was a cultural thing.

[43]

James: Mmmm. See it wasn't the job market or the things the city
      had to offer, it was the *family*. I'll bet you'll type that up.
Mary: [Reprovingly.] James!

And Carl Motto, a public official, used the simplest mode of attack, the unattributed slur. I did not know him, and had arranged to meet him at his workplace through the intervention of a mutual friend. I had trouble finding my way around in the large building, and walked into his office four minutes late, apologizing profusely. His stunning reply was, "I expected you to be late. That's what you're like."

I was amused and impressed by these spontaneous, witty lunges at my professional neck; how could I blame these men for protecting themselves from my intrusions? But they also drew blood: few researchers are immune to the suspicions that they have not really understood anything about their topic, that they are imposing their own distorting grid on reality. And these men, unlike the Nuer with Evans-Pritchard, shared sufficient culture with me to perceive this vulnerability and to attack it with skill and verve.

I was never, however, attacked on political grounds, although my informants and I often differed in our opinions. This was in part because I tried to avoid asking questions about controversial topics or else tried to approach them tactfully. I never asked anyone what she or he thought of feminism, but instead elicited concepts of gender in the course of taking life histories. I learned about racial attitudes through asking about other racial and ethnic groups in taking residential, school, and occupational information. I avoided asking about abortion, homosexuality, and international issues, even though such discussions might have created deeper intimacy in my relationships with informants. I could not risk the intimacy of hostility. An argument about abortion would have given me great insight into Clelia Cipolla's perspectives on women and reproduction. I would also probably have had no more interviews with her. In a village or a small town setting, I could have written pages of notes on the process of being ostracized—as Berreman (1962) did so insightfully in northern India—or observed others fighting one another over controversial topics. But it was clear that fieldwork strategy in an advanced industrial setting would have to be different. How many notes could I write on a simple negative phone call? I did not dare create this scene for intimacy for fear of having no one left with whom to talk.

But my informants had no such qualms: at the calm end of an evening's interview, Cetta Longhinotti suddenly asked me how I was going to vote on the Briggs initiative (which would have legalized the firing of known homosexual teachers). I was plunged into doubt, but probity won out: I had determined to try not to lie to informants. I told her that I felt strongly about the issue, that my husband John, whom she respected, was working against the initiative. The ensuing conversation taught me more about Cetta than all the ones past. It did not break our rapport, but I had to let Cetta take the lead.

They took it up often, proving to me repeatedly what contemporary feminist literature claims: that family issues are inescapably political issues. They intertwine with gender, race, and economic questions—all of the major questions of the day. Since I neither hid nor pushed my own perspectives, and since, in any event, I felt genuine empathy with these Italian-Americans, most of them, no matter which views they held, were eager to talk about them. Clelia Cipolla explained with disdain, "Of course, I'm not a union person, so I believe in giving time without being paid," while Joe Longhinotti spent an entire evening discussing his recent strike activity. Angela Caputo inveighed against racism, while Linda Mornese said matter-of-factly: "I *am* prejudiced—Chinese, Blacks, anything." And Carl Motto joked about his father's mother, "Other than doing things women were expected to do she didn't talk much," while Jim Bertini feelingly related an interaction with a married woman cousin: "We said Lucy, what's wrong? 'Nothing.' Why don't you get a job? 'Well, my husband likes his woman at home.' We looked at each other and said, Oh, man . . . It was depressing."

Still, it is likely that my perspectives influenced my interactions, that they evoked a resonance in some, drawing them out to tell stories, to explain opinions that they would not have related to a more conservative interviewer. Jim Bertini and Gus Brandis, both leftists, talked freely with me about politics and family relations. Nick Meraviglia, after some hours, brought up his Italian socialist relatives; receiving understanding and encouragement, rather than shock and disapproval, he then produced American Communist

[45]

cousins. And many women discussed with me their resentment of fathers, brothers, husbands.

It is probably also true that I unconsciously stifled responses that a different researcher might have evoked. I know, in fact, that this was the case for Cetta Longhinotti, Joe Cruciano, and Jarus DiVincenzo on the issue of race: while they were circumspect in talking with me, their *children* openly criticized them for their racist attitudes and fully reported a series of family interactions on the issue, complete with exact quotations. This is a strong argument for interviewing all family members in doing family research, but it is even stronger proof that one cannot do objective, nonpolitical research on political topics. I had very good rapport with these adult children, and therefore they shared with me their unease about their parents' politics; for a different researcher the process might have been reversed.

These Italian-Americans' insistence that political issues be discussed led me to consider the sources of ideology and their connections to symbols of family, ethnicity, and gender; their candor about personal economic issues led me to analyze the integration of concepts of class with these other social constructions of reality. In the following chapters I bring together a materialist analysis of a population divided by class, gender, and generation and an analysis of their varying constructions of those and other divisions, constructions that do not follow material divisions in a one-to-one fashion. In so doing, I describe one strand of the historically changing and synchronically diverse varieties of ethnic experience.

# [2]

# Italian Families, American Families: Immigration History and Settlement in California

> Household activities cannot be analyzed as separate from the socioeconomic relations in which they are embedded—Rapp 1979:177

"They come with a cardboard suitcase in one hand and a rosary in the other," said Tony Ripetto of the Italian immigrants of his parents' generation. He was repeating, however, not his relatives' stories of steerage and Ellis Island, but those retailed in popular books and films. What is the truth behind this sentimentalized picture? Who exactly were these immigrants? What was their background and why did they wish to leave? From which parts of Italy did they emigrate? How were households constituted in Italy and reconstituted in the United States? And how did immigrants come to participate in particular sectors of the developing American economy?

The answers to these questions are crucial to our understanding, not just of those involved in this period of immigration, but of migration, economy, and family in general. We tend today, for example, to conceptualize and judge contemporary Asian, Latino, and Caribbean migrants by referring to popular media images of the hard-working but backward European peasants of the second wave, peasants who were allowed to share the fruits of our superior democracy (Bryce-Laporte 1980). Differences in economic success among different migrant groups and their descendents then appear to be the result of better or worse behavior, usually family behavior, which is seen as determined by "ethnic culture."

Revising the model of European immigration to the United States helps to alter our perspective on successive waves of arrivals as well. A large part of the European impetus to emigrate arose from American economic competition with native industries and agriculture. Many migrants, far from being timeless peasants, had been skilled workers in these threatened industries. And developing American firms actively recruited Europeans as a docile labor force. Migration is a result, not the cause, of linkages among nations; it is part of a changing global economy in which the demand for labor itself migrates and alters with uneven capitalist development. Our understanding of contemporary Caribbean and Latino migration should thus be broadened to include the political economy of the hemisphere (Piore 1979; Portes and Walton 1981). This perspective, however, still leaves us with a complex of ideas linking ethnic family cultures with differential mobility rates. It does not directly explain why some migrant groups appear to do better economically than others.

To enter this question, we need to understand migrants' actual individual and family economic strategies,[1] and the contexts in which they created and implemented them. Focusing on the patterns of Italian immigration to the United States, and more specifically to California, and on the sorts of occupations, households, and kinship relations that these immigrants and their descendants chose and created will allow us to reexamine the issues of family culture and ethnic mobility with a broad historical and empirical background.


## From Italy to California: Italian Emigration in the Nineteenth and Twentieth Centuries

In considering the movements of Italian nationals within and beyond their country's boundaries, we must first note that the

---

1. I use "ethnic economic strategy" here in the tradition of Stack (1974) and others. The concept implies that immigrants perceive specific arrays of kin structures and occupations as more appropriate than others, and that they make decisions about which to implement according to these preferences and according to what they perceive will be possible in the new environment. These issues are discussed further in Chapter 3 under "A Model of the Interaction of Culture and Economy."

statistical evidence of their migration is extremely poor. The Italian state, unified only in 1861, relied on erratic and inconsistent local record keeping. United States statistics, while more centralized, were hampered by legislated changes in categorization, racism, and geographic ignorance—the U.S. Bureau of Immigration actually assigned Liguria to southern Italy. To complicate the issue further, illegal migration and repatriation were particularly high among Italians. Individuals circumventing periodic legislation against emigration debarked with illegal passports from Marseilles and other European ports and thus were not counted; scholars estimate that approximately one hundred thousand Italians emigrated clandestinely in the years 1869–75 alone. On the other hand, the majority of emigrants, for the entire period of heavy emigration, left intending to return. The evidence suggests that large numbers were counted as *new* emigrants and immigrants, by the Italian and American governments, as they left a second, third, or more times in their periodic returns and reemigrations.

Nevertheless, the number of emigrants to the United States was large enough (about 4.5 million between 1850 and 1930) that we may trace the broad sweep of their movements and the reasons behind them.[2]

First it must be noted that *internal* seasonal migration, following agricultural cycles, and then migration to western Europe to take advantage of the demand for industrial and other labor, were well-established patterns in many regions in Italy before the mid-nineteenth century upsurge of migration to the New World. Italians, even (or especially) Italian peasants, were by no means unaccustomed to the notion of labor migration as an economic strategy before the concatenation of domestic and international factors induced nearly nine million of them to leave, first for South America and the Mediterranean rim and then for North America, in the late nineteenth and early twentieth centuries.[3]

There have been debates over the relative importance of the domestic (push) and international (pull) factors in this wholesale

2. On Italian and U.S. record keeping, see Foerster 1919: chap. 1; Palmer 1965:27–42,89n.; and Thomas 1973:42–50. For estimates of migrant numbers, see Palmer 1965:46–48,337,344; Dore 1968:105; and Cinel 1979:71–94.

3. See Foerster 1919:532–33; Palmer 1965:44, 345–46; Mack Smith 1969:239; and C., L., and R. Tilly 1975:112ff.

[49]

population movement. They are in fact interrelated, two sides of the coin of the development and integration of the capitalist world economy (Thomas 1973; Piore 1979). In Italy, the sequelae of national unification included the breaking up of some Church and privately owned latifundia and their sale on the market, and the establishment and then abandonment of tariffs against certain French agricultural goods (1887–90). The new availability of land was an inducement for many to emigrate in order to accumulate purchasing capital. The short-lived tariff war brought French retaliation which bankrupted some Apulian, Calabrian, and Sicilian viticulturalists, harmed the silk industries of Lombardy, Venice, and Piedmont, and affected exports of rice, cattle, and cheese from the north. Emigration rose in these areas as a result of economic hardships and opportunities, but was spurred as well by long-term economic change originating in western Europe and across the Atlantic.[4]

The years following the end of the Civil War in the United States were marked by large-scale industrial growth and increasing demand by capital for inexpensive labor. Some sectors of capital experienced this demand strongly enough to order advertising pamphlets distributed in European countries and to go into partnership with shipping companies to increase European immigration. (The transportation of immigrants by ship was itself an immensely profitable business.) Thus the technological and economic development both of American industry and of the international shipping industry resulted in heavy inducements to Europeans to emigrate (Jones 1960:163–67, 182–86; Ward 1971:58–71).

At the same time, the growth of these industries and the coming to age of American agriculture led to the flooding of European markets first by American wheat and then by citrus and tropical fruit from California and Florida. This exacerbated the general agricultural depression of the 1870s and 1880s; it was felt most heavily in citrus-growing regions of the south and Sicily, and was a further

---

4. Briggs (1978:2–3) and Cinel (1979:83ff.) present evidence that in regions where there was land available to buy there were high rates of emigration, while in regions dominated by latifundia peasants tended not to emigrate and instead organized a variety of strikes and revolts in their efforts to effect political change. For the sequelae of Unification, see Jones 1960:199ff.; Mack Smith 1969:160–62; Cafagna 1973; J. and P. Schneider 1976:120ff.; and Cinel 1979:83ff.

spur to emigration. Finally, the competition of cheap consumer goods from industrialized western Europe undercut the smaller-scale, locally subsistent industries of the south and Sicily, and spurred the emigration of large numbers of newly unemployed artisans.[5]

These emigrants were overwhelmingly young and male, and tended to leave first from north and central and later from south Italy and Sicily, as the combined impact of these economic changes and the availability of information about emigration affected each area. At first the majority left for South America, some actually commuting annually between Argentina or Brazil and Italy in time for harvesting seasons at home and abroad. But at the turn of the century the proportions reversed and the majority, at this point largely migrants from the south and Sicily, came to the United States.[6]

In Italy, migrants' families accumulated their savings and bought transport animals, parcels of land, homes, and small businesses. Modestly prosperous returned *Americani* became a feature of town and village life. In the several years before the outbreak of World War I, migrants' remittances home were so large that they exceeded all income from Italy's already well-developed tourist industry (Mack Smith 1969:242). The Italian state encouraged these remittances and their accumulation in state-sponsored banks: they assured the balance of trade and were "an organic component of the structure of the development process" (Cafagna 1973:325). But that process, given the current economic situation, involved investment in northern industrial development and urban infrastructure. It did not lead to the improvement of agriculture or the quality of life in the south. Some industrial ventures failed, bringing down banks in their train; in one case 400,000 depositors, mostly returnees, lost their savings. Thus the state siphoned off the migrants' capital, accumulated for the purpose of investment in agricultural small-holdings, and doomed to failure their collective economic strategy of small-scale farming. The capital of southerners, the largest group

5. See Jones 1960:163–67,182–86; and Ward 1971:58–71 for American economic development. For its transatlantic effects, see Jones 1960:200; Palmer 1965:70; C., L., and R. Tilly 1975:114; J. and P. Schneider 1976; and Cinel 1979:135ff.

6. See Foerster 1919: chap. 13–16; Palmer 1965:43–46.

of emigrés, was diverted to the north, continuing the tradition of underinvestment that has lasted into the present.[7]

Gramsci observes in the *Prison Notebooks* of the 1930s that in this way the Mezzogiorno (southern Italy) was "reduced to the status of a semicolonial market, a source of savings and taxes," and traces the origin of the mystifying ideology of southern Italian racial inferiority to this period (1971:70–72,92ff.). Here, then, is the source of the train of misperceptions of southern Italians continuing into the present on both sides of the Atlantic. The so-called timeless peasants of the Mezzogiorno lived in an economy deeply pene-trated by developing capitalism even prior to the unification of the country (J. Davis 1979); the economic basis of their lives changed continually as national capitalism developed. And they reacted to these changes with a variety of economic strategies.

For these reasons, for personal reasons (such as avoiding ar-ranged marriages or military service), and because of perceived better economic opportunity, increasing numbers of migrants de-cided to settle permanently in the United States. Sons, brothers, and husbands arranged for—or acquiesced in the intention of—mothers, sisters, wives, and children to join them. The proportion of women migrants increased (Palmer 1965:345–46).

A note on Italian women migrants: as we must alter our concep-tion of the "timeless Italian peasant migrant" in general, so we need to recognize that women migrants, in particular, had backgrounds and skills far different from the cloistered peasant woman ster-eotype. The populations from which emigrants came had artisanal, shopkeeping, and home production (putting-out system) back-grounds as well as agricultural experience. This means that many women migrants had craft skills, entrepreneurial or domestic ser-vice experience, or familiarity with industrial labor (Noether 1978; Gabaccia 1979; M. Cohen 1978). The emigration era spanned more than seventy years—in those several generations the Italian state was formed and large-scale economic changes altered migration cycles and destinations, industry and agriculture, transportation and communication—changes reaching deeply into the lived expe-rience of all Italian women, north and south.

Women's official rates of labor force participation responded to

7. Schacter 1965; Cafagna 1973:292ff.; and Cinel 1979:105–19.

these fluctuations in the larger economy. They first dropped as agriculture became dominated by wage labor and as industry developed and women and child laborers were replaced with men, and then rose with the upturn in economic development after 1901 (C., L., & R. Tilly 1975:114; Cafagna 1973:298). And since migration became so ubiquitous and was, until the latter stages, so largely male, large numbers of women who would later migrate were left unchaperoned, autonomous—and responsible for themselves and their kin—for seasons, years, decades (M. Cohen 1978: chap. 2). Women migrants, then, varied greatly in skill and background, in relative autonomy and in employment history, depending upon their regional and family background and on their time of emigration. Their experiences in the United States, however, like those of their male compatriots, depended more upon what they found here than on what they brought with them.[8]

Italians arriving on the Eastern Seaboard and the industrial Midwest at the turn of the century and the first two decades of the twentieth century found themselves, in company with other southern and eastern European migrants, Catholic and Jewish, at the tail end of an earlier influx of migrants from northwestern Europe: Irish beginning with the Famine of the 1840s, Germans with the upheavals of 1848 and following, Swedes as a result of the agricultural crisis of the 1880s, and others. They thus entered at the bottom of a stratified white industrial work force. There were few opportunities to engage in agriculture. A small number of Italian emigrants joined a handful of planned agricultural colonies. Others attempted to do seasonal agricultural work in the South, such as the Louisiana sugarcane workers studied by Scarpacci (1979), but gave it up as un-

---

8. Yans-McLaughlin, in her research on Italian families in Buffalo (1977), has been the foremost proponent of the perspective that Italian culture involved notions that women belong in the home and must be well chaperoned. Scherini points out that Yans-McLaughlin's population originated from only one Sicilian town (1976:32). Historians Alice Kessler-Harris and Louise Tilly have both criticized Yans-McLaughlin for her assumption that "women are in a sense by-products of their culture" and because she "postulates a separation of cultural traditions from economic and social factors" (Kessler-Harris 1974:446; L. Tilly 1974:452). Finally, historian Miriam Cohen has documented the high labor-force participation rates of Italian women in most East Coast cities. She convincingly argues that Buffalo provided few employment opportunities for women; the local economy, rather than Italian culture, was responsible for Italian women's low employment rates there 1978:74ff.).

profitable when they realized that white Southerners wished to exploit them as they did Blacks.

In the main, then, Italians in the East and Midwest found themselves at the bottom rungs of the primary (mining), secondary (construction, manufacturing), and tertiary (peddling, hairdressing, shoeshine) sectors of the rapidly developing and nationally integrating economy (Foerster 1919: chap. 18). The economic and settlement history of their compatriots in California was strikingly different.

### Italians in California

Although the numbers involved are much smaller, the statistics available on Italians working and settling in California are as inaccurate (and sometimes nonexistent) as those on emigration from Italy. Parts of the 1850 California census were lost in a fire, and enumeration methodology, especially that designed for the foreign-born, was in any event very poor (Palmer 1965:vii, 106).

Added to this are two other factors making the present-day delineation of California Italian-American history difficult: the U.S. Census does not count as "ethnic" any individuals beyond those who are foreign-born (first-generation) or "foreign stock"—those who have at least one foreign-born parent (second-generation). Thus, because of the early settlement of some Italians in California, by 1920 the ancestors of some of my informants had slipped beyond the enumeration net. And while the 1950 Census captured the bulk of my middle-aged informants as second-generation Italian-Americans, it does not reflect the ethnic identity of their third-generation children, now in their twenties and thirties. The second unfortunate factor is that there has been very little work as yet done in California, as there has been in New England and the Midwest, in the tradition of the new social history. Thus there are few secondary sources on ethnic immigration and settlement to provide context for my California Italian-Americans' life histories.

Nevertheless, we can still trace the broad strokes of Italian migration to and settlement in California. This was in the beginning, as we saw in the last chapter, one of the major destinations for Italians in the United States, counting over a quarter of all immigrants in an era when California's population was only 1 percent of the national total. This stream, over time, slowed to a trickle: only 7 to 10 percent of all Italian-Americans now live in California (Tomasi and Engel 1970:27; Lopreato 1970:chap. 2).

The intervening 130 years encompass enormous population growth and economic development. The 1850 population of about 90,000 had shot to 22,294,000 by 1980, and a largely undeveloped, empty region developed first an exporting primary sector (mining, agriculture) and then nationally important manufactures (food processing, aerospace, semiconductors) and a tertiary intrastructure on that base.[9]

The first Italian migration to California coincided with the Gold Rush and the flurry of economic activity that it inspired (literally building San Francisco in two decades). Italians arrived, like others, to mine gold as individuals, but were soon driven from the mines by racist white miners, as were other Mediterraneans, Chinese, Latinos, and Blacks (Palmer 1965:135; Bean 1968:121–22). As increasing numbers of Italians (almost all northerners) arrived in the successive decades to the turn of the century, they worked largely in fishing and agriculture, mining, lumber and railroad work, and as traders in urban areas, especially in San Francisco. There were some early Italian capitalists, like Ghirardelli, Sbarbero, Fontana, and DiGiorgio, but the majority of Italians in California in this period shared the position of these capitalists' field and factory laborers: whether working for American or Italian bourgeois, or for themselves as growers of produce or as fisherfolk, they clustered in the lower rungs of the economic ladder.

These northern Italians, then, were overwhelmingly proletarian: the vision of an early northern community of *prominenti*, of capital-rich, opera-loving bourgeois and petit-bourgeois distinct from southern proletarians that is reflected in Gumina (1978) and others, is seriously mistaken.

There were major distinctions, however, as we have seen, be-

9. See McWilliams 1939; Palmer 1965:358; and Bean, 1968. California was not "empty" prior to white settlement in that it harbored an estimated excess of a quarter of a million Native Americans, who lived successfully at six times the population density of those in the rest of the landmass. This population, however, was so rapidly decimated and immiserated by epidemics, Spanish and then American exploitation, and murder that only about 20,000 Native Americans remained in California by 1900 (Bean 1968:4–11,166–70; Cook 1976:43,199).

[55]

tween these early immigrants in California and those in the Eastern Seaboard and in the Midwest. Italians were originally much more heavily concentrated in California than elsewhere; they formed part of a white proletariat distinct from substantial Asian and Mexican racial minorities, who were absent elsewhere; and they worked in greater numbers in the primary than in the secondary or tertiary sectors. This unique population mix meant that, for example, that Irish/Italian proportion was considerably different in New England than on the West Coast. In 1890, a generation past the peak years of emigration for the Irish but a generation *before* the Italian peak, Irish in Massachusetts swamped the Italian population by 33 to 1; but in California they predominated by only 4 to 1. By 1950, a generation past restrictive immigration legislation, first- and second-generation Irish and Italians were nearly equal in numbers in Boston, but Italians predominated by over 2 to 1 in San Francisco.[10] This difference is suggestive in terms of early access to and creation of ethnic occupational niches and political power for these competing coreligionists.

The significant presence of racial minorities, largely Chinese and Japanese in this period but including Mexicans and Native Americans, clearly acted to displace white racial animosities from white ethnics. The Know-Nothing movement, for example, which agitated strongly against Catholics, mainly confined itself in California to the harassment of Chinese (Bean 1968:174). Gino Angeluzzi recalled his father telling him of the boyhood game in San Francisco, circa 1903, "of tying the long hair of Chinese people in a knot and then running like hell!" [laughs]. Had Gino's father's family gone to Boston or New York, he would not in these early years have found a well-established lower status group upon which to develop feelings of racial superiority.

California, uniquely, offered the early Italians opportunities to work as fisherfolk, orchardists, truck gardeners, and viticulturalists. While it is true that these early workers were exploited by their compatriots, over time agriculture proved to be an important economic strategy for California's Italians. The relative absence of large-scale manufacturing enterprises meant that Italians were not induced, in the numbers that they were on the East Coast and in

10. Calculated from U.S. Census 1890, Compendium, pt. 2, pp. 602, 604; and U.S. Census 1950, Special Reports, pp. 255, 258, 295, 296.

the Midwest, to form a self-reproducing industrial proletariat. This allowed them to fan out into entrepreneurial ventures in numbers beyond their compatriots elsewhere. Decker, for example, finds that Italian males account for three times their expected proportion in the peddling/merchant class in 1880 (1978:172).

Among my informants, four families had one or more family lines that could be traced back to immigrants in the mid-nineteenth century. (Those who arrived before 1869 must, of necessity, have arrived by ship around Cape Horn rather than on the transcontinental rail journey [Scherini 1976:1].) Because of intermarriage among these early families, these histories fan out backward into seven distinct kin lines in the 1850s. The oral history materials are naturally fragmentary, but with them we can trace the representative economic adaptations of these early migrants.

Two of Nancy Ferrucci's great-grandfathers, both from the north, emigrated to California at mid-century. One established himself in fishing. His children worked in a variety of occupations (one was a waiter in San Francisco), but eventually focused on entrepreneurial activities outside of San Francisco, changing the commodities they sold in order to take advantage of changing consumer markets. They invested their profits in land and became affluent over several generations. The other great-grandfather abandoned his family in emigrating to participate in the Gold Rush; his wife and children emigrated later, also became entrepreneurs, and intermarried with the first kin line.

Jarus DiVincenzo's great-grandfather left a southern Italian seaport in the 1830s. After some years on the East Coast, he came to California in the 1850s, took advantage of agricultural wholesaling opportunities, and bought land.

Dorothy DiVincenzo's antecedents, Italian Swiss, settled outside of San Francisco at mid-century, bought land, and became successful farmers, intermarrying with other local farming families from the same region.

Gino Angeluzzi's mother's antecedents arrived in California from Sicily at mid-century. By the turn of the century the family owned property and small businesses.

It is unclear when Joe Longhinotti's mother's antecedents arrived in San Francisco from northern Italy, but it is likely that they were skilled workers there.

[57]

These Italian immigrant family histories fit into the more affluent segment of the overall group economic history described above. This may be due to sampling accident, to the fact that poor relatives are often "shed" from oral family histories, or to the repatriation of less successful early immigrants.

Repatriation rates, as I have noted, were very high. These family histories, and those of informants whose relatives emigrated later, suggest that there were two different patterns of Italian settlement in California, perhaps linked to different economic strategies. The Italy-based pattern seems most common: migrants arrived with little capital (that was left with relatives in Italy) and worked as proletarians in occupations requiring little investment. They sent the bulk of their savings back to Italy and periodically returned home themselves. They did not attempt to acquire American badges of status: proficiency in English, literacy, property, a high-status occupation. The America-based pattern, by contrast, involved liquidating Italian assets (notice how rapidly after immigration the above families acquired property), minimizing Italian ties and economic claims, learning English, investing in property, and attempting to secure high status for oneself and one's children through farming and entrepreneurial activity.

An interesting historical test of the Italy- and America-based strategy hypothesis is the attempt by Andrea Sbarbero in 1881 to organize the Italian-Swiss Colony in Asti as an agricultural cooperative. Sbarbero offered shares to Italians in California, but finding no buyers, abandoned the plan and organized instead a for-profit private firm. Both Sbarbero himself and Cinel (1979) note that Italian immigrants were unlikely to be interested in such an investment, as most intended to return to Italy. But both also go on to stigmatize immigrants as "unwilling to join cooperative ventures" (Sbarbero) and to speculate that "although unemployed, they preferred to live in the city" (Cinel).[11] This gratuitous vilification of those who pursued the Italy-based pattern is common, part of the popular insistence on judging migrants instead of assessing their economic contexts.

It seems likely that these Italian-Americans' antecedents were among the atypical early immigrants who intended to remain in the

11. Foerster 1919:369; Palmer 1965:267–81; and Cinel 1979:305–7.

Birthplaces of informants' antecedents

- ▲ Actual birthplace
- ○ Informant could specify no more than general region from which her/his ancestors emigrated.

No indication is given of concentrations of antecedents in particular towns or regions.

United States. My sample did not include any of those whose antecedents were unskilled laborers but who settled in California; it could *not* include those whose antecedents repatriated.

The second period of immigration to California, from the turn of the century to the cutoff by restrictive legislation in 1924, is the major period of Italian immigration both to the United States and to California, although California received smaller percentages of the total stream of immigrants from 1880 on (Palmer 1965:360). It is also the period during which most of my informants' antecedents arrived in California. As we are now considering fourteen separate and very detailed family histories, I will discuss them generally and follow only a few of them in detail.

Of the fourteen individuals or groups immigrating during this period, ten were from northern and four from southern Italy (or Sicily). This proportion compares fairly well with the California immigration figures for those years and with Cinel's estimate of a 60-40 proportion for the same period in San Francisco (Palmer 1965:365; Cinel 1979:29). (See map for regional origins of all informants.)

Most of these immigrants came straight to California from Italy, but some arrived after a period elsewhere in the United States. Lucia Mornese's mother migrated in 1913 to an Eastern Seaboard city as a northern Italian adolescent to marry her childhood sweetheart. When he died two years later, she moved with her child to San Francisco to live with his kin there. Lucia Mornese's father, meanwhile, had emigrated from a different northern Italian region to New York in the 1910s, where he had worked as a ditchdigger; he then made his way across country to San Francisco.

Candy Lombardo's paternal grandfather emigrated from southern Italy in 1905 and worked at a wide variety of proletarian jobs all over the United States before returning to Italy in 1910. He reemigrated in the 1910s, spent five years in California doing agricultural labor, moved back East, married, and worked with his wife for several years to accumulate capital. They then moved permanently to California in the late 1920s and opened a grocery store.

Joe Cruciano's father was born in the 1910s in New York of southern Italian immigrant parents. As a young adult, Joe recalls that "something happened in New York that my Dad never told me about, but he had to leave town right away. They put him on a train and shipped him off to relatives here."

[60]

Whether they came to California immediately, or after an interval spent elsewhere, these immigrants almost always came in a process of chain migration. One major pattern was that of a young man migrating to an area where kin or friends from the same village or town would lodge him and guarantee him work. He would then, after some years, return to Italy and marry, paying for the passage of his wife (and children) after yet another interval of work in California.

Clelia and Dom Cipolla's, Cetta Longhinotti's, and Tony Ripetto's parents and Gino Angeluzzi's father's parents settled in California in this way. But there were other patterns as well. Angela Caputo's mother defied her parents and emigrated from northern Italy with a women friend in the early 1900s, moving to San Francisco where her brother worked, but not to be under his chaperonage. Joe Longhinotti's father emigrated from northern Italy alone around 1910, lodged with village-mates, and married an American-born woman of the same regional origin as himself. And Joe Cruciano's maternal grandmother emigrated from southern Italy in the 1910s with five children and an intended bride for her son, whom she joined. All the adult women of the family went to work in the local food-processing industry.

The term *chain migration* describes a process, but it does not tell us the context in which that process takes place. In turn-of-the-century San Francisco, local Italian and American bourgeois wishing to inflate the labor market, lower wages, and break unions both used direct advertising, inducing immigration to California from Italy and the cities of the Eastern Seaboard, and urged Italian-Americans, through Italian-language papers, to recruit their kin and friends to the area (Giovinco 1973:chap. 6; Cinel 1979:318–19). The fact that migrants cushion the processes of transition for one another, and that they sometimes seem to move often and erratically, should not blind us to the fact that they must heed the imperatives and restrictions of capital's fluctuating demand for labor in order to live.

These migrants joined kin and friends all over Northern California: in San Francisco, Oakland, and San Jose, in the small towns north and south of San Francisco, and in the farming settlements of the Central Valley. And once settled, the bulk of them moved—often more than once—in the next several decades. Some moves were inadvertent, such as Gino Angeluzzi's father's abandonment

[61]

of San Francisco after the 1906 earthquake and fire, but most were strategic responses to the changing regional economy.

How were these immigrants connected to the California economy? Of the nineteen adults of the 1910s–1930s lineally connected to my informants, twelve worked either directly on farms or in occupations in the agricultural industry. Of those twelve, six worked consistently as farmers or farm laborers, four began as farm laborers or farmers and then moved into other occupations, and two worked consistently in canneries. The other seven were in small business or skilled work and, in two women's cases, spent brief periods in nonagricultural factory labor. Here we run into a statistical bog: the U.S. Census did not give regional ethnic occupational enumerations between 1900 and 1950. Palmer skips this period as well (1965:155). In assessing the fit between my informants' antecedents' occupations and those of Italians in California in general, we must rely for the present on scattered references. Cinel (1979) states that Italian-dominated truck farming was a major California industry by 1870. The 1900 Census indicates that nearly a third of all Italians then in California worked in agriculture; Palmer claims that in South San Francisco alone, in 1908, 1,200 Italians controlled 8,000 acres of truck gardening, Pecorini, in 1909, claimed that half of all California Italians were farmers or farm laborers. The 1920 Census indicates that nearly 4,500 Italians in California then were farm operators—that is, 5 percent of *all* Italians in California in 1920, not all employed adult males; the figure for farm laborers must have been many times higher. And it is clear that a significant proportion of the field, orchard, and cannery laborers employed by Fontana's, DiGiorgio's, Sbarbero's, and others' corporations in the

12. Tomasi and Engel 1970:60; Palmer 1965:126,220; Pecorini 1909; Cinel 1979:304, 325–30; and U.S. Census 1920, monograph 6, p. 109. Cinel claims, however, on the basis of his examination of the government records of his San Francisco sample, that only 4 percent of the San Francisco Italian population (employed, first-generation male immigrants) engaged in farming during this period (1979:193). Even given the likely urban tilt of a purely San Francisco sample, I doubt this figure. It looks particularly odd when we note that the 1950 Census, after thirty years of urbanization, mechanization, and the reduction of the farm population, indicates that 4 percent of foreign-born Italian men over forty-five in the San Francisco-Oakland SMSA were *still* farm operators and that another 2 percent were farm laborers. The percentages are unlikely to have increased over time.

1910s and 1920s were Italian.[12] Italians were also one of the major ethnic groups involved in the Wheatland agricultural laborers' riot in 1913.

These immigrants' economic lives, then, are probably fairly representative of the larger San Francisco Bay Area Italian population of the time. They were agricultural proletarians, cooperative or individual small farmers, small businesspeople, and skilled workers. (Had there been examples of unskilled laborers, the sample would be more representative.) Before following some of these families' economic experiences across time, we must first note a final wave of Italian migrants to California.

These are the Italian-Americans who, with the rest of the U.S. population, moved West from the 1930s on, but especially in the postwar era of the growing aerospace industry (Bean 1968:522–24). There is also the small number of Italians who managed to immigrate, often with the help of kin, after the passage of restrictive legislation in 1924, and especially after the liberalization of the law in 1965. The latter are enumerated in the U.S. Census and comprise some hundreds each year (Scherini 1976:7); the former are not. There was only one direct Italian immigrant in my sample, although my informants had kin and friends who belonged to this category, but five of the families had one or more members who arrived in California in the postwar years after a period—sometimes a lifetime—in another state.

They came, like Al Bertini, James Giovannino's father Michael, and Sam Lombardo, to take advantage of the booming California labor market for professional-managerial class occupations. And they came, like Nick Meraviglia's parents, simply to try out working-class life in a better climate. In all cases they came in a process of chain migration. Al Bertini moved with his wife, child, father, and fictive uncle in response to a job offer—and moved in with his sister and her family. Michael Giovannino and his wife moved for educational opportunity—but they moved to the city where the wife's parents lived. Sam Lombardo arrived in California after military service in the 1960s—and settled near his sister. Nick Meraviglia's father moved during World War II at the behest of his cousin, secured a job in a factory, and sent for his wife and Nick.

Whether they emigrated from northern or southern Italy, these migrants and their antecedents were already accustomed to living

[63]

within a national economy integrated into the world capitalist system. Italians migrated to the United States only after some decades of experience with seasonal, intranational, west European, and South American migration. The evidence suggests that the broad mass of immigrants were following an economic strategy of seasonal, cyclical migration to accumulate capital for investment in land, homes, or businesses in Italy. Throughout the period of emigration, but increasingly as it became clear that involvement in Italian farming was unwise, individuals and families remained in the United States. Sectors of both Italian and U.S. capital profited from this large-scale movement of labor; other sectors perceived it as harmful and tried to minimize it. Italians who settled in California encountered an economy in an earlier stage of industrial development than that of the Midwest–Eastern Seaboard. They worked largely in primary-sector occupations, and had the opportunity to farm. The majority of California's Italians were northerners, but they and the southerners were equally proletarian. Racial minorities were present in California in significant proportions, and were relegated increasingly to the lowest-status occupations. Racism against them probably siphoned off some of the oppression experienced by Italians elsewhere in the United States. Italians in California entered a population mix in which they were *not* perceived to be the lowest status group.

My informants' family life histories fit into this overall historical and statistical picture. (It seems likely, though, that many of the Italian proletarians of the 1880s–1920s were repatriates, and thus that their descendents are not in California today.) Immigrants came in small numbers in the decades of the 1850s, 1860s, and 1870s. The numbers increased in the 1880s, continuing to increase until the restriction of immigration in 1924. Subsequently, Italians migrated to California from the rest of the United States, especially in the postwar years.

Thus an Italian population not fundamentally different from others settled in a region economically and socially very different from the Midwest and the Eastern Seaboard. Differences in their experiences vis-à-vis their coethnics and those of their descendants elsewhere in the United States should be ascribed more to their destinations than to the resources they brought with them.

[64]

## Italian Families, American Families

The living arrangements of my middle-aged informants' families of origin, that is, households of the 1920s–1940s, exemplify what Modell and Harevan (1977) have called the malleable household.[13] Depending upon the material circumstances of immigration, and their adaptation to the changing California economy, individuals lived in nuclear or extended households, boardinghouses, or in groups composed of kin and nonkin. If we consider "family" in Stack's sense—"the smallest, organized, durable network of kin and nonkin who interact daily, providing domestic needs of children and assuring their survival" (1974:31)—we find that families at times extended beyond households. Kin and friend networks varied greatly as well, depending upon demographic circumstances, region of settlement, and economic arrangement. Women's roles also varied and altered over time as these families, like all American families, responded to the developing economy and changing society. In fact, because of the unique agricultural tilt of California's Italian-Americans, and the late development of California's economy, we can discern among these families, and across time, structures similar to the evolution from what Tilly and Scott call the "family economy" through the "family wage economy" to today's "family consumer economy" (1978).

Tilly and Scott coined these terms to describe changes in the relations among women's roles, domestic life, and work life for the broad mass of families over the course of the industrialization of western Europe. The family economy refers to the preindustrial rural agricultural and urban artisanal household which was itself a productive unit, including women, men, and children. The family wage economy characterizes the industrialized working-class household: production and reproduction are split with the rise of the factory system and women's lives are newly punctuated by movements into and out of the industrial labor market. Until the advent of child labor legislation, all family members work for, and pool, wages; there is little economic margin above subsistence. The

13. Modell and Harevan were concerned primarily with the phenomena of boarding and lodging in nineteenth-century American households.

family consumer economy refers to household patterns in the modern era as standards of living rise. Households can support children's or mothers' absence from market labor, and mothers become family-consumption administrators and child-rearing experts.

Tilly and Scott locate these concepts historically, but they also describe the variation in contemporaneous households with different economic adaptations. Family economy and family wage economy households, however, are not in any sense "throwbacks" or "primitive"; all these households intersected with the same capitalist economy.

## Five Families from the 1920s to the Present

From agriculture to aerospace, and now to semiconductor and service industries, California's economy has grown and altered over the course of the lives of those now middle-aged. The increasing population has shifted from rural areas to towns and cities, and urban development has transformed and built over the once agricultural and smaller-scale urban landscape in which these Italian-Americans live. Focusing on specific individuals as they move through successive households enables us to follow them and their kin as they adapt in varying ways and with differing resources to the changing economy.

### Dorothy DiVincenzo

I first met Dorothy and Jarus DiVincenzo when I visited their home one spring evening. We sat and drank wine in the breakfast area of a large and immaculate kitchen, and Jarus, courtly and eager, poured out his family history and local ethnic anecdotes while I scribbled notes with growing incomprehension. Only when I asked about the couple's children did Dorothy say more than a few words. I turned to her and asked about her own family; she quietly wrote out an old-fashioned genealogy so that I could follow her relatives over their century of residence in California.

My next visit was with Dorothy alone on a summer afternoon. In the daylight I could gauge the size and emptiness of the house,

1. Dorothy DiVincenzo: genealogy

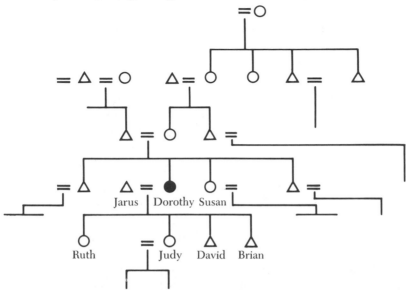

bought for a large family now grown up and away. Dorothy was still reserved in manner, but was unexpectedly clear and stern in her judgments of others—and herself—and was firm about her plans for school and work.

Dorothy DiVincenzo's Italian Swiss family, of which she is a third-generation member, lived in the 1920s and 1930s in two fluctuating, interconnected households.[14] The first, a farm household, consisted of Dorothy's mother's parents, a changing array of relatives, and, periodically, Dorothy and her brothers and sister. The second, in-town household was made up of Dorothy's nuclear family—mother, father, and siblings. A third household of Dorothy's father's father and his second wife was economically but not socially interconnected with the nuclear family household.

14. Given the proliferation of surnames in this work, I refer to women by only their married names throughout, and also designate their families of origin in this way. Family studies tend either to present all evidence namelessly, without distinguishing among various sources (as does Rubin 1976), or to focus on a few people as exemplifying a larger homogeneous pattern (as does Stack 1974). I did not want to follow the first pattern, and could not follow the second (I focus on variety, not homogeneity); thus I have compromised on the surname issue in order to reduce the burden on the reader's memory.

Dorothy and her siblings lived periodically with their mother's mother to help with farm work and—when they were very young—to be looked after. Their parents' house was small, and their mother worked outside the home during the day. Over the years, Dorothy's grandmother's own mother, her bachelor or widowed brothers, and their children lived on the farm, working when they were able and cared for when they were not.

These Italian-Americans, already at least one generation removed from the immigrant experience and English-speaking, were embedded in a three-generation, intraregional network in which many friends, as a result of intermarriage, counted as kin as well. Isolated on their remote farms from the larger society, and indeed from one another, they met at church and in periodic ethnically organized social gatherings.

The family as a whole straddled the family economy and family wage economy: Dorothy's grandmother's household was economically self-sufficient; her parents' household relied on the mother's wage packet and the father's small business profits.

These household, kin, and network patterns are clearly related to the material circumstances of immigration and economic adaptation. Dorothy's antecedents emigrated early, with capital, intending to settle in California. They prospered in farming because of the enormous San Francisco population growth of the latter half of the nineteenth century and the concomitant increased consumer demand, and they prospered in small business, catering to the increased needs of farming families. Well established, these farms and businesses survived the Depression intact. Women worked both at farm and household tasks, and in small businesses outside the home. The malleable household moved children where their labor could be used, and where their care was less of a burden. Because several generations now lived in the area and because of rural isolation, coethnic kin and friends formed a large, intermarrying regionally homogeneous network.

Dorothy DiVincenzo's nuclear family moved in the late 1930s. Her father, wishing to educate his children for further nonfarm mobility, had liquidated his business interests and invested in a business partnership in the South Bay. The family moved in shifts, Dorothy and her brother boarding first with other Italian families until their parents and younger sibs joined them. Dorothy's mother worked at the store, but when her husband sold it and started a different business, she became involved in the parochial school Mothers' Club. She hired a cleaning woman. The household had moved into the family consumer economy pattern.

Dorothy's grandmother sold her farm in the mid-1940s and moved in with a cousin and his family who had rented a house she owned. Until her death she divided her time between this home and that of Dorothy's parents.

Dorothy and her sibs went to the local college and lived at home until they married. Dorothy met Jarus DiVincenzo, also a third-generation, college-educated Italian-American (but of Sicilian origin) whose family was in business, and married him in the mid-1940s. Dorothy's brothers went to work for her father; her sister worked for an advanced degree. Dorothy became a housewife, and had four children in the following decade and a half. She and her husband purchased a home, and then a more expensive home. Their children went to parochial schools and then to college.

During this period the family's social network had two major components: nearby kin, and the parents of the children's Catholic school friends. Among kin, the family socialized most often with Dorothy's parents and her sibs (especially her sister) and their children. Dorothy's grandmother, with whom she remained close, often cared for her children. Until the family moved into its second home, which was farther away, Dorothy's father stopped by daily on his way to work.

Jarus DiVincenzo, during this period, was embedded in an acquaintanceship network of customers, coethnic businesspeople, and coethnic professionals. He participated in the partially overlapping network that his wife created through her Mothers' Club and charity activities, but his base was at work.

Dorothy's parents retired; they had considerable wealth, and status and power among their kin. They built a vacation home for the use of the relatives. Jarus, in his early fifties, retired as well, living off the income from his property.

### Angela Caputo

I was gloomily emerging from Angela Caputo's San Francisco apartment house one afternoon, wondering how we had managed

2. Angela Caputo: genealogy

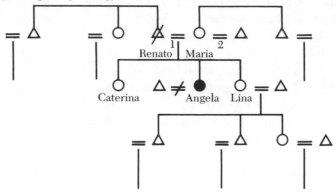

to confuse the time of our first appointment, when I found her struggling up the stairs clutching two overfilled grocery bags. She quickly took stock of the situation and, dumping one bag in my arms, shooed me back up the steps and into her apartment. She settled me at the table in the tiny kitchen with a cup of tea and, chatting about the date mixup and the dinner party she was giving that evening (tossed salad, stuffed zucchini, pesto), briskly put away the groceries and fed the cats prowling around her feet. We moved into the living room, which was formal and elegant, with silver and china pieces on tables and a breakfront of dark wood. Angela assumed an immediate intimacy, and answered all my questions readily and at length.

In contrast to Dorothy DiVincenzo, Angela Caputo lived, with her sisters Caterina and Lina, in a strictly nuclear household throughout the 1920s and 1930s. Her mother had emigrated to San Francisco without capital, as we have seen, around 1910. Learning English rapidly, she worked at a variety of nonfactory jobs: as a cook, a housekeeper, and for a short period as a seamstress in a small shop. Working first for wealthy coethnics from her region, she soon switched to Anglo employers to gain higher wages and less exploitative working conditions. Angela's father had emigrated earlier, from the same region of northern Italy, and had found skilled work in San Francisco after working in the mines. (It is likely that both young people sent money to Italy.) After the couple married, Angela's father strained the ties with Angela's mother's kin and friends. Family social life then revolved around his local farm and peddling kin across the bay. In order to support the famil, Angela's mother returned to work whenever she could secure adequate child care (no nearby kin were available). She established warm patron-client relationships with a succession of Anglo employers.

Angela's father invested his small savings in Transamerica stock (the holding company of the Bank of America) and became comparatively wealthy as the stock price rose in the 1920s. The entire family then returned to Italy and lived on this capital. When the stock price dropped after the crash of 1929, the family, suddenly impoverished, returned to San Francisco and both parents went back to work. Angela's father died, Angela's sister Caterina went to work, and Angela's mother's kin provided their lodging. Because Angela's mother cut ties to her husband's kin after his death, and because of the dislocations of their financial rise and fall, the household existed apart from its North Beach environment throughout the 1930s. The exception to this disconnection was the network of Italian-American school friends that Angela and her sisters built up. Over time, Angela's mother expanded her coethnic social network through these children.

Late, solitary emigration, urban settlement, and lack of capital determined some aspects of this family's household and economic arrangements. Other aspects were due to the dislike husband and wife felt for each other's resident kin. The social dislocation resulting from sudden wealth and equally sudden poverty took the household from the family wage economy to the family consumer economy and back again. Angela's mother found herself, through the fluctuations of American capitalism, elevated from a "breadgiver"—in Ryan's (1979) phrase—a working-class woman whose market labor was essential to the survival of her family, to a leisured bourgeois in Italy, and back to the breadgiver role, within a few years. Responsible for the family's self-presentation and unable to bridge the contradictions between present and past, she limited the audience for that self-presentation. Angela recalls that there was always a strong feeling that "our family honor had been impugned."

Angela Caputo's elder sister, Caterina, took on the major burden of supporting the family at the start of the 1940s. Angela's mother

[71]

retired and kept house while each daughter went to work full-time as she graduated from high school. When Angela was well established at a clerical job (handing her mother her paycheck), and the younger sister Lina had married and moved out, Caterina enlisted in the Women's Army Corps and spent the rest of the war years abroad. She sent home money to support her mother. After the war, when Lina and her husband had settled in San Francisco and he had taken over his father's small business, Angela applied to work for the federal government abroad. After some years, she returned home, but soon married a non-Italian and moved out of state. Caterina moved up the job ladder with her company, taking a management position. She bought a home in a suburb. Their mother remarried to an Italian man, and they bought a home in the suburbs as well. Lina by now had several children, and has remained a housewife.

Angela and her husband settled in San Francisco. Caterina and Lina's husband tried to assist Angela's husband, but his business ventures failed and the couple again moved out of state. They separated; Angela returned to San Francisco and moved in with Caterina until she could support herself.

Meanwhile, their mother's second husband died, leaving her an inheritance. She moved into an apartment close to Lina and her family, and ate with them every day. Lina and her husband added onto their house, and the mother moved in with them. After some years she became frail, and the sisters persuaded her to move into a nursing home.

During this period Angela and her sisters, despite their movements, centered their social lives on one another and on their mother. They wrote one another consistently and sent gifts when they lived apart. Angela and Caterina made friends through travel and work, but focused their social energies on their immediate kin network, visiting their mother together every Sunday.

Through the sisters' friends, their mother was drawn into a co-ethnic network. Her own kin died but she restored the link with her first husband's kin. She became very close to Lina's husband's mother.

The sisters' economic fortunes differed. Angela joined the clerical working class through her divorce, while Lina took on the affluence of her husband's family (her husband recently retired to live off the income from his property). Caterina invested in property and became well-off. All three sisters visited often with Lina's children, most of whom did not attend college but found well-paying corporate sales positions. One son took over the family business.

Angela's kin group, then, rose in economic position as the California economy expanded in the war and postwar eras. Angela and Lina linked their economic fortunes to their husbands'; one prospered, the other did not. Caterina never married, spending her energies on work and investing in property. The next generation has been similarly economically successful and, like Angela's generation, experienced this success outside of the educational mobility ladder.

### Lucia Mornese

I first met Lucia Mornese when she opened the door to her stucco San Francisco row house. I followed her up the carpeted stairs and into a small, heavily furnished living room. As I was setting up the tape recorder, I remarked that the steering wheel of my old car had displayed a new and alarming tendency to vibrate on the drive over. She shook her head at me, admonishing: "Young people are so fearless, they think nothing's ever going to happen. If you aren't careful, you'll never get your Ph.D." After I explained my project, she settled back into her chair and launched immediately into her life history. She talked easily, and willingly furnished dates and details. Later in the afternoon her mother came slowly into the room and sat down, silent, in a corner. Just before I left, Lucia's husband Salvatore arrived home early from work. He said he wasn't feeling well, subsided into an armchair, and listened with interest to the continuing interview. Lucia fussed at him to go to bed. When he lit a cigarette, she jumped up and came back with a small machine designed to vacuum the smoke from the air. It seemed to do little more than make a loud whirring noise. When I later transcribed the interview tape, it sounded as if a small plane had been in the room.

On a later visit I talked with Salvatore alone. Lucia had gone on a trip with her Italian-American women's group. Salvatore talked at length about his childhood, the war, and his work experiences. But

[73]

3. Lucia Mornese: genealogy

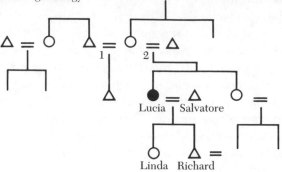

Lucia Salvatore

Linda Richard

he also wanted to know about my own work, and to engage me in debates about economic development and affirmative action. Late in the visit, we heard a noise in the kitchen; it was his daughter Linda bringing over the cat from her nearby apartment. He called to her to come in and meet me, but she shouted back that her hair was in curlers, and beat a swift retreat.

Lucia Mornese's family, like Angela Caputo's, was also composed of solitary, late-arriving emigrants who settled in San Francisco and lived in a nuclear household; but it had otherwise a very different history. As I have already noted, Lucia's mother arrived in San Francisco in the 1910s, a widow with a small child, to live with her husband's kin. She went to work in a factory, and her sister-in-law cared for her child during the day. She met and married Lucia's father, who was boarding with a coethnic family, and they set up a household, having Lucia and another child in the next five years. Wishing to escape the pollution of the factory, at Lucia's mother's urging they leased a small store from a friend, and worked in it together. The oldest child was boarded periodically with a farm family, at one point for two years, and Lucia and her younger sister were cared for by a non-Italian woman in her home for some years until Lucia herself was old enough to do most of the child care. From the late 1920s until the late 1930s, Lucia and her parents ran the store together, working in shifts. Lucia's brother, often away, found employment and left home early; her younger sister was seriously ill in the early 1930s, and convalescent for several years. At this point Lucia's parents did not remove her from school, but she stayed at home so often to nurse her sister and to spell her mother at her store shifts that her education was permanently disrupted.

The family's social network had many components. The original ties with Lucia's mother's first husband's kin continued, but because the parents worked long hours and took few holidays, Lucia often spent her holidays alone with these kin. Then there were the large numbers of customers, Italian and non-Italian, who frequented the store.

There were also, in the family's network, the farm families with whom the children had boarded, and especially the family with whom Lucia's sister had lived for some years. When she had a relapse of her illness, the mother of this family immediately came to help nurse her: "Well it was quite a deal for her to come. First they had to come down the mountain in this old model T, then she had to get on the train. Then she had to get on a boat. I saw her coming up the street—I was so surprised to see her. She sat there all night holding her hand and telling her that the chickens were waiting for her—and the dog was going to take her to the farm—and she pulled her through."

Finally, while Lucia's father had cut ties with his kin in emigrating, Lucia's mother kept up contact with her family in Italy (and would have returned to them when her husband died, but was prevented by the onset of World War I).

Because they began a small business with little capital, and because they had been running it only a few years when the Depression struck, Lucia Mornese's family could not bridge the gap to the family consumer economy. All able family members worked throughout the 1930s, and Lucia's mother had little time to spare for managing the family's self-presentation.

The 1940s greatly altered the structure and economy of the Mornese household. Lucia took an office job, and then qualified for a better-paying government clerical job. She persuaded her parents to sell out their business. Her mother bought an apartment building with proceeds from the sale and savings, and retired from market labor. Her father at first tried another business venture; when that failed, he went to work in the same sort of business he had operated. Lucia's older brother enlisted in the armed forces and married; the family disapproved of his wife, and further relations were strained. Lucia's sister took a technical training course, found a job, and remained at home, turning over her paycheck to her mother.

Late in the war, Lucia was transferred to Italy. There she met and married an Italian national of bourgeois background. Salvatore Mornese was anxious to live in the United States; although he knew that his economic fortunes would decline, he wished to leave an overbearing father and the disorganization of postwar Italy.

The couple returned to San Francisco and moved into one of the apartments owned by Lucia's mother. Lucia had Linda, and then went back to work, her parents providing child care. Salvatore at first could only find work as a ditchdigger: "My best friend, among the crew, he was a colored fellow. . . . The others, white, they laughed at me. . . . I wasn't very strong and he gave me a hand."

Salvatore learned English, and began to work in a series of clerical jobs. He took technical courses and was offered a better-paying position with a branch of a large firm that involved moving to the periphery of the Bay Area. He moved in advance of his family, boarding with the daughter of the same farming family that had cared for Lucia and her brother and sister in the 1920s and 1930s. The couple bought a house in a new subdivision filled with ex-servicemen who had settled in California during the war and had returned with their families to settle there. Lucia had a second child. At first she was lonely, not knowing how to drive and missing her kin and friends in San Francisco; after a few years she had learned to drive and made women friends within the subdivision. Her parents and her sister (who had married) and her new family visited often, staying for weekends in the cramped quarters of the tiny house.

After four years, Salvatore was transferred by his firm to southern California. The family of four moved again and spent several years isolated from kin and making few new friends. Lucia was bothered by the weather and persuaded Salvatore to quit his job and return to San Francisco. They bought a house in a section of the city with a concentration of Italian-Americans and enrolled their children in parochial schools. Salvatore found a job with a different firm and Lucia went back to work as well.

While Lucia and Salvatore were in Southern California, Lucia's mother, feeling isolated in San Francisco, sold her and her husband's apartment building and bought a small house near the sister and her family across the bay. When Lucia and her family returned to San Francisco, they then spent every weekend commuting to visit the parents and sister.

As the 1960s progressed there were further changes in household structure and economy for Lucia's family. Her father died, and her mother moved in with the family; the house was so small that the living room became the mother's bedroom. The family stopped entertaining. Linda went to junior college but soon quit and went to work, paying room and board to her parents. Her brother did the same a few years later. Lucia became very ill and was forced to retire and to apply for disability payments. Finally, Salvatore was fired by his firm a few months before he would have qualified for its pension program. With no legal recourse, in late middle age, he took another job and a substantial cut in salary.

After seven years at home past high school, Linda moved into an apartment with a friend—a few doors away. Her brother continued to live at home until he married in the late 1970s.

The Morneses' move into the family consumer economy was qualified by Salvatore's language handicap, and later by illness and corporate venality. The children's wages and mother's board payments allowed the family to retain its home, but the couple had experienced considerable immiseration by the late 1970s. Unlike the DiVincenzos and Angela Caputo's sisters, the Morneses were unable to accumulate sufficient wealth (or pension security) during their peak working years to weather the inevitable slowing down of middle age and the recession of the late 1970s.

The family's social network, as we have seen, was most affected by their moves away from San Francisco. However, through constant visiting, ties among parents and children and between sibs were kept strong. When the family returned to San Francisco, they entered a social network constituted through the children's school ties and augmented by social visits with some of Lucia's former school friends. These contacts were restricted after the arrival of Lucia's mother and a period of relative isolation followed. After the children had grown, and after Lucia retired from work, the family entered a new network pattern. There were two major components. Linda's roommate and her brother's new wife provided access for Lucia and Salvatore to new friends. Lucia began attending Mass with Linda's (non-Italian) roommate. The couple met their

[77]

son's wife's (non-Italian) kin and began to socialize with them. The second component was Lucia's new membership in an ethnic women's organization. Within that group she began to reconstitute her childhood, business-related Italian network. She also added Italian-American women from her neighborhood parochial school network by sponsoring them for membership. All of these social contacts, however, took place outside the home because of the constant presence and capricious behavior of Lucia's mother. The mother did, however, maintain contact with her kin in Italy. Now that she can no longer see to write, Lucia has taken over responsibility for these ties. At the time of my research the Morneses were visited by the affluent descendent of one of these relatives. He promised to provide for them during a prospective trip to Italy.

Lucia and Salvatore's children, unlike those of the DiVincenzos and Lina Caputo's, could receive neither higher education nor job sponsorship from their parents. Linda has a high clerical post in a large firm, and hopes to improve her position through further training. Her brother married a woman just finishing professional training, and so shares her secure financial status although he has only held temporary blue-collar jobs.

### Cetta Longhinotti

When I first drove into the Longhinotti neighborhood it seemed similar to the DiVincenzos'—newer looking, ranch-style houses with well-gardened front yards. But in fact the yards and homes were much smaller. Two bedrooms and a bath, instead of four bedrooms and two baths, were the norm. Joe and Cetta were on the lookout for me, gave me a gracious welcome, and ushered me into a living room decorated in formal style, with china ornaments on a shelf. That evening was spent again discussing the "old Italian community" and Joe's experiences—but Cetta seemed more relaxed in her own home, and spoke up when her children were discussed. Greg, their youngest child, dropped by during my visit.

Two weeks later I came to see Cetta alone. Joe excused himself to watch a baseball game in the bedroom. Cetta was nervous about the tape recorder, but soon forgot it and launched into a very personal account of childhood poverty and adult disappointment.

4. Cetta Longhinotti: genealogy

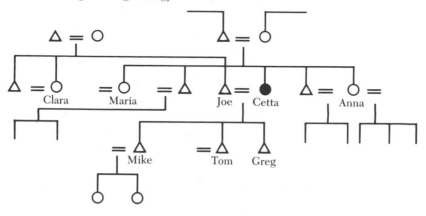

Cetta Longhinotti's father, a northern Italian, began working seasonally in the countries of western Europe as a young adolescent in the early years of this century. His father had died and the burden of support for his mother and younger siblings had fallen upon him. After some years, he began migrating periodically to the United States. He married Cetta's mother during an interim in Italy. She lived with his family until she migrated permanently in the early 1920s with her first child, Maria, to join him in an agricultural company town near San Francisco. Cetta's father taught Cetta's mother to cook, as she had done only farm labor in her own family in Italy. She then kept a boardinghouse for the many single Italian male workers in the town's processing plant. Cetta's father, still sending money home to his Italian family, managed to accumulate sufficient capital through the boardinghouse and through factory work to open a small business with a partner. The partnership dissolved—Cetta's father felt that he was being cheated—and the family, now with two children, bought an orchard in the Central Valley in partnership with another family of the same regional background. Cetta's mother worked in the orchard and smokehouse, the farm prospered, and the family, now with three children, was enabled to begin buying their own farm. The older children went to school and worked on the farm after school and during the summers. Cetta's mother, isolated on the farm, learned English slowly, and Cetta's father did the family's shopping in town and at the local *cooperativa*.

[79]

When the Depression struck, demand for farm produce dropped so sharply that Cetta's father could not make his loan payments. The bank foreclosed, and the family, now with four children, was forced to move into housing provided by charity. Cetta's father pulled Maria, the oldest child, out of school and put her to work in a store in a neighboring town. The family grew their own food, Cetta's father worked at temporary jobs, and the two older children found after-school occupations. Only at this point did Cetta's father end his remittances to Italy. After some years, he was injured while working on a construction job. The family then was forced to survive on the older children's wages, and on the seasonal field labor in which the mother and all the children, even the smallest, participated. The youngest child, Anna, who was then a toddler, remembers that she was given the job of carrying the water jug to her mother and siblings as they worked in the orchards, vineyards, and cotton fields.

Because Cetta's father and mother each migrated as single sibs, because they moved often, and because of the isolation imposed by farming life and later by poverty, the family's social network was never large. Cetta's mother was inhibited by her lack of English. The family's poverty, like that of the Caputos, kept it distant from the other Italian families in the area. Cetta was close to her godmother and her daughter, however, and this tie became more important as the years passed. The entire family also established patron-client links with their Anglo employers. The daughters were given their meals in the homes where they did housework and childcare, and these Anglo families later gave them wedding presents. Later, Cetta's father was offered a janitorial job through the intervention of the owners of the building site where he was injured.

Cetta Longhinotti's family, then, like Angela Caputo's, suffered both financial reverses and the loss of the male breadwinner's contributions during the Depression. Angela's mother, however, had a history of waged employment to which she could return. Cetta's mother, involved in the family economy pattern at the point when disaster struck, and isolated by language, returned with her children to field labor.

The family's fortunes improved during the war years. Cetta's father found a steady custodial job. The family grew most of their own food, and Cetta's father peddled the surplus, increasing the family's income. Cetta graduated from high school and could not find work in the farming town, so she moved to San Francisco to live with her godmother and her daughter and found a clerical job there. Her younger sister Anna lived with her during the summers, earning enough money in low-level clerical jobs to pay for her own clothing, schoolbooks, and medical bills. Maria had married out, one brother enlisted in the army, and the other was still living at home and working after school.

Through her godmother's daughter, Cetta entered a network of young San Francisco Italian-Americans. When her brother was demobilized, he came to live with her and expanded this network further. North Beach provided a lively setting for evenings spent at Italian restaurants, going to films, and attending Italian-American-sponsored dances. In this way Cetta met Joe Longhinotti, who was stationed nearby. They married, Joe was demobilized, and they settled in San Francisco. Cetta continued her clerical job and Joe entered GI Bill-sponsored training. When Cetta became pregnant, she quit her job. Joe went into partnership with Cetta's godmother's daughter's new husband, who was starting a bakery in a small town outside of San Francisco, an old food-processing firm's "company town." Cetta and Joe, buying a small home on the GI Bill, moved just before their first child was born. Meanwhile Anna, after living with Cetta and Joe for a year, also married an Italian-American. She became pregnant, and quit her clerical job. Anna and her husband remained in San Francisco, where he had a lower-management position in a firm. Cetta's parents periodically packed crates with produce and homemade goods and sent them by train to Cetta and Anna.

Cetta and Joe lived almost a decade in this small town. Cetta had two more children. She sent them to the local parochial school, and made friends with several Italian-American mothers of their schoolmates. She also remained close to her godmother's daughter—the partnership between the husbands facilitated frequent contact. Her neighborhood, too, was heavily Italian-American. Cetta kept in close contact with her sibs—especially Anna, on whom she relied for support and child care during her confinements. She periodically visited her parents in the Central Valley: "I'd pile the kids in the station wagon and Joe would have to fare for himself." All the

[81]

siblings met on holidays. Anna recalled that "one Thanksgiving we *all* converged on Cetta. We were laughing hysterically, pounding on the door. Joe pretended that he wouldn't let us in." Joe, like Jarus DiVincenzo, engaged in a large Italian-American network through his retail business. His status in that network, though, reflecting his lesser economic resources, was much lower.

As the town increased in population, supermarket chains began moving in and small food stores lost business. Joe and his partner decided to cut their losses and move to a more remote small town northeast of San Francisco. "We left that town with Safeway on our tail." Cetta and Joe bought a much smaller house—the three boys slept in one bedroom—and Joe and his partner opened a new store. But his partner, having more capital, also invested in real estate. Cetta and Joe met some Italian-American families through the local Catholic church, and Cetta remained close to her godmother's daughter—"She was like a sister to me." But the next five years were lonely, since they could not afford to phone or visit with kin, and the family was not in the habit of writing letters. "We had our first Christmas without my parents there."

Over this period the partners once again experienced super-market competition and decided to sell out. But Joe's partner had profited from his land investments, and there was difficulty over the division of the proceeds of the sale, as their contract with one another had only been verbal. Joe and Cetta moved to the East Bay, where Joe had grown up, and Joe tried to go into business on his own. When that venture failed, fearing loss of the larger home they had begun to buy, Joe went to work for a large bakery as a union baker. In order to buy furniture for the new home, Cetta had gone to work as a clerk in a large department store. After a few years Joe decided to sell their house and buy a smaller one, and Cetta remained at work of necessity since Joe's income had been cut significantly.

The children had by now all graduated from high school. The eldest, Mike, gained a foothold in a skilled trade, married a non-Italian, and left home in the early 1970s. He and his wife had two children, and she stayed at home with them. The middle child, Tom, moved out to do skilled work, but lost his job and moved home again. He found another and moved out again after a year. The youngest, Greg, began working for a large firm part-time as a high school student. When he graduated, he began working full-time and accepted unpleasant shifts and overtime work in order to rise to a managerial position. He continued to live at home until the late 1970s, paying no board and saving his salary. Then, with his parents' encouragement, he bought and moved into a house a few miles away.

During this period both Cetta's and Joe's fathers died. The widows sold their homes and began to live with their children, moving from one child to another. Cetta's mother lived with Cetta and Joe for six months, but she mainly stayed with her eldest daughter, by then a widow, who still lived in the same Central Valley town. When she became frail, the children decided to place her in a convalescent home (paid for by MediCal). The eldest daughter continued to visit her daily. Joe's mother, however, stayed off and on with Cetta and Joe for a period of years. This was an extremely difficult period for Cetta, when "things kinda got a little hairy":

> I never got along with her—she didn't hear well—and for some reason my voice just didn't carry with her [looks pained]. . . . I put her in the bedroom and slept on the living room floor. . . . This was when Greg was working at night, and she would wander around at night. . . . I told Joe to keep her in the bedroom so I could get some sleep. . . . The routine was this: Greg went to work around midnight and I cooked dinner for him just before he left. Then I'd clean up and it would be 1 A.M. before I got to bed. I got up at seven to go to work.

After some years when, as Joe's sister Clara said, "She sort of lost her little mind," her children also placed Joe's mother in a convalescent home.

Like the Morneses, but for different reasons, the Longhinottis experienced immiseration from postwar economic stability over the 1960s and 1970s. While Salvatore Mornese sought security in working for a large firm, and was betrayed and barred from his pension, Joe Longhinotti took entrepreneurial risks, and was defeated by lack of capital and corporate monopolization of his chosen retail industry. Lucia Mornese worked in order to add to her husband's language-handicapped income, and then retired after an illness. Cetta Longhinotti returned to work in middle age to enhance her family consumer economy, after more than fifteen years out of the job market. After her husband's business failure, she remained at

[83]

work simply to retain a lowered standard of living. But unlike the Morneses, the Longhinottis refused to ask for board from their adult children, and received no money for lodging their much poorer mothers.

Like the Morneses', the Longhinottis' social network was most affected by their repeated moves. Cetta more than once expressed to me her distress at being far from kin and moving away from friends. After they moved to the East Bay, although they were once again near kin and Joe's childhood friends, their contacts were restricted by Cetta's work and, like the Morneses, by the requisition of the living room for lodging aged mothers. Overwhelmed by work and by all her home responsibilities, Cetta never became friendly with her neighbors. "Other than to say hello I don't know a soul." During the two years I visited Cetta, her mother's condition worsened and she began to drive to the Central Valley to be with her every weekend. She gave up all pretension to a social life, seeing only her children and grandchildren and visiting with her sister Anna only by telephone.

At the beginning of her work career, Cetta was friendly with a group of women co-workers and exchanged gifts with them. By the late 1970s, however, these women had left her office. She did not make friends with their successors, some of whom were Black or Asian.

Joe Longhinotti's social network contracted with Cetta's. He belongs to an ethnic club but goes there seldom now, because "when you get up in age, when you come home you relax, and . . . [laughs]." He likes to attend ball games with friends, but "*she* doesn't like it, so I have to close my eyes sometimes." Joe is very close to his younger sister Clara: "I guess I used to play with her . . . even when she was born, what the heck, I brought her oranges. How in the hell she'd know I was bringin her those oranges?" He drops by Clara's house often, but Cetta and she are not friendly, so the two couples seldom meet.

### Gino Angeluzzi

The Angeluzzis' neighborhood was much like the DiVincenzos'— large ranch-style houses, big lots, tree-lined streets. The Angeluzzi

home, however, differed from the DiVincenzos', and from many in
its own neighborhood. It had an air of shabby cheerfulness, and its
yard was a mass of luxuriant growth. An obviously broken-down
Volkswagen bug stood at the curb. Gino Angeluzzi answered my
knock and led me to the living room in which decoration had been
overrun by the marks of family life—a television propped on a chair
for comfortable viewing, schoolbooks and magazines scattered on
the floor, battered upholstery. As Gino and I talked that afternoon,
several of his adult children and the family dog drifted in and out of
the room. A parrot, shut up in the garage, squawked repeatedly.

Gino's wife Teresa came home from work, and invited me into
the kitchen for a cup of coffee. Lucille and Edith, their daughters,
made the coffee, served it to us, and listened in on our conversation. Teresa and I riffled through a women's magazine together,
and settled on a article on inexpensive country-style decorating.
We jeered at its hypocrisy in filling the photographed rooms with
antique baskets and quilts. Teresa made an appointment with me
for an interview alone, and kissed me goodbye at the door.

Gino Angeluzzi's father arrived in San Francisco as a child at the
turn of the century. He and his sibs traveled from Sicily with their
mother to join their father and older brother, who had menial jobs
in the produce industry. Gino's father and his younger brother sold
matches on the streets. After the 1906 earthquake and fire the
family split up. Gino's father's parents and sisters remained in San

5. Gino Angeluzzi: genealogy

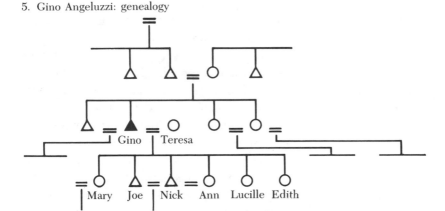

Francisco, and Gino's father and brother moved to join some Sicilians from their region who were living in the East Bay. The two brothers leased land and began to farm.

Gino's mother was born in the East Bay, the youngest child of a family with landholdings and already established in small businesses. Her mother died when she was still young. Her father remarried, but died soon after, and she found herself disinherited. An older brother supported her for a period, and she then went into low-paid wage labor.

The couple married in 1918 and worked, with Gino's mother's kin, on a large parcel of farmland which they leased as partners. Other, temporary farming arrangements followed, in which they worked alone or with kin on either side, coresiding with other families who worked the land with them. Gino's father lost farm property once through the bankruptcy of a growers' organization with which he had a contract. By the mid-1920s the couple had three children and enough capital to lease a large farm in the Central Valley. The children were put to work as soon as they were able, feeding farm animals and candling eggs. But there was need for more labor, so "my Dad picked up a hitchhiker and offered him a job. Then when he got home we found out he hadn't eaten for three days. He stayed with us and became almost like a big brother. He was Irish."

The family (including the Irish farm laborer) returned to the East Bay at Gino's mother's behest, to escape the climate. They were almost immediately impoverished by their new vulnerability as the economic dislocation of the Depression set in. Gino's father went to work with his brother, growing and selling fruit. (The father and the Irish laborer had an argument; the laborer moved out.) The family moved into a shack on the brother's property. But the brother died and his property was repossessed. Gino's mother went to work in the local cannery, his father began peddling, and all the children (there were now four) found menial after-school and summer jobs. Gino recalls that "things got real bad during the Depression—there were times where it was mustard greens and that was *it*."

As soon as they could, Gino and his older brother lied about their ages and took better-paying summer jobs in the local canneries. By the mid-1930s, the family was bringing in enough income so that Gino could afford to begin college. He wished to become a doctor and his entire family's economic effort was bent to the task of supporting him through his training. All his siblings went to work after high school, living at home and turning over their paychecks to Gino's mother.

The family, then, over the 1920s and 1930s, straddled the patterns of family economy and family wage economy. When the family lost its access to land, wage labor in the canneries was available to Gino's mother. Her children were old enough not to require child care and she was able to work from then on without interruption.

The family's social network changed over time. Gino's father seldom saw his parents and sisters after he and his brother moved to the East Bay. There they entered a network of Sicilians originating in the same region. Gino's father met his wife through this network, and the couple remained within it until they moved to the Central Valley, where they became isolated from others by distance and by the constant necessity of farm labor. When the family moved back to the East Bay, they reentered the Sicialian network, but like the Caputos and Longhinottis, they minimized these ties for a time because of their poverty. "We didn't mingle too much in those days."

The family remained by choice in the family wage economy pattern throughout the 1940s as all members bent their economic energies to assist Gino through college and medical school. In the mid-1940s, increased wartime demands for produce enabled Gino's parents to lease land and return to farming. When Gino went to college near San Francisco to finish his bachelor's degree, his mother activated old kin networks and found him cheap lodging with her brother's daughter's family. Gino worked part-time during the school term and full-time in the cannery during the summers, handing over his paycheck to his mother. His first year he managed to collect unemployment for nine months "until they closed the loophole."

Gino was accepted in a Catholic-connected medical school on the Eastern Seaboard. "I had fifty dollars for the deposit, but my mother said 'Trust in God.'. . . . Later I found out that my Dad sold his truck and my mother sold the house to help me."

While in medical school, Gino worked as a medic in a factory, and on the "graveyard shift" (overnight) in a convalescent home. In his third year he fell ill and his sister took the train East to nurse him.

Gino's non-Italian roommate was a year ahead of him in the

[87]

medical school program. His sister, Teresa, came to his graduation; she and Gino met, and they were engaged within a week. She moved to be near him and went to work as a nurse. They married, Gino graduated, and they took the train, filled with troops, back to California. Teresa was by this time pregnant: "We sat on our suit-cases in the aisle all the way to Oakland! Oh God was I nauseated!" (laughs).

The couple lived at first with Gino's parents (two of his siblings were by now married and living in the area). Gino then started his internship in a hospital two hundred miles away. Teresa worked as a nurse until late in her pregnancy. The close contact with and support from Gino's family continued. Teresa said of one of Gino's sisters: "She *gave* us a car! We used it for two years. She said we needed it worse than she did."

Gino finished his internship and the family of three moved back to the East Bay to open practice. At first they rented a house; after two years they managed to buy one; and after a decade they could afford to move to the affluent suburb where they still live. Teresa had five more children over a fifteen-year period. She returned to work after Gino became ill in the early 1970s. All of the children have had at least some college education. Several of them are pro-fessionals or married to professionals. They all live within a few hours' drive, and most see their parents more than once a week.

Gino's sisters married men—one Italian, one not—who were modestly economically successful as well. Neither woman worked outside the home after her first pregnancy. Gino's parents stopped leasing land as they became older, but Gino's mother continued to work seasonally in the local cannery, and Gino's father worked with Gino's brother in his business, until shortly before they died. The parents had provided for their funeral expenses and for the pro-ceeds from the sale of their house to be divided among their chil-dren. "Even in death they gave to us."

The family's network altered over time. When they first settled in the East Bay, Gino and Teresa visited mainly with Gino's kin. As their children grew, and as Gino's practice increased, their social world was composed more and more of the parents of their chil-dren's parochial school friends and of other local doctors and their families. They continued to see Gino's kin often, especially his parents. Gino's mother provided all their child care, and Gino's father gardened for them and brought over his own homegrown produce. After the parents' death, ties with siblings became more attenuated, especially as nieces and nephews began to marry and have families of their own and no one's home could accommodate the entire kin group at holidays.

Gino's family of origin was thus enabled by the war economy to support him through his professional training. Gino himself is acutely aware that he has not been able to provide consistent "middle-class" financial support for his own children. Because Gino had professional insurance, though, and because Teresa was able to return to work, Gino's illness did not cause the family immiseration that the Morneses' and Longhinottis' reverses did.

## Economy, Family, and Culture

These families' economic adaptations had powerful influences on kin forms and functions. Farming, wage labor, small business, and professional-managerial occupations all had concomitant effects on perceptions of children's and women's roles and on household size and structure. Farming and small business allowed the family economy pattern; wage labor, depending upon its remuneration (and the number of household workers), correlated with the family wage or family consumer economy; and professional-managerial occupations ensured the latter pattern. This analysis suggests that there is no monolithic Italian *family* pattern. Instead, there seem to have been a variety of materially determined kin and social network patterns, and a variety of ethnically determined economic *strategies* correlating strongly with chain migration and with established ethnic occupational niches (cf. Denich 1975). Her antecedent's early migration and rural settlement created one childhood network pattern for Dorothy DiVincenzo. Late, solitary migration and rural settlement created another for Cetta Longhinotti. Running a small business involved becoming the center of a local Italian population for Lucia Mornese's and Dorothy and Jarus DiVincenzo's parents; working in service occupations for bourgeois non-Italians involved very different network patterns for Angela Caputo's mother, and for the adolescent Cetta Longhinotti and her sister Anna. But the choice of particular occupations and the relative success of economic strategies were profoundly affected by large-scale economic changes. Focusing on the Depression and World War II eras illustrates the historical character of the interpenetration of family and economy.

The experiences of all these families, but especially those of the impoverished Longhinottis, Caputos, and Angeluzzis, bear a close relation to those of other American families during the Depression. Milkman (1979) relates that women in working-class and impoverished middle-class families tended not to lose their jobs. Sexual segregation in employment ensured that men did not cross over into female occupational sectors despite the strong contemporary public feeling that employed women were taking jobs away from male breadwinners. Thus Angela Caputo's mother was able to find work as a cook-housekeeper. Unlike many women who entered the labor market for the first time during the Depression, the wives and mothers of these Italian families were already working in the 1920s. It was their daughters, the adolescent Caterina Caputo, Lucia Mornese, and Maria Longhinotti, who were thrust early into paid labor. Milkman also points out that it was as unpaid domestic laborers, rather than as market workers, that women truly "took up the slack" during the crisis: they canned, sewed, and otherwise labored to produce commodities for the household that had been increasingly bought on the market throughout the 1920s. Cetta Longhinotti and Gino Angeluzzi related at length their mothers' sewing skills and creative use of cheap ingredients to put nourishing and delicious food on the table. Gino remembered that "alot of people thought my folks had money—it was the way my mother dressed us. We never ran around begging . . . . they wouldn't go on the breadline. What's that guy say, 'Whatsa matta, you got no shame on your face?' Well, she had shame on her face."

The Depression also temporarily reversed rural-urban migration as families returned to farms for economic security and assured food supplies. Among these Italian-American families, urbanites did not move; the Morneses instead boarded out their children in the summer for country air and food. Rural families, even though they lost their cash-crop farming, as did the Longhinottis and Angeluzzis, still practiced subsistence farming and foraging to supplement their diets.

Milkman also presents evidence that families experiencing immiseration withdrew from social networks (1979:524). We have seen the same effect among the families of Angela Caputo, Cetta Longhinotti, and Gino Angeluzzi.

These families, then, and the others in my sample responded to the Depression in ways typical of other American families of similar class status.

The Second World War brought economic growth to California as it did to the nation as a whole. Federal spending raised personal incomes to three times their prewar figure (Bean 1968:426). Farmers prospered as the government guaranteed a market for their produce, and war industries sprang up, creating a high demand for labor. The economic fortunes of these families reflected the war prosperity. Both Dorothy DiVincenzo's and Jarus DiVincenzo's families benefited from increased consumer demand for their retail commodities. Dorothy, her brothers and sisters, and Jarus were all able to attend college during these years. (The men attended before or after military service.) Angela Caputo and her sister Caterina both gained higher-paid clerical positions through wartime demand for labor, and Caterina parlayed her experiences into a series of increasingly better-paying managerial positions after the war. Lina's husband gained administrative skills in the military that he put to use in his family's business. Lucia Mornese, Cetta and Anna Longhinotti, and Gino Angeluzzi's sisters all benefited, like the Caputo sisters, from the demand for clerical labor. Cetta Longhinotti's and Gino Angeluzzi's families returned to farming, a strategy that lifted Cetta's family from poverty to working-class status, and allowed Gino's to send him to medical school. Finally, Joe Longhinotti's bakery training and the DiVincenzo, Caputo, Longbinotti, and Angeluzzi family homes were sponsored through the GI Bill.

While these five families (and other families in my sample) had common experiences in particular economic eras, they were also differences related to their place in the economy. Household economic strategies were not always successful; hard times were not equally hard on all. The Depression caught Cetta Longhinotti's and Gino Angeluzzi's parents just as they had initiated a new farming strategy, while Dorothy DiVincenzo's (and Clelia Cipolla's) parents were better placed to weather the drop in demand. Angela Caputo's father risked his savings in stock investments; like many

[91]

others, he was impoverished with the fall of the market, while his kin had withdrawn their capital and invested in property just in time. The entrepreneurship of Dorothy DiVincenzo's and Jarus DiVincenzo's (and Nancy Ferrucci's) antecedents profited them greatly. Lucia Mornese's parents merely got through the Depression intact.

In recent decades, Joe Longhinotti's entrepreneurial risks were blocked by the monopolization of the retail food industry. Salvatore Mornese's bid for security through a steady job with a large firm was undercut by that same firm. At the same time, Tony Ripetto and Joe Cruciano's father (and Nick Meraviglia's parents), all unionized workers, are receiving adequate pensions.

Large-scale economic shifts are not, however, the whole story. Institutions alter in connection with them—they are influenced by them, and condition their trajectory. In the 1920s, children were still a significant factor in the U.S. labor force. Extension of compulsory schooling, child labor laws, and changing values have removed them from work force participation. Parent-child relationships have altered as well, and there is less emphasis on children's lifelong economic duty to their parents. This shift is reflected in these Italian-American family histories: in the households of the 1920s and 1930s, children's labor was relied upon and adult children automatically lived at home and handed over their wages to their parents. By the 1950s, no children under sixteen engaged in market labor, and by the 1970s, only Linda Mornese and her brother continued to pay board to their parents.

Appropriate roles for women altered as well. In the 1920s and 1930s even those women in families with property, such as Dorothy DiVincenzo's mother (and Nancy Ferrucci's), worked outside the home or on family farms or in family businesses. By the 1950s and 1960s, after the onslaught of postwar propaganda concerning women's proper place at home, and after two generations of declining self-employment, the family-administrator ideal of the housewife seemed appropriate to Dorothy DiVincenzo, Angela and Lina Caputo, Lucia Mornese, Cetta Longhinotti, and Teresa Angeluzzi. But Dorothy's sister and Caterina Caputo as well as other older women in these families continued to work, just as did other American women—Rosie the Riveter, statistically, became Rosie the Secretary, not the Housewife (Ryan 1979:190ff). And by or during the

1970s, mirroring the historic movement of increasing numbers of American women into the labor force, all of these housewives except Lina Caputo had returned to work. Finally, the households changed in composition over time as a result of the demography of immigration. Few of the earlier households, being constituted by immigrants, had to accommodate aged parents—they remained in Italy. All of the later households did, differing in method as a result of their own and their parents' financial resources.

Variations in household form and function, and their simulatenous embeddedness in a changing economy, provide clues to understanding the role of regional origins in the lives of these Italian-Americans. Intense regional and linguistic solidarity and mistrust of outsiders, or *campanilismo*, has been claimed as an Italian-American trait. The reality is far more complex. For these family histories, all of the marriages of the 1910s and 1920s were among men and women from the same region (in the DiVincenzo case, of the same regional origin). But the relative regional homogeneity of their networks varied greatly. Dorothy DiVincenzo's family, the wealthiest and the furthest from immigrant experience, was extremely campanilistic in its associations. Angela Caputo's family, of Piemontese origin, was in fact related to non-Piemontese—Angela recalls her "nice Toscano" uncle—and its network included Italians of every regional origin. Lucia Mornese's family's experience was similar: her parents associated with Italians of all regional origins. The Longhinottis' social life, although they were rural like Dorothy DiVincenzo's family, mirrored that of the urban Caputos and Morneses. The Italian farm families in their area had a variety of regional origins. Cetta's family learned Toscano as a lingua franca to communicate with these regionally diverse Italians at Sunday gatherings.

Gino Angeluzzi's mother's family experience bore a resemblance to the DiVincenzos': they were removed by generations from immigration, they spoke English, and yet they associated and intermarried largely with others originally from their own village. However, even though Gino's mother's early experiences were campanilistic, the family's friends throughout Gino's childhood were so various that he can understand "Napoletani, Romani, Toscani—every one except Genovesi."

Campanilismo, therefore, is a product of settlement patterns and

[93]

ethnic mix. It is variable, like other components of culture, not fixed, like the alleles determining eye color. When there are a large number of Italians of a particular origin living near one another, and when they have significant common economic interests, campanilismo may be used, like any other ideological formation, to assert solidarity and control. Cinel cites considerable evidence that the Genovesi of South San Francisco did precisely that, shutting other Italians out of their highly lucrative truck gardening ventures. Only when Lucchesi, in numbers and well organized, challenged this hegemony did they allow them into their organization. This pattern was later repeated as Sicilian immigrants attempted to break into, and later won control of, the Genovese fishing monopoly (1979:301–12). Once again, a component of "Italian culture" varies greatly according to material circumstances.

The arrival of Italian immigrants in the United States, like all other historical migrations, was part of a larger global political-economic process. The upheavals attendant on Unification, the competition of European goods and American foodstuffs, the development of international transportation, and the intense demand for labor in industrializing America all contributed to the broadening and diversion of the preexisting emigrant stream to U.S. soil. Italians, largely northerners, arrived in California earlier, and in greater proportions, than those who settled in the Midwest and the Eastern Seaboard. These migrants, while they worked in the largely primary-sector jobs of a not yet industrialized region, were as thoroughly proletarian as their compatriots who labored in factories and construction. They found themselves, however, in a very different population mix: the presence of Asians and Mexicans deflected racist sentiment from them and from other European immigrants. The expanding regional economy and its agricultural tilt, as well, provided farming and entrepreneurial opportunities not available farther east.

So-called timeless Italian peasant immigrants were in fact artisans, entrepreneurs, and early industrial workers as well as agricultural laborers. This holds true for women as well as men, and there is evidence that Italian women on the East Coast had higher labor-force participation rates than has been thought.

The narrative of five Italian-American family histories illustrates

[94]

the interpenetration of kinship and economy. We have seen the influence of occupation on household form and function, the economic conditioning of household strategies, the evolution of family role expectations, and the material conditions underlying the expression of campanilismo. These varying Italian-American family histories, so closely connected to the developing California economy, help us to see beyond the vision that many have read into Gans's *Urban Villagers:* that Italian-American "family culture" creates an ambitionless, self-reproducing, urban working class.

But what evidence is there that these families are really representative of California Italian-Americans? And are there differences in Italian-American economic fortunes in different American regional economies? The next chapter confronts these questions through focusing on the aggregate outcomes of the intersection of economic strategies with the changing political economy: on the historical issue of ethnic social mobility.

# [3]

# "The Family Is *Sopratutto*": Mobility Models, Kinship Realities, and Ethnic Ideology

> Interpretation of the present requires assumptions about the past. The actual choice is between explicit history, based on a careful examination of the sources, and implicit history, rooted in ideological preconceptions and uncritical acceptance of local mythology—Thernstrom 1964:239

Having related these family histories to one another, and having connected them to the changing California economy, I was puzzled by the findings of historians working with the issue of ethnic social mobility. Rather than being concerned with the questions of how immigrants integrated themselves into regional occupational structures, historians of nineteenth- and twentieth-century mobility have focused on judging ethnic groups vis-à-vis one another. The students graded in this ethnic report card system differ; but the general structure of evaluation is consistent across studies: the higher the proportion of second-generation men holding white-collar jobs, the higher the ethnic grade. In addition, it is assumed that ethnic family structure is largely responsible for the relative white-collar outcome: differing "cultures" determine the structures and values of ethnic families, and they in turn determine the economic status of the men associated with them.

These presumptions, which incorporate our national myth that anyone who works hard enough can "make good" in the United States—and that everyone's primary goal is individual enrichment—seem unwise in the light of the complex economic realities of the migration and settlement experience. But it is not enough to criticize the premises of these historical mobility studies. We must assess their methods and findings: we must meet them on their own ground.

## Mobility Models and Empirical Reality

### The Dominant Model and Its Empirical Support

Several recent mobility studies compare Italian-Americans to other white ethnic groups. Glanz (1971) compares Jews and Italians, giving the former group high and the latter low marks. Kessner studies the same groups in New York City. Analyzing city censuses, he finds that Jews were more mobile than Italians and that Italians tended to concentrate in jobs demanding heavy physical labor. He ascribes this to Italians' peasant background, which "equipped them for this kind of hard work and solid, if somewhat stolid, accomplishment" (1977:59). Kessner's sources on Italian families indicate the perspective with which we are already familiar: Italian society is characterized by "amoral familism" and Italian-American parents are portrayed as selfish and lazy, pressuring their children to support them, since "few harbored aspirations for themselves or for their children" (1977:95). Jews are portrayed, in contrast, as striving and forward-looking because of their family and *shtetl* background.

Barton (1975), using parish records to study Italians, Rumanians, and Slovaks in Cleveland, found that Slovaks "remained largely in the working class" because "the Slovak community created social institutions emphasizing the value of order and maintaining the continuity of the ethnic group." Italians, while also largely working-class, had a group "of young and ambitious leaders who cultivated the memories of the village but also encouraged expectations of upward mobility and success." Some Italian men attained middle-class status, but they "consistently failed to pass on their status to their children." Rumanians, on the other hand, "present the classic rise of an immigrant group. The secular orientation of their culture, the alacrity with which they adopted an urban small family life, and their consistent use of education as a means of upward mobility

[97]

facilitated their rapid gain of middle-class status" (1975:172). Barton's study focuses, we can see, far more on the good students than on the bad. But his orientation is the same: family structures and values determine the white-collar success of the sons who grow up with them.

The most influential of the studies in the report card genre is Stephan Thernstrom's *The Other Bostonians* (1973), which examines immigrants *en bloc,* in comparison to native-born Bostonians, and arrayed against one another.[1] His results in the latter exercise are extremely impressive (see Appendix, Tables 1–3). There seem to be large variations in economic success among groups in the 1950 Census data Thernstrom uses. These differences appear in the job categories in which each group clusters, in the resulting proportions of white-collar workers, and in the patterns of mobility between fathers and sons.

Thernstrom uses three basic measures to assess economic status and relative mobility among British, Irish, Russian, Italian, Swedish, and German men in Boston in 1950. He considers how closely a group's spread among different occupations matches that of white men in the city as a whole, each group's proportions of white-collar versus blue-collar workers, and each group's percentage of high-income workers. Thernstrom also looks at years of formal education for portions of his sample. These measures indicate that there are great differences among the groups in the sample. There are high correlations among white-collar status, high income, college education, and Jewish or Protestant backgrounds (Thernstrom infers religious background from ethnicity). Italian and Irish men, in particular, seem to be concentrated in low-skill and low-status occupations in the first generation, and to remain in them in the second (although Irish do move into the clerical and sales category). This low occupational status correlates with a low level of formal education in both generations, and contrasts starkly with the Russian group. Second-generation Russian men have the highest white-collar and high-income proportions, even though their "fathers" (first-generation men) have a lower educational level than Irish "fathers." Thernstrom invokes Jewish cultural values to explain this mobility:

1. Thomas Sowell's recent (1981) study is yet another extension of the report card genre. Interestingly, not only his admirers (Thernstrom 1981) but also his critics (Jencks 1983) accept the presumption that groups can and should be ranked by income and judged accordingly.

Despite their lack of education, Jewish immigrants moved very rapidly into white-collar callings, particularly as proprietors of small shops and manufacturing concerns, and this, of course, put them in a far better position to educate their sons than any of their Catholic *rivals.* The special Jewish commitment to education . . . stands out. . . . This seems to be a clear example of the way in which the cultural values of a group can shape the career patterns of its children in a distinctive manner. (1973:173, my emphasis)

To explain the low scores of the Irish and Italians, Thernstrom refers to their peasant origins:

. . . and this, it is likely, gave them a distinctive value system that was passed on from generation to generation via the family. Particular attitudes toward education, work, thrift, and consumption patterns were inculcated in the Irish and Italian family, and these influenced the occupational placement of children reared in such families. (1973:168)

These family cultural explanations seem very plausible, especially when the statistical evidence is so impressive. But I found both explanations and statistics difficult to reconcile with the family histories that underlay Gino Angeluzzi's professional or even Joe Longhinotti's craftsman status. I could not connect Thernstrom's image of the Italian family—stolid, inward-looking, preventing the mobility of its children—with my clear evidence of an array of economic strategies, including risk-taking and planning for the future, and a variety of gender and household structure patterns. It did not seem that the answer lay in the differing Italian immigrant populations in California and the East Coast. Perhaps then there were differences in regional economy and society. I decided to reexamine Thernstrom's statistics, and to duplicate his tables using San Francisco Bay Area Census materials.

There are difficulties with Thernstrom's method that he notes himself. He does not consider women at all. He denominates men of Russian origin "Jews," including, it is likely, many non-Jews, and leaving out numbers of non-Russian Jews. He arbitrarily calls the two Census age categories "fathers" and "sons." And he arrays all groups by presumed, rather than known, religion (1973:7, 140–41, 172). These difficulties, however, seem to be outweighed by the startling clarity of his results.

There are other, less apparent, difficulties that Thernstrom does not mention. First, the Census categorization of occupations misrepresents the American occupational structure and emphasizes a sharper dividing line between white- and blue-collar jobs than actually exists (Conk 1978). Second, and most important, is the question of the immigration history and demography of the ethnic groups being compared to one another. Simply put, since groups arrived at different times and in vastly different numbers, to take a "snapshot" of men of a certain age and generation across groups is to compare the fundamentally noncomparable. The 1950 samples of English, Irish, Swedish, and German first- and second-generation men are of very late, atypical immigrants and their sons. The peak migration years for these groups were in the middle to late nineteenth century. The Russian and Italian samples, on the other hand, given their early twentieth-century migration peak, are of highly typical migrants and their sons—but there are about twice the number of Italians as Russians in each generation.

Differences of generation and number may have affected the economic statuses of these men in a variety of ways. Migrants of different periods encountered different labor markets. Their numbers might swamp or might constitute an insufficient challenge to particular occupational niches. Later migrants might benefit from the occupational opportunities, union strength, or ethnic professional networks created by earlier compatriots. Or they might find themselves excluded from these benefits by earlier arrivals from other areas. The quality and availability of local housing stock and school accommodations would be conditioned by similar processes as well.

Let us assume, however, that Thernstrom's use of these data gives *some* indication of ethnic stratification in Boston in 1950. The question then remains: Is it the ethnics (as Thernstrom would have it) or is it Boston? That is, to take the two most comparable groups, did Italians and Russians have the same divergent economic outcomes in other areas, or were there instead regional differences in ethnic occupational and income stratification? In order to answer this question, I duplicated Thernstrom's Boston measures for the San Francisco–Oakland Standard Metropolitan Statistical Area in 1950, and considered the same measures for both regions in 1970 as well.

## San Francisco and Boston: A Comparative Test

These duplicate measures show very different patterns in every regard (see Appendix, Tables 4–9). First, and most striking, there was in 1950 and 1970 simply less ethnic stratification in San Francisco than in Boston. There is a much lower percentage point spread in proportions of white-collar and high-income workers for both generations. That is, much more similar proportions of men in each group "do well" in San Francisco than in Boston. Relatedly, the very dissimilar representations of men across the occupational spectrum in Boston are in San Francisco considerably evened out— especially the "managers, officials, and proprietors" category that Thernstrom finds so important to Russian (Jewish) mobility. In San Francisco, *all* groups commit a significant proportion of their members to this category, and the evenness of the commitment increases in the second generation. A "generation" later, in 1970, Boston second-generation male ethnic differences hold up, with Russians maintaining over twice the proportions in high-status occupations as other groups. The 1970 figures in San Francisco show nearly identical percentages in the category across all groups.

Second, all white ethnics do better economically in San Francisco than in Boston. The white-collar, high-income, and college-education measures are all uniformly higher, and only part of the high-income measure can be explained by higher prevailing overall incomes in the West.

But not only do the ethnic groups do better in relation to other whites—they are more evenly spread across occupations and have more nearly equal incomes. There are still in San Francisco, as there are in Boston, distinct ethnic occupational emphases. Italians in particular tend to have the highest blue-collar proportions and the lowest percentages in professional and technical occupations and related low levels of formal education. And, as the Angeluzzi family history would lead us to guess, they were still heavily committed to farming in 1950—first-generation men at four times the level of white men in general, and two to four times the proportion of other white ethnics.

There is still evidence of a possibly distinct Italian economic strategy—involving farming, small business, skilled crafts, and service work (some of which was in highly lucrative cooperative scavenger companies). What varies by region, though, is the ability to carry out that strategy, and its income results. Italians in Boston, even into 1970, have by far the lowest proportion of high-income workers. In San Francisco in 1950, depending on generation, they are middling or lowest—but the difference between lowest and highest, a gulf in Boston, is in San Francisco reduced to a few percentage points. By 1970, San Francisco Italians, less than half of whom have white-collar jobs, and who have a uniquely low proportion of professionals, tie with the British for second-highest proportion of high-income workers. The Russian group, fully three-quarters of whom hold white-collar jobs, and who have double the expected proportion in professional occupations, have only 12 percent more high-income workers than the Italians and British.

I also looked at 1950 Census information on ethnic women for both Boston and San Francisco. The findings parallel those for men (see Appendix, Table 10). Labor force participation rates, which vary widely from group to group in Boston, are higher in San Francisco, and vary little by ethnic group. Moreover, since a higher proportion of San Francisco women are married, the participation rate differences are clearly not related to the need of single women to support themselves. Women's decisions to work outside the home, like men's choice of occupations, appear to be less ethnically organized in the West Coast city.[2]

This critique of Thernstrom's model of ethnic mobility and its supporting data is purely technical. In a willing suspension of disbelief—ignoring the evidence against comparing these groups, and against the utility of Census occupational data—we have considered precisely the same measures for San Francisco/Oakland. This comparison indicates that differing regional political economies intersecting with particular ethnic economic strategies, rather than the

---

2. The information on ethnic women strengthens the regional-difference finding in two further ways. First, since the income figures used for ethnic men include women's incomes, and since women's aggregate incomes are always lower than men's, the San Francisco ethnic women's higher participation rates *depress* Western ethnic incomes relative to Boston. In other words, San Francisco white ethnics had even higher collective incomes, relative to their Boston counterparts, than they appear to have had. Second, as the participation rate for Boston Russian women is by far the lowest among ethnic women in that city, Russian income figures are overstated relative to the others. The Russian group is not as economically successful, even in Boston, as Thernstrom would claim. See also Dublin 1979b.

family cultures of workers, are the important explanatory variables for overall ethnic occupational class systems. The Boston ethnic class ladder, with its tight correlations among education, white-collar jobs, and income and its Jewish-Protestant-Catholic hierarchy, seems to have more to do with Boston than with ethnicity.[3]

What are the regional differences in social history that would account for these very different patterns? California's heavily agricultural economy, late industrialization, and unique racial configuration suggest that the answer includes both differing economic opportunities and a very different climate of racial and ethnic intolerance. Farming was a springboard to mobility for Dorothy DiVincenzo's and Gino Angeluzzi's families (as well as for many others in my sample). The farming strategy was unavailable to Italians in Boston. Many others, like the Morneses and Caputos, chose small business or were self-employed craftspeople. Self-employment, perhaps because of Boston's much earlier economic development and thus greater corporate control, was significant only among Russians there by 1970. All ethnic groups in San Francisco had a sizable commitment to that strategy. I suggest that differing stereotypes of "good" and "bad" businesspeople and differing networks interacted with and influenced this regional occupational difference. This is a far more plausible explanation of these distributions than Thernstrom's contentions that the Boston Irish "lacked any entrepreneurial tradition" or that Boston Italians lived in a "subculture that directed energies away from work" (1973:140, 169). Variation between areas again gives the lie to "family culture" explanations and points to the importance of regional influences on ethnic populations.

Probably most important, though, was the early presence in California of distinct racial groups (Asians, Mexicans) who experienced intense economic oppression. These groups filled the most proletarian jobs and suffered the most from white ideological constructions of themselves as dirty, incompetent, lazy, and ambitionless. Italians, Irish, and French Canadians filled these slots in Boston. Italians in particular were suspected and despised as poor citizens throughout the 1920s and 1930s because of the heavily publicized

3. There have been a number of critiques of parts of *The Other Bostonians*, but none to my knowledge of this section on white ethnicity and mobility in the recent period. See Miller 1975; Alcorn and Knights 1975.

Sacco and Vanzetti case and Italy's role in World War I (Ehrmann 1969; Whyte 1981:273). West Coast concern over Italian loyalty during World War II was muted by the collective hysteria over Japanese-Americans, a situation largely absent on the East Coast.

In the discussion of his findings, Thernstrom does consider a variety of exogenous factors—discrimination, background handicaps, settlement concentration, family sizes—but he concludes that they have contradictory and therefore minimal importance. In the end he relies on culture and family:

> . . . part of the explanation [of differential ethnic mobility] . . . was not simple prejudice or even passive structural discrimination but objective differences in qualifications to perform demanding occupational tasks. . . . It can be said that immigrants from both Catholic peasant societies and the Jewish communities of Eastern Europe brought with them distinctive habits and attitudes that were slow to disappear and that influenced the occupational trajectories of the two groups long into the future. (1973:258, 175).

We now realize that the assertion of "distinctive habits and attitudes," at least for Italian peasants, is deeply flawed. We may suspect it for other groups as well. Like others, Thernstrom relies on poor models of the European backgrounds of immigrants, and on popular perspectives on American ethnic family cultures. These presumptions lead him to compare ethnic populations that are non-comparable, and to interpret his findings as resulting from cultural differences rather than from the social history of Boston.

## Critiques of Mobility

The model of mobility from which Thernstrom proceeds is ubiquitous: it is the most common perspective on the issue among social scientists as well as historians (see Blau and Duncan 1967; Lipset and Bendix 1959). It proceeds from the assumptions of neoclassical economics and posits a *Homo economicus* who consistently acts in order to maximize his economic advantages, an economy governed by competitive market forces, and therefore a "fair field" for economic actors who are handicapped only by their inherited disadvantages—and here is the opening for familial culture.

One of the many critiques of this model emphasizes looking at humans as wholes—beings with a variety of interests beyond narrow economic advantage. Henretta, for example, stresses that the model makes the "hidden assumption that all groups have economic success as their primary aspiration" and ignores the "evidence of wide divergence among definitions of success and the ideal social order" (1977:170,173). He points out that, according to Handlin (1974), Boston's Irish immigrants, rather than investing their savings, sent money back to Irish kin and gave it to the Catholic church; Henretta sees this phenomenon as an example of specific cultural values taking precedence over mobility. It might be better seen as a model of mobility encompassing nonresident kin, and we have seen its importance among my informants' families. Indeed, it is curious that precisely the two Catholic groups castigated by Thernstrom and others for poor familial values are those known to have drained their U.S. kin networks of capital, for years and in some cases generations, in favor of supporting their European kin. This phenomenon has not gone unremarked—Zenner (1970) has noted the importance of remittances in migrant networks—but the connection between differential remittance sending and differential mobility for European immigrants to the United States has not been sufficiently investigated.

Historians have stressed other contextual issues in studies of particular groups' economic experiences. Property mobility—the decision to buy a home rather than to attempt to launch one's children in careers—has been cited by Thernstrom himself as important (1964), but not for groups in Boston (1973:170). Dawley (1976) has stressed the importance of the struggle to maintain labor autonomy among Lynn artisans at the coming of the Industrial Revolution. And Dublin (1979a) focuses on the precise economic and social motivations that induced young women to leave New England farms to become part of the American industrial proletariat. Varying investment strategies, struggles against deskilling, and variations in women's work strategies clearly differentiate populations embedded in the same economy. These factors and others emerge in importance when we shift our perspective on mobility from the assignment of ethnic report cards to the investigation of the meaning of mobility from the inside out. How do people conceive of mobility? And which kin do they see it encompassing?

We cannot answer these questions, however, with the assertion that a particular group has "strong cultural values"—as do, for example, Yans-McLaughlin (1977) and Golab (1977). Concern for cultural values alone is no corrective to the neoclassical mobility mode. It is in fact complementary to it. The same model can be and is used both to blame the victim or uncritically to celebrate "cultural" behavior. Kinship fits into the model easily: families are seen as transmission belts for culture—for unchanging perceptions of the world and of proper behavior. Families are praised or blamed for their members' mobility experiences, or they are celebrated for their "cultural cohesion." It is all part of the same model. And culture can be seen to fuse with *Gemeinschaft* and *Gesellschaft:* either one has culture and heritage, or achievement and assimilation. This pendulum construction swings continually through the same arc. It cannot accommodate the flexibility and dynamism of individuals' and groups' actual negotiation of ethnic identity and economic life. We must abandon it.

We need instead to step back from mobility models, from "implicit history," and to look at the U.S. economy as a whole—at the points at which migrant groups entered (and are entering) it, at their regions of settlement, and at the changing ideological constructions of ethnic and racial groups and of the white population at large.

Second-wave migrants entered a capitalist economy undergoing rapid industrial growth (with its attendant periodic slumps) and technological innovation. The scale of development and transformation—and the mass labor struggles of both centuries—brought improved standards of living for the population as a whole. The growth of firms and of the state encouraged a vast expansion of clerical and professional-managerial positions. At the same time, this growth and transformation has not changed the general division of wealth: "The long-run growth of total income in the United States has made it possible for the *absolute* level of income of the poor to increase even without any change in their *relative* position in the overall distribution" (Edwards, Reich, and Weisskopf 1978:297, their emphasis). Neither taxation nor government spending has altered this general picture (Ackerman and Zimbalist 1978:302–6). In fact, the apparatus of state welfare serves more to maintain and discipline a reserve army of labor for the needs of capital than to enable individuals to escape poverty (Piven and Cloward 1971).

The U.S. capitalist system has been expansive and progressive—it has grown rapidly, labor has become more productive, old occupations have been altered and sometimes made obsolete, and new ones have been created. Nonetheless, class divisions have been maintained and reproduced, while the racial and ethnic components of these divisions have changed over time.

Mobility historians have therefore been considering the movements of regional white ethnic populations across these class divisions (and, of course, have also charted their rising standards of living). That is, most mid-nineteenth-century and later European immigrants to the United States at first constituted part of the industrial proletariat. Mobility historians have been concerned with their differential movements as through economic expansion, their own struggles, and replacement from below, they became more broadly represented across the class spectrum, assimilating to the class distribution of the white population as a whole. These same historians attribute faster or slower ethnic group movements into the *petit-bourgeoisie* and professional-managerial class to varying familial cultures. I argue that we should consider the encounter between different ethnic economic strategies and the economic structure and ethnic/racial mix of particular regions of settlement, as well as the changing national occupational class structure. We must shift our explanatory focus.

These are not particularly original suggestions. Marxists and radicals have been making them for some time—but about racial minorities rather than about white ethnic groups. The fairly early movement of segments of some white ethnic populations into the *petit-bourgeoisie* and professional-managerial classes has confused the issue for many scholars. Some have tended to ignore white ethnicity altogether, preferring to focus instead on the much clearer history of racial oppression in the United States.[4] Others focus only on working-class white ethnics; or going further, they assert that all

4. Indeed, scholars with a global perspective define the term *ethnicity* in such a way that only U.S. racial groups fit within it. Cf. Giddens 1973:111–112; and Wallerstein 1975:369.

white ethnics *are* working-class, despite evidence to the contrary.[5] Taken together, all these tendencies have the effect of leaving the field of ethnicity and economy clear. They create a vacuum that has been filled with the dominant, neoclassically derived model of ethnic mobility. What should we put in its place?

## A Model of the Interaction of Culture and Economy

The following schema is designed to apply to any group immigrating to the United States, and its descendants, whether its members are defined as "ethnic" or "racial" by the society at large. (It does not, however, apply to Native Americans or to the majority of Blacks whose antecedents arrived in America through force.) The ordering of the topics is a chronological one, but each topic should also be seen in historical context.

### Migrating Strategy

Individuals of the same group may have very different intentions in emigrating. They may intend to settle in the new area for life; or to migrate seasonally for part or the whole of their working lives; or to make several lengthy stays, accumulating capital for investment in the native country, as did the majority of Italian emigrants to America. Changing circumstances may influence migrants to shift from one pattern to another, but adherence to any one pattern proves nothing about an individual's or group's inherent human worth.

Individuals, however, almost always migrate as part of a group process, as part of an international movement of labor in response to economic change (Piore 1979; Portes and Walton 1981). In looking at any one group's migration, we must consider that process. We should also investigate the manner in which the process takes

5. Sennett and Cobb (1972) exemplify the tendency to focus on working-class white ethnics. Historians have worked increasingly in this tradition in recent years. Cf. M. Cohen 1977, 1978; J. Smith 1978, 1981; and E. Ewen 1979. Greer (1974) asserts that all white ethnics are working-class. See also Argersinger 1982 for a critique of recent work in American ethnic history.

place—the demography of migration strategies. Men or women alone may migrate; couples alone; men and women separately; or entire kin networks, in a process of chain migration. This demographic component, in conjunction with the available housing stock and with particular economic strategies, has a large influence on household structure and functioning, and thus of the different "timeless ethnic family cultures" perceived by outsiders.

### Occupational Class Structure

The first arrivals of any particular wave of migration generally have specific types of work in mind. They may have actually been contacted by industrial or agribusiness employers: Joe Cruciano's antecedents, for example, were originally induced to leave their village by a labor recruiter for a wealthy Anglo agribusinessman. On the other hand, the Irish arrived in New England coincidently with new demands for labor and increasing militance on the part of the native-born American work force in the textile mills (Dublin 1979a:chap. 8).

Successive migrants will tend to take jobs already held by co-ethnics. They will be excluded by nationality from a greater or lesser number of occupations, depending on the social climate, including ethnic/racial mix, and stereotyping. The strength and type of union organization, and whether or not members of the group are used to break unionizing efforts, will also affect the level of job discrimination against them.

### Racial/Ethnic Mix

Migrants settle in different regions, each having different racial and ethnic populations, and each population being already occupationally segmented and socially stereotyped—both by the society at large and by one another. Members of the dominant society, affected by migrants' cultural markers, by international politics, by already existing ethnic/racial stereotypes, and by the occupational niches most migrants enter (factory work, agricultural labor, student status), construct an image—or array of images—of the group as a whole. As part of this process, the migrant group constructs an image—or series of images—of Americans as well. The migrant group and all the other groups with which it is in contact—and they may be simultaneously migrating groups—also construct mutual images of one another. These products of boundary interactions are continuously renegotiated over time as economic, demographic, and political factors change.

## Cultural Resources

This category is less crucial than the dominant mobility model asserts; the model, as well, misconstrues the operations of culture.

Migrants, at the point of arrival, have an array of skills, a set of perspectives on the world and social relations (including perhaps an affiliation with an organized religion), and a set of concepts of appropriate and inappropriate behavior. All of these factors are constantly changing as individuals and networks interact. Nevertheless, they partially determine the first occupations migrants take, the first households they construct, the first extraethnic friendships they form; and these anchoring institutions have an effect on those that follow them. We can thus conceptualize culture as a process channeling options for immigrants, not as a grid determining their behavior.

## Cultural Markers

The recognizably foreign aspects of migrants' bodies, behavior, and material culture—appearance, language, dress, food, demeanor, household arrangements—provide the majority society (and other migrant groups) with interpretable elements for the creation of ethnic and racial images. These elements break down somewhat into innate and chosen categories—such as Asian features versus Asian food—and migrants are thus more or less able to abandon them if they wish. The balance between ascribed and achieved partially determines the majority society's treatment of immigrants as racial or ethnic. The majority society may also use particular markers, such as dark skin or Spanish speaking, to assimilate new migrants into already constructed stereotyped racial groups. Thus Nicaraguans are perceived as Mexican or Puerto Rican (depending on region of settlement) and West Indians are perceived as Black Americans (Bryce-Laporte 1980). There are, as well, "ghost markers": asserted but largely or totally nonexistent traits. The Japanese historically ascribed an extra bone, a foul smell, and a birthmark to the Burakumin, a racially Japanese but socially stigmatized group (DeVos and Wagatsuma 1967).

## Networks

Group immigration history determines the number, age, and sex structure of a migrant population in any particular region, and these factors, as well as migration strategies like chain migration, have an effect on the sorts of networks that migrants form in the foreign country. Especially important is job recruitment through migrant networks: it not only smoothes the route to employment, but helps to establish the opportunity structure that each group perceives it must work within. Cultural resources also affect the institutional components of migrants' networks: religious and political organizations, benevolent societies, kin and fictive kin institutions, unions.

The majority society's response to these formations, however, places limits on the sorts of networks immigrants and their descendents will form. Racism may prevent or slow union organizing or prevent extraethnic friendships. Firm owners may encourage or try to prevent ethnic networks in their work forces. And state initiative and the general social climate may encourage or prohibit various sorts of ethnic associations.

## Negotiation and Renegotiation of Ethnic Ideologies

Over time and over generations, and affected by racism, international politics, and their place in the economy, groups evolve more or less deeply held ethnic identities; the character of the ethnic images constructed at groups' boundaries alters as well. This continuous renegotiation of ethnic ideologies both affects and is affected by the level and type of political mobilization that groups practice.

[111]

This array of ethnic images is not a mere ranking of groups: instead, it is a series of sets of ascribed *qualities* that have profound implications for the possible economic and social strategies that individuals may choose. Nonethnic whites, for example, may hold equally strong negative stereotypes about the Jews, Italian-Americans, and Puerto Ricans with whom they are in contact. But these different stereotypes, involving among other factors very different estimates of occupational competence, will have profoundly different effects on their behavior, and on the self-images of the denigrated groups.

All of these factors must be taken into account in considering the past and present linkages among ethnicity, kinship, and class. When historians and social scientists fail to recognize their importance, they make egregious blunders in their portrayals of ethnic life. Thernstrom and others have been beguiled by a misleading sense of expertise—since we have almost all grown up in families—in perceiving distinct, endogenous family cultures. In order to avoid ideological preconceptions and uncritical acceptance of our own local mythology concerning ethnicity, kinship, and class, we need to disentangle and to study all of the historical and material factors that condition their interconnection.

## Kinship Patterns and Ethnic Ideology Today

We have seen in the last chapter how some Italian-American families responded to and were changed by changing economic and social conditions. Moreover, the evidence on family mobility leads us to doubt that there have been particular ethnic family structures that have determined the mobility experiences of their members. Instead, there have been clear tendencies for different groups to follow different sets of economic strategies, strategies that have been reified over time by the construction of internal and external ethnic images.

Attention to these varying historical processes can help to disentangle local mythology concerning ethnic family structures. We have seen the cyclical and common influence of the developmental cycle of domestic groups on some Italian-American families: an Italian household (to use Cetta Longhinotti's life) consisting of a young man and a pregnant woman differs markedly from that of a middle-aged couple, their coresident adult son, and the husband's elderly mother. Much work on ethnic families glides over these differences by exalting the "extended family"—usually meaning that the elderly live with their married children and that lineals and laterals see one another often, if they do not actually live together— but this use of the concept of ahistorical.

In the first place, permanent emigration itself is an enormous *disruption* of kinship systems. These working-age emigrants of the 1850s to the 1920s, my informants' antecedents, removed both market and domestic labor power from the control of family heads as soon as they stopped sending remittances to Italy. This meant particularly that the care of the ill and the elderly—remembering that emigrants were overwhelmingly healthy and young—fell to other kin in Italy. It also meant, as we have seen for Lucia Mornese's and Angela Caputo's mothers, that the child care that elderly relatives might have provided had to be secured elsewhere. That first generation, now aged parents, that we have observed sleeping in their daughters' living rooms, calling their daughters-in-law daily, being visited in nursing homes—these elderly are receiving care that they have never themselves bestowed. My second-generation women informants repeatedly stressed their consciousness of this fact. Lucia Mornese said of her co-resident mother:

> She gets on everybody's nerves. . . . I think it's because they never took care of their own mothers. This is what Rose and a few of my friends who have mothers this age say—they never had to do it so they have no idea what it's like, to get yourself tied up, to have someone telling you how to live your life. . . . She keeps saying, "Oh, I should have stayed with my mother, I loved my mother," . . . and I say, "How do you know, you were twenty-six years old! . . . . I can just see *your* mother telling you what to do when *you* were fifty or sixty!"

In the second place, the "extended ethnic family" will have varying personnel depending on the demography of immigration and the generational distance of its members from that experience. The point at which emigration occurred and its demography, so crucial, as we have seen, to economic strategies, have also had consequences for the kin networks of the second, third, and fourth gener-

6. Dorothy DiVincenzo: schematized oral genealogy

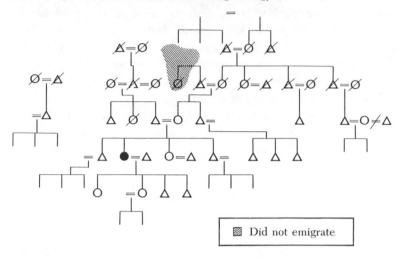

☑ Did not emigrate

7. Cetta Longhinotti: schematized oral genealogy

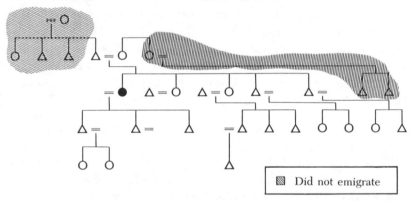

▨ Did not emigrate

ations today. If we consider, for example, the oral genealogies of Dorothy DiVincenzo and Cetta Longhinotti (that is, all those relatives known without consultation of records or with other family members), we see the effects that one's antecedents' point of emigration have on the shapes of kin networks (diagrams 6 and 7). The two women are in the same age group, and both are grandmothers; this ensures that at least four generations of relatives are personally known to them. As it was Cetta Longhinotti's parents but Dorothy DiVincenzo's great-grandparents who were emigrants, however, Dorothy is aware of six generations to Cetta's four. More important,

Dorothy knows her great-grandparents and grandparents' lateral descendents—second and third cousins—while Cetta, whose parents emigrated without siblings, does not even have cousins in the United States. The final effect of these widely divergent points of emigration is the contrast between Cetta's continuing knowledge of Italian kin (they have exchanged visits in the past decade) and Dorothy's ignorance of Italian kin. (Although some of Dorothy's relatives have spent time and money in reestablishing contact with their kin in Italy, these relatives are not personally known to her.)

These divergent personal genealogy shapes—Dorothy DiVincenzo's rectangle and Cetta Longhinotti's triangle—determine the numbers and types of kin available to the two women with which to form kin networks, or "extended families" in the popular usage. Again it is clear that "ethnic culture" has a highly complex, and highly *mediated,* influence on ultimate family structures. This example illustrates the crucial and varying role of the material circumstances of immigration history on possible kin structures at various stages of these domestic groups' developmental cycles.

In some ways, however, the developmental cycles of these families have all altered similarly, and altered in common with those of most Americans. Power relations based on age and gender seem to have declined in importance. Specifically, parents assert less control over their children's lives, and women in domestic groups, especially daughters, have increased parity with men.

While writers have tended either to acclaim or to decry these alterations in basic familial roles, it is more interesting to try to understand them.[6] Smelser (1959) and Zaretsky (1976), building on the work of Marx and Engels, and supporters and critics following them, have elucidated the role that developing capitalism has played in stripping the family of its productive functions, and thus of the authority roles within it. Feminist scholars have stressed the systematic effects of historical alterations in patriarchy (working in conjunction with capitalism) on familial gender and age dynamics. These scholars generally hold that developing capitalism and developing systems of male dominance have interacted in complex ways across time. Women are vital actors in this historical evolution, not only reacting to their changing positions but also acting within the

6. These changes are the subject of a large literature, including Weinstein and Platt 1969; Shorter 1975; and Keniston 1977.

boundaries of their class and era in order to maximize power and autonomy for themselves—and often, as well, for their female kin and friends.[7]

A major theme in the literature on white ethnic families is their "stability"—in opposition, presumably, to the families of minorities and nonethnic whites. Stability here is in part a code term for patriarchy: what is claimed is not only that ethnics remain married and care for their aged, but that women remain in the home and "do their duties," that parents discipline their children strictly, that Lasch's (1977) nostalgia for the authority of the father is here satisfied.

My field materials lead me to believe that this claim is as baseless for Italian-Americans as are the other claims about ethnic families we have found wanting. It is in part a result of the confusion of the present with the ethnographic present—the use of old family studies as if they represented contemporary life. It is in larger part the result of the confusion of ethnic symbols with ethnic behavior.

If we return to the five family histories of the last chapter, looking specifically at age and gender expectations, in every case the dynamics have altered considerably. Dorothy DiVincenzo lived with her parents and was under their discipline until she married at the end of her college years; even as a young wife and mother, she was involved in a close round of daily and weekly visiting, much more so than her nearby brothers. "I think they felt freer with a daughter." Dorothy's own children left home after each had finished high school; those who attended college were supported generously. There was a great deal of tension during "those difficult years" as Dorothy's daughters asserted their rights to make their own decisions, especially sexual decisions. But emotional and financial support were not cut off.

There is another, seldom mentioned aspect to the evolution of youthful and female independence: with the loosening of parental discipline has come freedom from certain parental responsibilities. Both Dorothy's mother and grandmother willingly cared for Dorothy's children, but "I wouldn't take care of my grandchildren like that. . . . She [grandmother] never thought of complaining."

7. Examples of this trend in analysis include Darrow 1979; Gillis 1979; Clawson 1980; and Folbre 1980.

Angela Caputo's family's experiences have been similar. Angela's mother depended heavily on the emotional and financial support of her "three girl-es" after her widowhood: "Oh, we were *obedient* children." She refused to allow Angela to join the Red Cross during World War II, keeping her at home. She prevented Caterina from marrying during her young adulthood, delayed Angela's marriage, and passed judgment on Lina's fiancé before she could marry. But Lina's children, although close to their parents, left home early and made their own work and social decisions. One son "went through the hippie bit, the drug and fleabitten bit." And Lina's daughter, when she decided to marry, presented Lina with a *fait accompli* as to partner, date, wedding list, and place, and asked her mother to make her wedding gown as well as to organize the wedding itself.

The Mornese household experience differs from those of the DiVincenzos and Caputos in that both adult son and daughter remained at home long after high school and gave their parents board just as Lucia and her sister did. But investigating beneath the surface of this structure, we find that again, youthful and female independence have grown in the generational transition. Although Linda and her brother Richard remained very close to their parents, Lucia and Salvatore placed no restrictions on them, and did not try to induce them to follow any particular educational, social, or career plans. Linda went to junior college, then decided to quit and go to work on her own; Richard changed jobs frequently. Finally, and most surprising, Linda openly had affairs and spent weekends with a long-term boyfriend while she was still living at home. "They never said anything."

Thus, the close contact between parents and children—Linda's proximate residence, Richard's frequent visits, the social outings planned for parents, children, and children's friends—are the product of choice in the absence of authority. Nevertheless, Linda has made it clear that she will not continue the family pattern of care of the aged: "I told her I was *never* having her living with me! No, I don't feel that in this day and age you should be burdened in that way. Although I have been watching over them now—I feel I have to—when they're old or senile or semisenile—I can't do this forever!"

The Longhinotti family experience fits in with the changes described for the DiVincenzos and Caputos. Cetta and Joe, however,

have no daughters, so we cannot trace increasing female independence. Greg, the youngest son, lived at home for six years after
high school, paying no board and saving money to buy a house,
even though Cetta and Joe were far from well-off. Cetta has attempted to be more authoritarian with her sons, and with her
daughter-in-law, than have the other mothers we have considered.
She has not succeeded, however, in enforcing their attendance at
Mass (they all stopped at adolescence), or attendance at catechism
for her grandchildren, or in preventing one son and his girl friend
from living together for several years before marrying.

The relations between the Angeluzzi parents and children resemble those of the Morneses. Gino says: "I can't get rid of
them . . . . they're still hanging around . . . . everybody comes
over, I'm busy all the time. . . . It's just like people say well you
ought to sell this house and move into a smaller one—what for? If I
don't have the space, the kids won't come and stay with us." Gino
and his siblings, especially his sisters, were strictly supervised;
Gino and Teresa's children are not. Gino and his siblings let Gino's
mother manage their wages until they married and moved out;
Gino and Teresa support their adult coresident children and their
educational ventures to the best of their ability.

I have stressed so far the ways in which these Italian-American
families are like other American families as well as the ways in
which specific immigration histories, rather than merely being Italian, influenced the personnel of kin networks. There are many
areas of the United States, however, in which most Italian immigration happened in a relatively short space of time, consisted largely
of individuals from one or a few areas, and in which most Italian
immigrants worked at one or a few sorts of occupations. In these
cases, the demographic and thus kinship consequences of the actual
history of immigration would appear to be due to "cultural values."
It is for this reason that I have repeatedly stressed the variations in
family form engendered by variations in timing and type of immigration. And it is for this reason that I claim that most aspects of the
family forms of Italian immigrants and their descendents are no
more "cultural" than is the fact that recent Cuban immigrants do
not have coresident grandparents. But within these historical and
demographic parameters, is there anything particularly Italian
about the way these Italian-Americans constructed their kinship
and network relations?

[118]

The religious institution of symbolic kinship, godparenthood, has been seen as a vital extrakinship link among a variety of groups worldwide (Davila 1971), and as a significant institution for Greek-Americans (Chock 1974). It was strikingly unimportant in my informants' lives (with the single exception of Cetta Longhinotti's relationship with her godmother). Most men and women could not remember their own godparents or cogodparents, and men repeatedly referred me to their wives for information on cogodparents and godchildren. Women, when they could remember the names of their godchildren, recounted their gifts to them in a dry, formal fashion; it was clear, in most cases, that there was no special relationship between cogodparents or between godparents and godchildren, and that gift giving slowed and ended as the children grew into adolescence.

Nonreligious fictive kinship, which is used in both sporadic and institutionalized ways among humans globally (Goody 1971), was an unpatterned but constant theme in my informants' lives. Pina Meraviglia became a "mother" to the boy and girl she cared for in the 1940s and 1950s, and is a "grandmother" to their children today. Linda Mornese's roommate calls Lucia and Salvatore "Mother" and "Father." Clelia Cipolla sees the Italian woman who has done her housecleaning for two decades as a "sister"; Lucia Mornese sees the daughter of the woman with whom she boarded in her childhood summers in the same way. And Jim Bertini grew up with a coresident fictive uncle and an elderly Italian neighbor who became his "surrogate grandmother." These Italian-Americans, then, are like other Americans, in that while they emphasize blood ties in ideology, in reality they use fictive kinship to sanction the intimate nonkin ties they form.

Close relations with consanguines' affines' consanguines (CACs)—for example, a sister's husband's sister—which Yanagisako (1975) found to be of importance in the lives of Seattle Japanese-Americans, seemed in my study to correlate with limited available kinship personnel due to immigration history and/or small completed family size. Al Bertini, divorced and with only one child, has become close to his son's wife's family; Lucia and Salvatore Mornese have followed the same pattern. And the Meraviglias have close relations with Nick's mother's sister's children, their affines, and their children, all of whom emigrated in the 1960s with Nick's mother's assistance.

The social networks of these Italian-Americans did reflect their

[119]

The Varieties of Ethnic Experience

ethnicity. These white ethnics were in general predisposed to like and to socialize with others of their own group; my own ethnic credentials were essential in securing first interviews. But their social networks—even the kin components—were by no means 100 percent Italian, and they varied in their ethnic composition from individual to individual, and across time.

Symbols of ethnicity, and the manipulation of those symbols, were all-important among these Italian-Americans, but particularly among the men. It is here, rather than in child-rearing patterns or husband-wife relations, that class becomes an important focus of analysis. Individuals used the prism of ethnicity to explain their place in the economy and in society to themselves and to others. They portrayed parents and other relatives variously; they celebrated or decried ideas of ethnic behavior; and they drew social boundaries and described the interactions that they perceived taking place at these sites in a variety of ways.

Both Joe Longhinotti and Salvatore Mornese, for example, reflected on their working-class status to me as the result of *not* behaving venally, and identified venality with successful Italian-Americans. For Joe Longhinotti, his successful ex-partner symbolized a certain way of dealing with people that would lead to financial success through denying human values:

> He was a good businessman . . . that's the way you make that extra dollar and that's the way you make big money, if you step on somebody's foot and you could care less if you hurt em—people can do it and I can't do it but that's life you know. I'd rather be the way I am—sincerely—if that's what money's all about I'd rather go the other road, because people have a tendency—especially . . . I hate to admit it . . . Italian people for some reason . . . their background . . . it was tough to make money and they have a good life, and they have a tendency to hold that money . . . and pretty soon they want more . . . and then all they want is more, more. And they neglect alot of themselves while they're living and they can afford the best and they don't spend it cause they want—they're *strinti*—*van'alla banca*—they gotothebankgotothebank. It's in their blood. My father educated me in that . . . always lead a good normal life. He never was a rich man but he got more outta life than the people who really had money, cause he always told me, I'll never forget—*Don't put money in your head.* Enjoy yourself in your own way. We're in this world for a short period of time.

Salvatore Mornese's reactions to well-off Italian Americans, while they focus more on consumption than on production behavior, strike the same key:

> We don't see eye to eye. . . . most of the people I know they brag too much. . . . They did very well in the United States, they throw it around, they are *smart,* well I really don't care. They are always on the same argument they got a new car and a beautiful home. Fine. So what? What does it prove?

These two men attribute to wealthy Italian-Americans stereotyped behavior usually used in American racist slurs against wealthy Jews and against *nouveaux riches* in general. Their manipulation of symbols of ethnicity differs markedly from that of those Italian-Americans who have achieved affluence. Joe Cruciano was happy to report on the path by which he had climbed to economic success:

> It was a pretty tough little neighborhood [in his Central Valley town]. . . . I was probably set apart from the majority because I went to a Catholic school. . . . Of course there were only two children in my family—we were considered rich. . . . The only thing my dad ever asked of me was to graduate from college—because my parents only went to the tenth grade. . . . I always knew I wanted to be something or somebody and make some money—even when I was a kid on the West Side—unfortunately I haven't achieved it yet [laughs]. . . . It's always from knowing somebody—that's how you get ahead in this world.

When Joe courted his wife Sally (who is of German ancestry) during their college years, her family objected strenuously to the marriage: "Her grandmother, she probably thought I was an organ grinder with a monkey." In the early years of their marriage, when Sally was "having babies like you wouldn't believe" and Joe was having trouble establishing himself in his profession, there was a fight with Sally's mother. Joe says, "I told her to go and never come back. There was silence for a year. Then she finally saw that maybe I *wanted* three kids. Sally had a nice little house, nice little car . . . they're takin a few trips . . . maybe he's not such a dumb Italian after all."

[121]

For Joe Cruciano the focus is on "Anglos" who assume that Italian-Americans cannot be economically successful. The ruthlessness of business and boasts of conspicuous consumption, the focal themes of Longhinotti's and Mornese's complaints, are here celebrated as part of an Italian-American success story. Joe Cruciano, like Joe Longhinotti, identifies with his relatives: but for Cruciano, the lives of his Italian antecedants indicated his future success—his father was "a pretty strong and smart guy," his uncle was "pretty progressive" in investing in land, and his aunts were "incredible— they were doctors for us." For Joe Longhinotti, instead, his father's life and advice indicate the superiority of *lack* of economic success: "Don't put money in your head."

It is ironic that working-class Italian-Americans distanced themselves from a sector of their ethnic group, while an affluent coethnic seemed to identify with his group as a whole. But class differences also must be perceived *generationally*. There was a division among my middle-aged informants between those whose parents were wealthy, or wealthier than themselves, and those who had achieved considerable upward mobility from their parents' positions. Those with well-off parents spoke about them matter-of-factly, or with some fear; they were people of a similar or better social position who had power over their descendents. Clelia Cipolla evaluated her deceased father-in-law: "He held the family together—perhaps with an iron fist, but he held it together. There was fear and love and respect. He didn't demand it, he just got it. We *knew* what we were supposed to do . . . [whispers] we *knew*. It was *his* home and his family."

In stark contrast, those with poorer parents generally tended to discuss them with the familiar language of self-aggrandizing sentimentality. That is, they praised their struggles against poverty and their self-sacrifices for their children from the comfortable position of economic independence. Maria Fante said of her working-class father: "I looked up to him, he was a fantastic man." Tony Ripetto, Gino Angeluzzi, Al Bertini, and Cetta Longhinotti all spoke of the sainthood of their mothers, their struggles to clothe and feed their children.

But there is a contrapuntal theme to this chorus of praise: those with education or high professional positions tended, also, to make fun of their working-class parents, and of older immigrants in general. They mimicked their accents, joked about their beliefs and behavior, and told stories and jokes with old immigrant protagonists. Gino Angeluzzi described a wedding of some cousins he had recently attended, switching halfway through into the persona of an old immigrant woman:

> It's an Italiana family . . . from a nice-a Italiana family . . . hissa folks hadda few dollars, you know? [laughs].

And he described an incident of decades ago:

> One old guy came to me:
>   "You father Aldo?"
>   Yeah.
>   "You mother Maria?"
>   Yeah.
>   "Ahhh, I know you folks a long time! We come over this country onna boat."

Angela Caputo mimicked her mother's accent, passing into and out of it as she described her mother's feelings about her "three girl-es," or her reading an account of Enrico Caruso's plight after the 1906 earthquake. "He poosh-ed and he pooll-ed his suitcase up the street." She also found the constructions of "North Beach Italian" amusing, laughing heartily over "*I gatti faitano*" ("The cats are fighting").

There are a number of Italian immigrant jokes in circulation in these professional Italian-American networks, jokes turning on the themes of the naiveté of immigrant parents and the protection that their sophisticated children extend to them.[8] One joke describes a loving son taking his immigrant mother to the opera, at the climax of which she screams, "Loook out, heesa gotta knife!" Another describes a heavily accented immigrant petitioning a judge for "citizenashippa," but worried about his poor English. The judge leans over and exclaims: "Donju worry. In thissa court, you gonna get your citizenashippa!"

But these jokes also contain themes of resentment and hostility

8. These jokes were collected during an earlier period of fieldwork from individuals who were members of my later informants' networks.

toward the immigrant elderly who are, after all, not social assets to their children. A Sicilian question and answer:

How do you kill the Italian people?
Grow *coluzzi* [mustard] on the freeway dividers.

This joke turns on the known foraging abilities of Italian-Americans: informants of working-class background, especially those in the East and South Bay, consistently told me that their parents or neighbors had gathered mushrooms, medicinal plants and edible greens in the orchards and wastelands. (Recall Gino Angeluzzi's memory that some Depression meals consisted solely of *coluzzi*.) In the joke, the former survival skills of the immigrants are transformed into outmoded instinctive reactions: the elderly wander onto the freeway and are killed by passing cars.

A story of Joe Cruciano's summarized and transcended these reactions. He told it at an after-dinner gathering with his wife Sally and Sam and Edith Trento, a neighboring couple of identical background (Southern Italian man and American woman). The narrative was obviously part of a stock repertoire, as Sally Cruciano had urged Joe to "tell it again" so I could hear it:

Joe: I was a big college guy . . . and of course I was tired of goin to
   funerals because I had such a big family, members of the
   family would pass away, and the same ritual every time: the
   people would go up and cry and talk about the whole life of
   the individual, but they would do it in Bruschitan: [singsong]
   "I remember when you and I picked poppies"—and they'd go
   through the whole life you know. I thought, geez, this is
   barbaric. I couldn't understand why people did this. So my
   aunt passed away, and we musta had five hundred people at
   the Rosary, so Aunt Rini goes up and she goes up to the coffin
   and she starts in with the "You're my sister and I remember
   when we were doing this and" . . . She looked, she was in
   such a frenzy that I was pretty afraid for her, I thought she was
   pretty old—she must have been fifty then. . . .
All: [Laughter.]
Joe: I figured, geez, she's real old, she's gonna *die* up there. So I
   went up there and I grabbed her—I went up and put my arms
   around her—the big college guy goes up and he goes, "Come

[124]

on Aunt Rini, I'll take you back." And she goes, (mutters harshly) "Go siddown, I'm alright." And she goes right on with the old ritual!

All: [Loud laughter.]

Joe: And she filled me with a state of shock. I walked the hell out of there and I figured—hey, my family's alright.

Sam: [Mimicking Aunt Rini's actions theatrically, wailing and flailing his arms, stopping to mutter to an invisible Joe: "Go siddown. Go siddown."]

All: [Continuing laughter.]

Joe: That's when I started to grow up, from that day on.

The point of Joe's narrative is that Aunt Rini, unlike the mother at the opera or the Italians gathering mustard, has a sense of distance from her role, and through it maintains her authority over Joe. The story embodies and fuses both sentimentality and distancing mimicry.

Clearly there are wide variations in the ways that these Italian-Americans make use of their ethnic kin and ideas of ethnic behavior to discuss and rationalize their own social and economic positions. Symbols of ethnicity are also manipulated in interpreting the meaning of ethnic family life; and this practice goes beyond the interpretation of immigrant parental roles. In the first place, most of my informants believed the majority scholarly opinion that there is *an* Italian-American family. They had no agreement with one another, however, as to the nature of that institution, beyond the relatively meaningless assertion that Italian-American families are "close." Just as they used varying ideas of Italian-American economic behavior to explain and justify their own economic positions, so they manipulated the emotionally resonant symbols of kinship to justify their own family behavior.

Clelia Cipolla and Cetta Longhinotti identified proper Italian-American family behavior with Catholic orthodoxy (which incidentally underlined their authority over their children). Carl Motto asserted that Italian-Americans support their parents, "right or wrong." Gus Brandis, in contrast, introduced the theme of family solidarity in connection with his father's refusal to attend his daughter's religiously unauthorized second wedding. For Gus, his *father* had denied family solidarity: "Basically I kind of look askew [sic] at situations where the family has been put second to anything—for

[125]

instance, the Church. Basically from my experience the family is *sopratutto* [all important]."

Another family theme was the symbolic meaning individuals attributed to the care of aged parents. Angela Caputo, whose mother was in a nursing home, expressed extreme guilt that she was not caring for her in her own home: "Among our relatives and friends, we are maybe the sole ones [not to keep their mothers at home]. . . My sisters and I stand alone in doing this." On the other hand, Cetta Longhinotti, in an identical situation, expressed great pride in the self-sacrifice of her weekly visits to her mother, and identified her behavior with Italian-American family values: "You have to do it." The social context of kin behavior is crucial to individuals' interpretations of its ethnic meaning.

The great malleability, the almost arbitrary nature of the meanings attached to symbols shows up clearly in the ways in which parents and children manipulated family symbols against one another and the ways in which individuals changed symbolic referents over the course of my research.

James Giovannino expressed sardonic pleasure in the way his father's insistence on the facade of a close Italian family—family dinners, special Italian foods, wine—"blew to hell" when he abandoned his wife to marry another woman. For James, the meaning of Italian family unity was "sticking up for each other—the kind of thing I never got from my father."

David DiVincenzo, at the beginning of my research, identified Italian-American family roles very negatively:

> Being a real Italian man is being a bastard, authoritarian. You're sensitive about your masculine image and hard on your kids. . . . A real Italian woman is Catholic—she suffers for her family, she's a martyr.

Near the end of my fieldwork, two years later, David had changed his mind about Italian men and spoke positively about his father and grandfather. And he had altered his identification of the meaning of Italian-American women's roles as well:

> I would say if the image I gave before [of Italian-American men] was a negative one, I really take that back, but I do still recognize the

negative aspects, but especially—this may sound sexist—among Italian-American women. I mean they've gone through a lot of shit, that's probably what's wrong, but a lot of guilt or sacrifice and stuff, I mean I find it pretty common, I don't find many women my mother's age who have moved from that stereotype. . . . My mother, you could say she's very adaptable, but in another way you could say she's Uncle Tomish in the sense—she has values but she's very noncritical so you don't always know where she stands.

Dorothy DiVincenzo herself saw her role as the necessary mediator among her husband, her parents, and her children.

Joe Cruciano saw himself as a man who had wanted many children and financial success, and who had both. His children, however, felt strongly that his financial success directly interfered with proper fatherly behavior. His son Rick said: "There was a certain point when my father started really making it—he was much less involved with the family from then on." And his daughter Clare perceived the first flush of affluence: "They were going out to a lot of parties and buying a lot of things—mostly they were going out with the people my Dad was doing business with. . . . The main thing I noticed was my parents being supertired . . . in a bad mood . . . or just not there."

In this chapter I have suggested that the connections between mobility and ethnic kinship are far more indirect than has been commonly thought. Rather than perceiving the economic and family lives of American ethnic populations in the United States through the prism of our own local mythology, a giant authoritarian classroom, we need to uncover their actual intersections with the changing economy—and their varying and evolving perceptions of the ethnic meaning of their economic and kinship lives. Some Italian-Americans, it has been shown, themselves see their families as good classrooms, proper launching pads for success in American society. Others feel that mobility involves improper family behavior: "Lead a good normal life. Don't get money in your head." In order really to understand these Italian-American constructions of economy and family, we must not confuse ways of seeing, theirs or ours, with patterns of behavior. The uses to which these women, men, and children put symbols of ethnic behavior and family vary according to context and intention. There is, however, a missing segment in this picture: between these Italian-American families and the larger society is the network of locally known coethnics, the "Italian community."

# [4]

# "It's Kinda an Old Immigrant Thing": Economy, Family, and Collective Ethnic Identity

> One cannot study the relationship between work and family if it is assumed that the connections are only tangential. Functionalist analyses must be replaced by perspectives which examine how people reconciled the two worlds—Pleck 1976:188

## The Myth of Community

One afternoon, when I had been doing fieldwork for a year and a half, I received a telephone call from a woman on the East Coast. She had gotten my name from another researcher in the area. She was going to be in San Francisco for a few days in the next month and wanted to know if I would "give" her some "community women" to interview. A very uncomfortable conversation ensued. I tried to tell her that there wasn't a "community" for these nonexistent women to represent. I explained that Italians were settled *all over* Northern California, in the smaller towns and in the suburbs, not just in San Francisco's North Beach (which had mostly Chinese residents by now anyway); but I supposed she might be able to interview some women living in San Francisco involved in voluntary associations, or one of the handful of upper-class women engaged in philanthropic projects. She replied in frustration that she was looking for "*key* community women." Running underneath her statements, almost bubbling up, was the opinion that if I could not come up with these key community women, pronto, I must either be selfishly hoarding them away, or must not know "the community," must not, in fact, be doing good research. She, after all, had a grant to pay for her long-distance phone calls, her airplane trips, her tapes and transcriptions. The money conferred legitimacy: it was for finding and interviewing these women; therefore, they must exist.

I thought about the women with whom I had ongoing contact. What would Cetta Longhinotti, who had just said about her neighborhood, "Other than to say hello I don't know a soul," who worked forty hours a week and drove hundreds of miles to visit her dying mother every weekend—what would Cetta have to tell this interviewer about community?

Or Lucia Mornese, who was retired and therefore had more leisure and who was, after all, active in a women's auxiliary ethnic organization? I thought about the organization's most recent project—a bus trip to Reno. Lucia did *know* many more Italian-American women than Cetta, but were her acquaintances representative of a community? They mostly didn't live in "ethnic neighborhoods," they were not pressuring City Hall, and none of my other San Francisco informants had even heard of them. No, I thought not.

Finally I thought of Angela Caputo. She was much more involved in the various recently organized San Francisco ethnic projects, like the Italian museum. She had more formal education; I had in fact met her at a local college class on Italian-Americans. Was she a community woman? But Angela lived alone in a large apartment building; she had spent most of her adult life outside of California, and, aside from her relatives and board members of these organizations, I knew, because I had taken the time to interview her over and over, and to chart them, that there were very few Italian-Americans in her social network. What community did Angela represent?

### The Ethnicity Industry

It took some time before the unease I felt as a result of this phone call faded. I finally realized that I had had a close encounter of the usual kind with the ethnicity industry. In the language of this industry, all Americans with any racial or ethnic identity are working-class or impoverished, live in "ethnic neighborhoods," and form part of the "X community." All members of all of these communities are "proud of their heritage" and all are, of course, organized into tightly knit hierarchial organizations. This last criterion is essential: it makes it possible for politicians to understand the feelings of the "X community" by having one meeting with the head of one organization. It is also the rationale for foundation and government grants for a variety of studies and projects—like the one in which my long-distance caller was involved.

This vision is continually renewed in writings on white ethnicity and working-class life in America:

> Social life in white ethnic neighborhoods is largely rooted in the family. . . . Most people know or at least recognize one another. There is a sense of community integrity and group identity. (Seifer 1973:8)

> The pattern of Italian-American life is continuous with that of their ancestors. Its verities continue to demonstrate that family, community and work mean survival and that outsiders are threats to the neighborhood stability which is necessary to the close-knit life and culture of the people (Gambino 1974:343).

> Within the geographic boundaries of the Italian Quarters the *connazionali* gave life to a closely woven community within which the Italian way of life flourished (Gumina 1978:37)

My caller's request reflected one major development within this complex of premises: the effect of feminism. It has finally become merely common sense to investigate the opinions and feelings of women, apart from men, about their ethnic/racial identities, their home lives, their jobs. But in assuming that all ethnic women were living in organized communities, she and others closed themselves off from seeing these women's actual lives. Why is this idea of community so compelling, and where does it come from?

## The Evolution of Community

Concepts of community are as old as social science itself. Since the time of Rousseau and his critics, the idea of community has

[131]

implicitly or explicitly contained the images of equality, order, and civility—and of narrowness, hidebound tradition, and ignorance. And equally, since Rousseau, the community model has been drawn both as an imagined opposition to the perceived social disorder or *anomie* of modern life and as a stolid backwater, a prior social stage from which civilization would deliver us.

Until relatively recently, this dichotomy was largely tied to opposing concepts of country and city, and to what Wrong has labeled "the conservative critique of modernity" (1976:77). Country/community represented an imagined peaceful and changeless feudal order, while city/crowd evoked social disorder, danger, and the challenge to established class divisions. This way of seeing mystified the political-economic unity of country and city in developing Europe and the United States—the constantly changing and increasingly capitalist nature of agriculture, and the interpenetration of urban and rural financial interests. The movement of country people off the land and into the city was the result, not of the mystical pull of evil city ways, but of centuries-long practices of land appropriation and of shifts in the entire industrializing economy (R. Williams 1973).

Ironically, the popular European and American image of country people being lured from the unchanging pastoral landscape into the teeming maw of city life was reversed in our popular image of the coming of second-wave migrants to the United States. Ignoring the unity of the Atlantic economy—the enormous effects of American trade on European economies and the energetic recruitment of migrants by American industrialists and transport interests—Americans focused instead on European political disorders and perceived the Atlantic migration solely as a flight from Old World despotism to American democracy. We saw the European countryside as in upheaval and the American city as the passive, entirely benevolent, and even vulnerable recipient of its refugees: "Give me . . . the wretched refuse of your teeming shore." The "refuse" of Europe, in this vision, came from a disordered world, and thus lacked community; that was an American possession which, depending on political perspective, we saw migrants as either acquiring or threatening to destroy.

Over time, this vision dissolved into another. European migrants were seen, finally, as like other urbanizing country people; and like them, became the subjects of theoretical dispute. Theorists from Durkheim and Tönnies to the Chicago school of sociologists of the 1920s and 1930s had developed a vision of the simple, humanly satisfying, face-to-face, traditional rural community that was giving way to the complex, anomic, modern urban world of strangers (Hannerz 1980). The profound Enlightenment ambivalence about community was carried forward: was it a priceless heirloom being shattered, or a less-civilized vestige that must give way to modern life? European immigrants and their children, highly visible in the Midwestern and East Coast cities that scholars were studying, caught the full force of this ambivalence. They did have community, after all, and they must forsake it. They must assimilate. They were not assimilating fast enough. Assimilation is an ordeal, something precious is lost, and we must understand and help them. And finally—some assimilate faster than others. They have superior families and are socially mobile. The others, urban villagers, carry on their peasant past: they have community. We have traced the path to the mobility historians.

The final, most recent twist of this ideological braid derives from a number of converging sources: the white ethnic renaissance, the gentrification of inner cities by young white professionals, the intensification of grass-roots organizing efforts by former student activists turned "community activists." We newly see "ethnic community" as good after all, something to preserve and extend (Wrong 1972). It gives life and charm to cities; it can be a focus for progressive organizing; it keeps the crime rate down. We can have our cake and eat it too: we can keep the country in the city.

Community, we can see, has always been an ideological construction. What is new is our unitary cultural emphasis on its virtue and necessity. This emphasis leads to a nonmaterial, a conceptual, definition: we are no longer talking about small settlements, about limited groups of people who see one another daily over a lifetime. We mean instead that *someone* perceives "togetherness" in a social network, or group of networks or even a social category, and thus labels the individuals in that network or category as a community. At the same time, this transposed definition retains, metaphorically, its original material connotations: daily face-to-face contact, organization, groupness—*Gemeinschaft*. This metaphorical use of community is now in common folk, scholarly, and especially political parlance: we

[133]

hear of the Black, gay, women's, or press community. In each case, thousands of people, unknown to one another, living often thousands of miles apart, take on the folksy cachet of peasant women meeting at the village well, or of shoppers in an American ethnic market arguing over *baccalà* or gefilte fish. Labeling a human collectivity a community confers upon it a hoped-for alliance of interests, solidity, tradition.[1]

We have unveiled one mirror to discover that it reflects yet another: the metaphorical use of community relies in part on images of American white ethnic communities that are themselves metaphorical. The idea that immigrants recreated the behavior and traditions of their original villages and towns in the New World urban setting, like the earlier image of a changeless European countryside, is simply false. Migration is an enormous disruption. Even when material conditions in the host country allow it, the demography of migration and new economic roles prevent the reestablishment of former household and social structures. And even when they are residentially segregated, when they do not yet speak English well, migrants must and do interact with the dominant society, and reconstruct their identities accordingly.

Finally, and most important, the material basis of ethnic community, residential segregation, has been misspecified and misunderstood. The myth of community has prevented us from assimilating the extent to which the Little Italies, Little Polands, and Jewish quarters (and ghettos, barrios, and Chinatowns) have undergone continuous alteration. Different groups have moved in and out; neighborhood boundaries have altered; businesses have opened and closed; and the immigrants *themselves* have changed house, street, neighborhood, city. This is a pattern that has been present since the nineteenth century, as Thernstrom shows for Boston:

> The familiar ghetto model of the immigrant experience is thus seriously misleading. The extent to which foreign-born newcomers typically huddled together in neighborhoods composed largely of their fellow countrymen has often been exaggerated, and even where there were highly segregated ethnic neighborhoods there was little continuity of the *individuals* who composed them over time. Just as

1. This is not to quarrel with the political uses of language, but to distinguish between movement building and the description of social reality.

there was a radical distinction between the visible portion of the community immortalized in the local newspapers and the masses of ordinary citizens, so too there was a distinction between what was most visible in the ethnic subcommunity—the groceries, restaurants, bars, churches, meeting halls, and the rest—and the nature of the ethnic community defined in a more comprehensive demographic sense. There were indeed Irish, Italian, Jewish, and other ethnic neighborhoods that could easily be discerned, but the vast majority of anonymous immigrants who lived in them at one census were destined to vanish from them before ten years had elapsed. (1973:232)

Thernstrom relates this enormous and consistent internal migration to the changing demands for labor in a rapidly developing economy (1973:228). The residents of today's as well as yesterday's ethnic communities, then, are most often either relatively recent arrivals or atypical late-stayers whose small businesses or pensions force or allow them to remain. Seeking coziness and stability, we have expanded their numbers and proclaimed their lengthy residence; when the fantasy slips and we see neighborhoods in flux, we cry out that ethnic communities are endangered. In so doing we falsify history and create misconceived nostalgia for worlds we have never lost, because "if there is one thing certain about the organic community, it is that it has always gone" (R. Williams 1960:277).

The dead hand of the community myth lies upon the living reality of past and present American ethnic life. Wrong concludes that "the error lies in conceiving of community as a kind of end in itself, apart from the particular activities and functioning that actually bind people together, and apart from those values that constitute a truly shared vision of life. As Ortega once pointed out, 'People do not live together merely to be together. They live together to do something together'" (1976:78).

## Economy, Family, and Collective Ethnic Identity

This economic emphasis—questioning what that something is that people "do together" that creates community—provided the key to my understanding of these Italian-Americans' evocations of collective ethnic identity. Some of them did, indeed, believe in an "Italian community," but what they meant by it seemed to vary as

[135]

much as did their notions of the Italian family. I began, slowly, to understand the differing material perspectives from which they constructed ideas of ethnic community. Work and family were the major material forces in their lives, and as I considered them, I began to see that work, family, and collective ethnic identity exist- ed in relation to each other.

The key lay in the social component of total *work process*—in the social relations engendered and maintained in the course of doing one's job. Work process is usually discussed in terms of workers' relative power and autonomy over their own work activities, or in terms of the effect of work organization on their relations to one another at the work site.[2] I found, looking beyond the workplace, that social relations on the job, relations within households, and ideas of collective ethnic identity varied in concert. Viewing oc- cupations in this way, as covarying parts of larger social clusters, I divided my informants across ordinary income and status lines into three large categories: small businesspeople, workers in large firms, and independent professionals.

It was among men and women who had small business connec- tions (either their own or their parents'), or were independent professionals with largely ethnic clientele, that I found pride in the number of Italian-American acquaintances they could name, well- developed ethnic maps (that is, they thought of areas in terms of ethnic neighborhoods), and the claim to membership in a commu- nity. On my first interview with Jarus DiVincenzo, I handed him a list of sponsors for a local Columbus Day event. Even though he did not belong to the organization that put on the event, and had not attended it, he enthusiastically ticked off each name on a list, giving minute particulars:

> I went to parochial school with him. *That's* a big family. Now here's his brother. He was David's [oldest son's] pediatrician. Now, Richard Caputo—he brought *me* into the world. Now Jack Trentini, he's a friend of my wife's father. His brother owns a sports team. John Barbuto, he's a twin—he has winery interests. These ones are all my customers.

2. See Braverman 1974; Burawoy 1979; Edwards 1979; and Zimbalist 1979 for analyses of changing work processes in the United States.

When I accompanied the Longhinottis to a local ethnic dinner, Joe happily surveyed the auditorium entirely filled with diners and proclaimed, "On my neighborhood night, I'll know four hundred by name." And Louis Baca, skillfully eluding my questions about his family while holding court in his North Beach store, named other, past Italian-owned businesses and minutely traced their family connections to present and past politicians. He also, like the others, gave me his personal vision of local Italian-American history, the contributions of each regional group, and his personal ethnic map:

> I was born on Telegraph Hill when the City was sane. The cops ran the town. It was controlled—we had no racketeers out here, thanks to the Irish. . . . You went in a restaurant [during Prohibition], they served you your wine in a mug. The Genovesi, they were famous for being window washers and scavengers. The Tuscans ran restaurants and were bootleggers. The Milanesi, Piedmontesi, and Venetians, they were the artisans. The Sicilians, they were fishermen. They were fine people, but they were poor and got kicked around.

Joe Longhinotti had his own list of Italian-owned Oakland businesses, and the kin and other connections of each owner, in his own version of ethnic life in the 1920s and 1930s in the East Bay:

> In the old days, parents made their children work for their education. It was a good clean life with hard work. Oh, they'd drink their wine—but it wasn't the party life—a picnic was a party. Those picnics up at Valenti Park, with the music and the food. And here comes your Irish people, they liked the music and the wine, being that they were born and raised. . . . Most of these people was Genovesi, Piedmontesi, or Lucchesi. You take a Genovese, a Jew, a Greek, and an Armenian—you gonna have a hell of a time who beats who. The Genovesi—they make buck, they save two.

Lucia Mornese discussed her parents' store and the intricate networks for which it served as a node:

> In Saint Peter and Paul's, they had the Salesian Boys' School—and that's also where they had Salesian Boys' Club and that's where Joe

Alioto and Judge Molinari and other well-known Italians were connected to that. They used to come in my father's shop—when I worked there at night some of the fellows would come and they'd do my homework for me! . . . . Even when my children were in school, we saw parents that I had known as a little girl, we had sorta grown up together—they would say, "Oh, gee, your father, I'll never forget him. You know I was hungry so many times and he used to give me hotdogs and put it on credit and never made me pay for it." And my children would say, "Everyone seems to know Nonno and they say how generous and kind he was." And I say, "Yeah, that's why he never had any money" [laughs].

Nancy Ferrucci was more enthusiastic about her San Jose store-keeping antecedents:

They were just plain starving. They came over here and put down their roots. They were all good cooks—everybody made wine, and ravioli on holidays. We always had Sunday dinner together. . . . We had a tremendous Italian trade in the stores, and of course we dealt with each other and that helped business. But the church reflected the neighborhood—there were always Mexican people, so we learned how to eat that, too. We were social—we entered floats in parades—there was a New Year's Eve bash. . . . The Irish are analogous—of course, if you're Irish, you're next to being sainted.

Note how the speakers' ethnic maps include Catholic non-Italians present in the area, and how their Italian regional portraits contradict one another.

These materially based visions of community are transferred to children, where they live on as ideology. But there seems to be a difference between those children who can benefit directly from their parents' and lateral relatives' local networks and those who cannot. The former have a full-blown "community" ideology and make active use of these networks, while the latter concentrate on contact with relatives. David DiVincenzo is thinking of returning to San Jose to take up his father's business offer:

It'd be tough to do that [move away] cause what my family is in a broader sense of just people I know there that are really related to my family, not just in a blood sense but in past things. It's a tempting

[138]

thing to be around there, cause it's so easy. It's a really comfortable place, not just because it's pretty wealthy or whatever—but—you can survive that if you have friends—but it's just cause you can work through things easier—like I got a job with my friend's father . . . and you know you can just automatically wield some power just cause you know people who know your parents. . . You know people know your name and stuff. You know it's a classic home turf-type thing.

In contrast, James and Mary Giovannino are seriously considering moving back to the Central California town where their parents still live:

We might go back. There are a lot of appealing things, one of which is the family. Of course, I have little chance of a job there.

Linda Mornese lives a few doors from her parents and drives her father to work every day. But her economic interests lie outside:

In fact recently my boss said I was being transferred fifty miles away and before he was finished I said I'm *not going*—so that was it, I didn't go. Family—definitely.

And Greg Longhinotti, too, sees staying in his area in nonmaterial terms:

I don't want to move far away. I try to see my family as often as possible. I like getting together with them . . . try to stop by the parents' house once or twice a week.

These young adults, all of whose parents have or had small business or ethnic professional connections, but not local networks and material resources sufficient to constitute a business or professional entree, do not see themselves as part of an ethnic community—do not, in fact, claim the existence of one at all. When asked about the characteristics of Italian-Americans, they describe their relatives. For them, family is not only community writ small, but the only ethnic community structure extant.

In this respect they resemble middle-aged individuals in one of the two other economic-sector categories: working-class and professional occupations in which ethnicity plays no material role—corporation lawyers, bankers, secretaries and technical workers for large firms, blue-collar workers in industry, public school teachers. Different as these occupations are, they share one attribute: work process is so organized that stressing ethnicity brings no material rewards and may actually be harmful.

Joe Longhinotti's career shift, from independent baker to baker for a large supermarket chain, shows this difference. When Joe had his own bakery, he had a significant Italian clientele with whom he could speak Italian. "It helps you in the business." His doctor, his insurance agent, and the parents of his childrens' school friends were all customers. Now that he has been forced out of business by the competition of supermarket chains, and gone to work for one of them, he is transferred from one location to another, and cannot count on having the same co-workers, much less coethnic co-workers, from one year to the next. He has little contact with store customers. An outgoing, friendly man with theatrical tendencies, Joe can no longer afford to burst into Italian song at work. Where the exigencies of work process once enhanced ethnicity, they now militate against it.

Another way to observe this occupational contrast is to look at intergenerational occupational changes within families. Dom Cipolla's father started a florist wholesaling business in a small town near San Francisco in the 1910s. It was successful, and his sons either joined it or started their own florist businesses in nearby areas. His youngest son, Dom, however, chose to pursue college and an advanced degree and is now a middle-level technical worker for a large San Francisco corporation. For most family members, work, kin, and coethnics comprise an interlocking social whole. Even their small town, now overrun by San Francisco and essentially a commuting suburb, is heavily settled with Italian-Americans originating from their region; older women in the family have not even needed to become competent in English. But for Dom Cipolla, work and kin are two discrete universes: none of his co-workers is part of his kin network.

Dom's wife's family history parallels his, on a lower-income scale. Clelia Cipolla's father came from Liguria in 1920 to South San Francisco in order to work as an agricultural laborer on land leased by one of his male relatives. Eight years later, he returned to Italy to bring back his wife and Clelia, then five. The family remained on the leased land until it was sold by the owners in 1950, Clelia's father working in the fields and her mother cooking for all the workers. All social life involved other Italian ranch families. The parents had so little contact with non-Italians that they never learned English. Their son and daughter, however, went to college and received advanced degrees. Each entered a profession where day-to-day contact was largely with non-Italians. Clelia married and remained in the area; when her children were born she quit her job and reentered kin and ethnic social life. "This may not surprise you Micaela—but five days out of seven I walked with the children to mother's after I had finished my housework. It was a pleasant walk, and we would visit with mother's friends on the way. One day a week we visited my mother-in-law." But now that her children are in college and her parents have died, Clelia has resumed work and has only peripheral contact with coethnics. "I miss this." Her brother has a technical position in a large corporation, and has been transferred to the East Coast.

Because Clelia and her brother have clearly achieved social mobility relative to their parents, we might be tempted to ascribe their loss of occupational ethnic networks to that process. But Clelia's husband Dom's family, owning rather than leasing land and in a more lucrative business, are more economically successful than either Clelia or her brother, or Dom himself. It is not mobility itself, but certain changed work-process patterns that mobility may entail, that determine the loss of work-based ethnic networks.

It is also, as has been seen with David DiVincenzo, not just the passage of time and generations and the changed residence patterns erasing "ethnic communities" that determine the presence or absence of ethnic networks and a sense of ethnic identity. David's "classic home turf" is a linked series of sprawling suburbs, and he is a fourth-generation Italian-American.

We can see this phenomenon more clearly by comparing the work lives and social networks of David and of Joe Longhinotti's son Greg. They are both in their mid-twenties, both went to parochial schools, their parents live in comparable suburbs (Greg's in a much smaller house) surrounding defunct Italian settlements in two cities, and each has one parent with a generations-long family connection to that Italian settlement. There are four main differences between them: David has interrupted his connection to his parents' area by college attendance and travel in Europe, while Greg has remained in or near his parents' home since high school; David's father's small business was successful, while Greg's father's was not; David's father is now retired, with property and investments, while Greg's is a worker with only a salary; and David now has college experience and the option to enter business through his father's resources and contacts, while Greg has worked up to the lower supervisorial rung of a large firm.

The "class equals culture" premise (as in Greer 1974) would predict that Greg's social network would be highly ethnic, while David's would not; the ethnic succession model (as in Gans 1962) would assume that suburbanization has ended ethnic behavior for both families.

In fact, Greg, like other Italian-American workers in large non-ethnic firms, although feeling his ethnic identity strongly, identifies it with his family life: "The main thing is how you're brought up . . . the closeness of the family. . . . I'm definitely proud I'm Italian. . . . It's mainly the love that you get from the family."

And Greg's personal network bears this out. On a weekly basis, he sees co-workers (almost all non-Italians), non-Italian male friends, a non-Italian girl friend, and his parents. He sees his siblings several times a month and his uncles, aunts, cousins, and grandmother only on family occasions. There is little connection between his friends' parents and his own parents. But most important is the lack of connection between his social network and his economic well-being (see diagram 8). Greg's father used his acquaintanceship with Greg's original supervisor to secure his first position with the corporation; none of his friends or relatives has been of economic use to him since. His siblings are skilled workers witn no financial connection to him. Some of his uncles and aunts have higher economic status and more resources than his parents, but they are also all workers for firms—there is no longer any business connection in the kin network. Greg sees this as a lost opportunity: "We've all made a few mistakes in our lifetime, I'm sure—especially when we [his father] were gonna get that deli. That would've been great! But it didn't work out."

David, as we have seen, has a broad community vision of his ethnicity that transcends family. At the beginning of my research

8. David DiVincenzo and Greg Longhinotti: schematized kin networks.

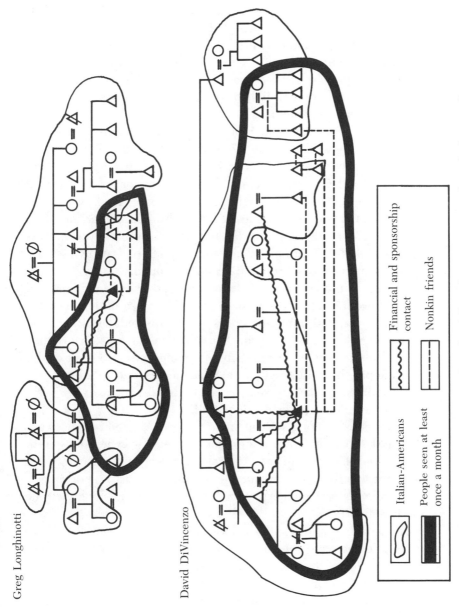

Greg Longhinotti

David DiVincenzo

| | Italian-Americans | | Financial and sponsorship contact |
|---|---|---|---|
| | People seen at least once a month | | Nonkin friends |

Only lateral relatives living in area are indicated in full; nonkin contacts are indicated schematically.

he casually typed up a list for me of more than fifty Italian-Americans of varying ages living in his area. When we later considered the list name by name, he could place each person's family in broader business, professional, and school contexts.

David's actual social network reflects this vision (see diagram 8). He sees not only his parents and siblings but also his mother's siblings and parents at least once a month. The nonkin component of his network is mostly Italian-American and is extremely large. There are many connections between the kin and nonkin components of his social network. Financial and sponsorship connections are very strong within his family: he receives significant amounts of money from both his parents and his mother's parents. They are also significant outside his family: he was hired for his most recent job by the Italian-American father of a close friend. Entrepreneurial capital and expertise are available from his father, mother's brothers, and mother's father. His brother wants to go into business with him. So the kin and friend components of David's network involve career sponsorship and economic support.

We saw in the last chapter that Greg's and David's mothers had very different personal genealogy shapes because of demographic and immigration-timing differences. While these differences, however, mean that David has a much larger *potential* kin network than Greg, they do not determine any other differences. David could, for example, have salaried parents and uncles who could not provide the business and personal contacts that his relatives do, without his genealogy shape altering at all.

Even, then, among Italian-Americans only in their early twenties, and separated from emigration by several generations, ethnicity *may* play a major material role. Greg feels his ethnicity but does not live it—his economic life militates against it. For David, the easiest path to financial success runs through his highly ethnic social network.

This analysis is implicitly historical: it suggests a causal link between the changing economy and changing patterns of kinship and ethnicity. There are two major post-Civil War economic developments in particular that have changed the face of the U.S. economy and set the stage for these new linkages.

One is the progressive rationalization of industry—of the workplace and of work process in particular—which is part of the maturation of capitalism in the United States. Gutman (1977) has clearly traced the thrust of this process in the middle and late nineteenth century.[3] Employers, concerned to control increasingly large labor forces, fought to eradicate what Gutman calls "preindustrial work patterns"—artisanal work processes, ritualized eating and drinking breaks, and ethnic holidays—through which workers asserted control over their work time and process. As the U.S. work force was repeatedly reconstituted by waves of first northwestern and then southeastern European immigrants (and Blacks, Asians, and Latinos in certain regions), owners continually restarted this process on each new group. They also took advantage of cultural divisions to prevent union organizing by deliberately mixing nationalities at particular work sites and by using one group as strikebreakers against another (American Blacks were used in this way as well).

Harry Braverman in *Labor and Monopoly Capital* (1974) takes up these changes in the U.S. economy and their effect on work process at the point where Gutman leaves off. Braverman traces the rise and effect of an ever more sophisticated "Scientific Management" movement on industrial work process: the breaking down of a single, skilled productive process under the control of one worker into many small, unskilled pieces of work where each worker does the same task repeatedly. He traces the simultaneous rise of "management" positions—the great expansion of office work in connection with industrial production—and finally the movement of scientific management into office work: the deskilling of clerical work (the separation of executives from secretaries and clerks), and the proletarianization of segments of the clerical sector.

The other process that has shaped the U.S. economy is the rise of that class variously labeled the middle class, the new *petit bourgeoisie,* and the professional-managerial class: the expansion and legitimation of the preexisting professions—medical, legal, and teaching—and the creation of new ones—social work, criminal justice, mental health work, public relations; and the creation and expansion of management positions in private industry and, soon after, in the public sector (Walker 1979).

Italian-Americans in California were less heavily affected than their Eastern Seaboard and Midwestern coethnics by the exigen-

3. See also Bernstein 1966; Edwards 1979; and Montgomery 1979.

cies of industrial control of work timing and process, and more affected by nascent agribusiness practices. But they shared with them, in the second and successive generations, the process of fanning out into various service, industrial, clerical, management, and professional occupations, increasingly under the control of large firms.

We have seen that regional economy rather than ethnic culture seems to determine patterns of self-employment. And yet the vision of the "authentic" Italian shopkeeper or firm owner persists, in histories which focus on that class, in mass media images of Italians as purveyors of salami and pizza, and in the images that Italian-Americans themselves hold strongly. David DiVincenzo voiced this contradiction between ethnic image and the ethnic reality when he discussed his recent clerical job: "It's a smaller company—I think a lot of Catholics would rather work in that environment . . . yet there's thousands of Catholics who work for huge corporations! [laughs.] Yet I think it's kinda an old immigrant thing."[4]

Much as the thrust of recent economic change is toward monopolization and corporate control of all workers, including those in the professional-managerial class, there are still niches in the economy (just as there are for small businesses) for independent, professional work: small medical, legal, and technical practices; teaching in prestigious universities; and the management of small firms. So we might divide this class into that portion working under corporate control in a stratified environment and that portion whose jobs are characterized by autonomy and self-management. This division would cut across income measures: the young attorney at the bottom of a wealthy firm with a hundred employees might earn more than her counterpart in a storefront practice with two partners, but would be classed in the less autonomous, "proletarianized" portion.

Labor under these varying conditions intersects with ethnicity in radically different ways. We have noted how Dom Cipolla's techni-

4. David used the term "Catholics" here to denote the descendants of Italian, Mexican, Irish, and German immigrants in his home region. This interview occurred late in my fieldwork; David had been living for a period with his parents, seeing old parochial school friends, and had come to the conclusion that there was a Catholic way of life with which he identified. This perspective had nothing to do with church attendance, but with the search for social justice with which he was then concerned.

cal work for a large corporation cuts him off from the enveloping kin/ethnic network of his family's small business and forces him to present himself as ethnically neutral for the bulk of each working day. But there are other ramifications to this occupational choice: like Joe Longhinotti and other nonprofessional, lower-paid workers for large firms, Dom Cipolla cannot in any way involve his family members in his work. The last chapter described the nearly automatic involvement of family members in small businesses and the consequent extension of family networks into ethnic networks. But part of this pattern of family work involvement also obtains for many independent professional Italian-Americans.

Joe Cruciano's wife worked in his real estate business for some years after their children were out of grade school; each child has also worked in the office for varying periods. The middle son, Jim, who lives at home and has gone desultorily to community college, will "probably go in with his Dad"—a business opportunity that would be beyond his reach outside of the sphere of kinship.

Gino Angeluzzi's wife and two of their daughters have worked in his general medical practice. One daughter has gone to work in the records department of a hospital, and Teresa Angeluzzi now heads a convalescent hospital.

The independence that makes the employment of family members possible, and sometimes economically necessary, also usually allows these professionals the option of stressing or deemphasizing their ethnicity in the workplace. Gino Angeluzzi can afford to joke about his multiethnic practice: "Some days—everybody in the waiting room was Italian. I said to this guy, You be the interpreter" (laughs).

An extreme sample of this "optional ethnicity" involves the use that some Italian-Americans make of Mafia symbols. Joe Cruciano, as an independent professional, felt very free to exploit them. His wife, Sally, described an annual golfing vacation that he organized:

> For years we had what was called the Mafia tournament . . . guys that were really close and been in the same frat. They were all Italian except one guy who was part Italian, and one who was Persian. We always went, once a year, to Monterey, or whatever, and had this husband-wife tournament. And then that night we'd have the awards, and they'd be violin cases.

[147]

Nick Meraviglia, working for a large firm, on the other hand, has worried about material harm resulting from the same sort of Mafia joking from members of the Rotary Club that he had joined for business reasons. Nick was forced to manage his emotions in the direction of lightness and humor:

> But if I had become, I am sure, in any way, shape, or form ill at ease or offended, I think it would have taken on a serious nature, whereas I threw a little humor into it, and just sort of. . .

Here Pina, Nick's wife, broke in:

> The Rotary Club dearly loved you, dear—those little old men!

And Nick replied:

> Well I know but remembering that insofar as Italian members of the Rotary Club were concerned in that town, you could count em on one hand. . .

Forced by his work situation to deal almost exclusively with non-Italians, Nick could not stress his ethnicity. His Italian surname alone made him vulnerable to suspicions of organized-crime involvement. Ironically, Joe Cruciano also felt concerned about his self-exploitation of Mafia imagery, for fear that recently acquired clients with genuine past crime connections would not understand. His wife, Sally, said:

> No, we don't have the tournament anymore. It surprises me he didn't tell you about it. The only reason he may be reticent about it is that he's very friendly with Renato now, and he would be offended.

The overlap among some work-process characteristics, such as relative independence and small work sites, cause similarities in kin patterning and ethnic identity for these small businesspeople and independent professionals. But there are differences in work process as well between these two groups, the most salient being the relation between worker and customer. Small businesspeople often function as information brokers among their customers. They display posters announcing neighborhood and ethnic events; they act as repositories of useful knowledge; they "have the gift of gab that pleases the public," as Joe Longhinotti said. And it is in their material interest, as I have stressed, to act as conveyers of information about their customers—to see them as forming a community.

Professional workers, on the other hand, deal with paying customers in the transformed role of "client." Part of the professional worker's obligation to her client is to keep silence about the client's legal, medical, or financial business. Thus stories about clients are not shared with family and friends (and anthropologists) as are stories about customers. Italian-American informants who were professionals felt an understandable reluctance to name their coethnic clients, which carried over into discussions of coethnics in other relations to them as well. Gino Angeluzzi straightforwardly told me that the "so-called Italian" Bank of America turned down his loan application when he was starting his career. He was forced to turn to "somebody my brother knew—he owned property—his kids are millionaires." But he would not name the man, even though he knew I would change all names, and in any event it could not harm the lender's reputation to be known as a benefactor. Joe Cruciano, in the midst of a discussion of Italian-American families, referred to two families where the father was too domineering, but would not name them. And Nick Meraviglia shied away from questions about his past and present coethnic colleagues. These interactions do not seem to form a pattern until they are compared with the ease and fluency with which other men, nonprofessional workers and small businessmen, talked about friends and acquaintances. Part of the professional ethic is that one is being paid to keep confidences.

This work process difference is reflected in ideas of ethnic community. Except for self-defined ethnic brokers who were active in voluntary associations, all these professionals, even those for whom I knew coethnic friendships were important, identified ethnicity with their own families. When they were asked specifically about Italian-American characteristics, they referred consistently to close families and to the characteristics of members of their own families.

Diagram 9 pictures the varying influences that work, kin, ethnic friends, and ethnic identity have upon one another in these Italian-Americans' lives. It is probably not coincidental that the "work overlap" circle shrinks as we move from occupational and work

9. Impact of work process on kinship, friendship, and ethnic identity

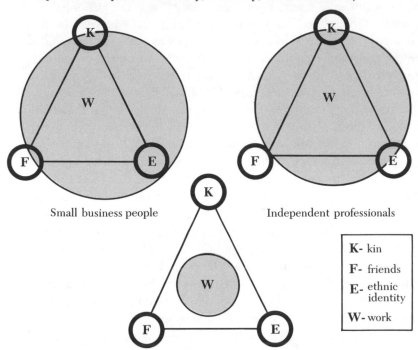

Small business people

Independent professionals

K- kin
F- friends
E- ethnic identity
W- work

Working-class, professional, and managerial workers for large, multiethnic firms

settings predating the Industrial Revolution, through those whose rise coincides with it, to those that have come into being with advanced capitalism. This is not to claim that small businesspeople lead preindustrial home lives. It is rather to suggest, as Marxists have explained, that the capitalist era has experienced stages in the organization of production, those of earlier periods coexisting with the most recent. Similarly, those occupations characteristic of earlier stages allow individuals the "free space" in which to maintain home/work intersections disallowed by more "modern" occupations.

It is important, however, not to assume romantically that the linked home/work lives of these Italian-American small businesspeople were or are necessarily more satisfying than others. Informants themselves complained about the stultifying effects of small business life. David DiVincenzo expressed pity for his father because he had been forced to work with his own father in the family store. And Lucia Mornese complained that store shift work kept her family separate: "I think when I was twenty-one I got them to sell the business. I thought it was time we had a family. . . . I told my husband, 'I don't want you going into business because I don't want the children going through what I had to.'"

Nevertheless, retailing with an ethnic flair carried a special cachet. The one exception to Italian-American professionals' tendency to keep confidence about coethnic clients and friends was that many professionals, in stressing their ethnicity to me, detailed their connection as customers to coethnic small businesspeople, usually grocers or restaurateurs. Nancy Ferrucci gave me her shopping list for her family's monthly trip to North Beach to stock up on Italian foods and mentioned several local Italian food stores she patronized. Gino Angeluzzi explained, at length, the superiority of produce bought at the local Italian-owned grocery to supermarket food. Food, in the American context, is often heavily freighted with ethnic symbolism. The Italian purveyors of Italian foods can therefore be seen as consummate ethnics. To prove one's connection with them is to claim an ethnic identity.

## Work Process and Types of Ethnic Solidarity

The community that these Italian-American professionals lay claim to through their connections to ethnic shopkeepers, and the community vision that the shopkeepers themselves expressed, bear a striking resemblance to Emile Durkheim's conception of organic solidarity. Mechanical and organic solidarity, or solidarity through likeness as compared to solidarity through interdependence, were developed as contrast concepts characterizing the social glue of simple versus advanced societies, but are now used in looking at social parts like schools or factories.[5] The community ideal expressed here involves the fanning out of coethnics throughout the economy in such a way that they provide a broad range of goods and services for one another. Joe Longhinotti describing his coethnic

5. See Merton 1965 and Giddens 1977 for discussions of Durkheim's theory and its modern uses.

customers as doctor, banker, insurance man, and Jarus DiVincenzo naming businesspeople and professionals from a list of Columbus Day sponsors, celebrated a broad coethnic interdependence. This is not quite the same vision as the well-known "small-town America" model used by Gans and others to describe urban ethnic "communities": the small-town ideal primarily stresses daily face-to-face interaction. This concept could instead be summarized as "We take care of our own" and, implicitly, "We don't need nonethnics." Joe Longhinotti repeatedly, in naming various business and professional figures with whom he had relations, would say with mock surprise: "He happened to be Italian."

This community model, articulated by members of the *petit bourgeoisie* and claimed as well by quasi-independent members of the professional-managerial class, also bears a resemblance to the romanticized ethnic community of popular journalism and advertising: the "exotic" ethnic stores are, after all, the most visible and the most useful component of ethnic presence for nonethnic, gentrifying young professionals. They provide the illusion of *Gemeinschaft* along with quality goods and services.

But from the new social history's emphasis on working-class labor struggles there arises another kind of community vision, one to which informants alluded but which figured little in their present lives. Large numbers of coethnics gathered at one point, engaged in one activity, felt solidarity with one another by virtue of their sameness rather than interdependence. Large, ethnically homogeneous work sites most often provide this setting; church and other voluntary organizations may also do so. It was (and is) this kind of solidarity that union organizers used in order to unite workers for strike action. As Gutman relates:

> An old Jewish ritual oath helped spark the shirtwaist strike of women workers in 1909 that laid the basis for the International Ladies Garment Workers Union. A strike vote resulted in the plea, "Do you mean faith? Will you take the old Jewish oath?" The audience responded in Yiddish: "If I turn traitor to the cause, I now pledge, may this hand wither and drop off at the wrist from the arm I now raise." (1977:65)

Coethnic job recruitment and collective action against discrimination or oppression also involve mechanical solidarity. And it is to this kind of solidarity that ethnic brokers appeal when they call for heightened activity in voluntary ethnic organizations. The motto of one local group is:

> Let's unite, work, and strive
> To keep Italian culture alive.

And the master of ceremonies at a different voluntary organization dinner proclaimed: "The more you do for Italian people the more you'll benefit. Because we have to have the Italian clout in this country—we're a big ethnic group."

But aside from the small business class, and aside from these expressions linked to voluntary organization activity—activity only peripherally touching my informants' lives—I found little evidence of work-related mechanical solidarity in the present. References to its past existence came from two sources: from those who had grown up in the Midwest or Eastern Seaboard in families connected to industrial labor in factories or mines; and from those whose family work roots were in California's agricultural labor— field and orchard piecework and the assembly lines in the canneries.

Nick Meraviglia remembered the Italian coal miners' mutual benefit society fund-raising party for his family after his father had been injured in a mining accident in his small Midwestern town:

> They came up with this fund-raiser which consisted of a dance and serving *porchetta* out into a little hamburger bun. It was the most flavorful, delicious *porchetta* you could have. . . . Of course I didn't have to pay because it was my dad's benefit—there was less money for the family, but I was getting my due share!

Joe Cruciano recalled his father's roots in New York City before his emigration to California:

> He worked for this mattress company. All the men in the area did. The women didn't work like they did out here.

Similarly, Al Bertini's family and neighbors all worked for the tire manufacturer in their Midwestern company town. James Giovannino's father's family were connected to the railroad yard in their Midwestern city.

[153]

Because California industrialized less heavily and far later than these Midwestern and Eastern areas of heavy Italian settlement, and because in California Asians and Mexicans filled many of the low-paying positions that Italians and other Europeans filled in the Midwest and East, the state harbored fewer industrial settings for Italian-American mechanical solidarity.[6] Agriculture and its allied food-processing industries did, however, provide these settings. Gino Angeluzzi worked summers in the local cannery from fourteen on:

> I lied about my age. Verdi, the assistant superintendent, his daughter was in my class, I was kinda in her group—which helped.

Gino's mother worked in the same cannery until her retirement, sitting at the fruit-cutting lines alongside her *cumbares* (literally cogodparents, but used for friends), the same women with whom she would gather to make *occidati* (dried fruit bars) each Christmas season.

Joe Cruciano remembers the fieldwork/cannery migration cycle his relatives and coethnics followed during his boyhood in the 1930s:

> The Bruschitans [people originating from the same village] would make the tour. First they worked the peaches in Kingsburg; later they went up to Sunnyvale to work the cherries at Libby's [a cannery]; then to Stockton for cherries and asparagus; then a lot of people went up to San Leandro.

Of course, as we noted in Chapter 2, agricultural work was very isolating for many California Italian-Americans. Sheer geographic distance as well as social distance kept many families from feeling consciousness of kind with others. Gino Angeluzzi's family farmed a fifty-acre spread in the Central Valley for four years in the 1920s. They saw other families only at Mass on Sundays, and left immediately afterward to do chores. When Gino's parents had to travel on

6. But also, because my sample was necessarily small, and because I was not sampling for this type of work experience, I did not contact Italian-Americans connected to many present and past industrial settings, such as the automobile, aerospace, and semiconductor industries in the present South Bay, and chocolate and cigar manufacturing in San Francisco's past.

farm business, there was no one with whom to leave the children. Gino remembers

> the time they couldn't get back in the evening and then my little sister developed a cough. It was dark and we heard every noise there was. We all crawled in Mother's bed. Cough, cough, cough. We kept giving her honey with warm water. . . . Finally my folks showed up in the morning.

Cetta Longhinotti remembers her social isolation during the Depression in a farming area heavily settled with Italian-Americans:

> We were the poorest of the Italian families. I felt inferior at school because Mother couldn't speak English. There was a clique of children from wealthier families. They had birthday parties at each other's homes. I was ignored. They had expensive clothes but we had hand-me-downs. I guess this is why I hate patchwork [smiles].

Her younger sister Anna noted the lingering effects of this social distance during her childhood in the war years, when the family finances had improved somewhat:

> On Sundays we would maybe visit another Italian family. All the women would be gossiping, all the men would play bocce, and the kids would be just running wild! And my father would bring a jug of wine. We never stayed for dinner, because there were five of us, that's too many. My parents could never afford to have that many to dinner to reciprocate. But I know the other families would stay.

Durkheim's concepts of solidarity are of course ideal types, highlighting tendencies rather than clear-cut distinctions: even a single family's division of labor produces cooperative "organic solidarity" through interdependence, and the most "organic" network of businesspeople and professionals are, and see themselves as, like one another. Like other concepts of this sort, they prove their utility through illuminating social reality—inchoate, seemingly unrelated phenomena acquire relation and meaning when arranged on new conceptual grids. Here we see Italian-Americans experiencing a sense of likeness, of interdependence, of isolation from one another; and these perceptions are dependent, as Durkheim originally understood, on their economic connections or disconnections. But conceptualizing two types of solidarity accomplishes more here: it produces implications about ethnic identity, models of community, and the connections of these cognitive phenomena to material reality.

Different kinds of ethnic solidarity are invoked by different actors. Businesspeople articulate the organic vision of the economically interconnected ethnic community; independent professionals lay claim to this vision through their connections to ethnic businesspeople, but also see Italian-American ethnicity as constituted by close, emotionally expressive families. Technical, professional, and skilled workers for medium-sized and large firms tend to invoke this family-structure vision as their model of ethnicity.

The overall picture thus is one of the invocation of familial sameness by all, with this invocation overridden for the shopkeeper class by the broader model of ethnic community. Independent professionals also indirectly lay claim to the community model. Ethnic brokers, those who make it their business to interpret ethnicity both within and outside the group, make use of the family vision, and of individually based mechanical solidarity, while other forums for the expression of ethnic mechanical solidarity seem to have declined.

This picture reflects the Northern California ethnic economic reality. Working-class Italians are no longer thrown together in large numbers at work sites (unlike, for example, Latinos and Asians), and so do not invoke work-related mechanical solidarity. Shopkeepers and independent professionals are able in their work to stress their ethnic identity and are reliant on ethnic clientele for economic success. They provide the leadership and the rhetoric of ethnic voluntary associations (and the advertising revenue for their newsletters), and they invoke both family and individual types of mechanical solidarity in public statements, and thus can appeal to ethnics from a broad class spectrum. In private, shopkeepers celebrate and stress their organic community with one another and with ethnic professionals—"It's good for business"—who also lay claim to it through their connections with businesspeople.

Work process influences the ethnic and kinship components of networks, and through them, ethnic identity. The evocation of

[156]

kinds of solidarity—that is, collective ethnic identities—is dependent, not only on class, but on the sorts of occupations ethnics hold across broad class categories. Changing American capitalism has not, as simplistic analyses have held, destroyed ethnic identity; neither is ethnic identity unconnected to economy, persisting mysteriously, as the *Beyond the Melting Pot* model would have it. Humans create and negotiate their ethnic identities, responding to their individual and collective economic positions. Through negotiation and renegotiation, they change the positions themselves. But the changing economy and the positions it creates are the bases from which individuals act.

And families themselves are situated within the economy. This is the case not only in the abstract sense of the influence of developing capitalism on changing Western families, and not only in terms of families' class statuses, but also in the particular forms of intersection that the occupations of each family's breadwinners allow between the worlds of work and home.

Economy, family, and ethnicity, seen from within, form a seamless web. Looking at them from the perspective of varying work settings within the changing economy enables us to turn over the tapestry and to trace its threads.

# [5]

# *"Abbondanza Youself!"*: Abuse, Boundaries, and Ethnic Identity

> The selection of ethnic identity as a means of organizing the
> meaning of social action . . . depends heavily upon the con-
> text in which the social action takes place—Mitchell 1974:31

For these Italian-Americans, ideas of collective ethnic identity
are tied to particular types of work experiences. But individuals use
the idiom of ethnicity as well to interpret their experiences of class,
of kinship, and of generation. We need to investigate more broadly
the ways in which they define themselves vis-à-vis other ethnic and
racial groups, and vis-à-vis the majority white society. Over the
course of my fieldwork, two major contexts of ethnic self-definition
emerged among my informants: ethnic discrimination and abuse,
and mass-media images of Italian-Americans.

## Ethnic Discrimination and Abuse

Like members of other ethnic and racial groups, Italian-Americans do not need to seek out prejudices against themselves among
the citizenry at large: they need merely go to the library. A conception of culture as a monolithic grid that determines both identity
and behavior, combined with researchers' concerns with ethnic
economic success, have encouraged a scholarly climate in which
groups are ranked relative to one another—and in which Italian-
Americans are usually placed at or near the bottom of the ladder.
Consider the following two-decade span of deprecation. Strod-

beck (1958) and Rosen (1959) "prove" that Italian-Americans have "low achievement motivation." (Rosen puts "Negroes" and French-Canadians in the same category.) Gans asserts the Italian "need for display" as the source of Italian-American success in the entertainment industry (1962:83). Shibutani and Kwan find that Italian-Americans are "fatalistic" and "regard intellectual interests as effeminate" (1965:64–65). Thernstrom compares the Census occupational rankings of Irish, Germans, Italians, and "Jews" (emigrants from the USSR) and, in evaluating the results, falls back on values: The Jewish "high value on education," the poor values of Catholic schools (1973:174). Sowell asserts that Italian-Americans' "traditional peasant culture" is a "barrier to higher education" (1975:86). And Epstein accepts the premise that Jews are "workers" who carry with them "the values conducive for middle-class success," as opposed to the Irish, Italians, and Blacks of Warner's (1941) "Yankee City" (1978:68).[1]

These considerations of ethnic identity are in fact the now familiar exercises in self-aggrandizing sentimentality and racist denigration. The concern is not with how members of particular groups participate in the social construction of reality differently, but rather in how different "cultures" can be praised or blamed for their presumed connections to mobility rates. The scholarly and the public climate are related, and I was not surprised to receive strong reactions from my informants to my questions about discrimination and abuse. Their experiences and their styles of reporting, however, varied considerably. I asked specific questions about job, group-membership, and friendship discrimination as well as exposure to ethnic slurs. As would be expected, older informants had had more experience with job and group-member discrimination than did younger ones. Experience with ethnic slurs cropped up across generation and class. As I began to know individuals better and to converse with them in the company of others as well as alone, an interesting pattern emerged. Many of the middle-aged who had originally answered my questions with a flat denial—"Discrimination, I never experienced," offered Nick Meraviglia—would, over

1. Epstein uses Warner's study in apparent ignorance of Thernstrom's (1964) widely known critique of Warner's work on social mobility in Newburyport—a work that was already over a decade old when Epstein was writing.

time, offer more information: "Yes. I remember my dad mentioning about the Masons being prejudiced against Italians."

Later, Nick described the emotional process he had undergone in dealing with ethnic slurs on his professional job:

> When I joined the office in the new location I became a member of the Rotary Club, and of course there were very few Italian members. So the minute I came on board, they started referring to me as the Godfather of the county. I didn't take it seriously—I laughed at it. OK? You want to call me the Godfather, self-proclaimed, fine. That would go on every week—"Here's the Godfather, here's the Godfather." Until finally the newspaper over there made reference to the fact that there's a strong Mafia foothold in that county. So I said, "Hey! Humor will go up to a certain point. Let's sort of cut this thing out." Well, they were obviously aware of it because all this didn't happen anymore. It was getting too close to home.

It was more than mere annoyance at ethnic joking. Nick clearly felt that he was also quashing totally groundless rumors of his involvement in organized crime:

> But if I had become, I am sure, in any way, shape, or form ill at ease or offended, I think it would have taken on a serious nature, whereas I threw a little humor into it, and it just sort of. . .

Joe Longhinotti, a skilled worker, at first also denied experiencing any discrimination. When I asked about accusations of fascist activity in the 1930s (when there were many open Mussolini supporters in the area), he replied, "In those days it never entered my head, because I wasn't in school." This reminded Joe of more recent history:

> You remember when we had that problem with Savio here at Cal? [Maria Savio was one of the leaders of the Free Speech Movement of 1964–65.] He created quite a problem around here—they jumped on it—why would an Italian. . . After all that's knockin on your school door there, but if I recall it was riots there, wasn't it? People say, "Look at that Italian he's starting something at Cal"—he stuck out like a sore thumb I guess.

After this reflection, when I asked Joe again about discrimination in his childhood, he said:

> Like I say they used to give you that trade name, that name Dago. And Spaghetti.

These narratives contrast strongly with the following ones. Al Bertini, the affluent professional who so thoroughly enjoyed himself at my expense in Chapter 1, responded to my question about discrimination:

> Lemme give you the actual facts. This is when I was at [another company] and I was the regional manager. They had this tremendous personnel department that works out of [a different city]. People in the personnel department are psychiatrists and all this other junk. . . Anyway, I was called once—it was about the time I was getting dissatisfied—they may have sensed it down there. I received a call from a senior vice president. He was a Southerner—by the way, I'm not down on Southerners—I definitely feel that they're more stupid . . . and have the ability to be prejudiced, no matter what [laughs]. Anyway, he wanted to talk and have dinner—so we went to Ghirardelli Square. I spent from about four to ten that night with him, very informal, he did it extremely well. In the course of that time, he told me a lot of things, many things he didn't know he was telling me. The crew that I had hired in my county—strangely enough, every one of my managers was Italian. Now . . . did I hire Italians. I say no, it's not the case. These people I hired were exactly what I wanted—personable, knowledgeable—I wouldn't have moved all this way if I didn't have these people doing their jobs. I really mean it. So as we were walking around and talking he made remarks like, "By the way, these guys that you hired, did you go to school with them?" Well I didn't even go to school out here! In spite of the fact that he had all my records he blew that one . . . "Are they relatives?" this sort of stuff. [None of them were.] Well, we got through that. Then he actually made the statement, flat statement. . . He said I was volatile, and he said in corporate structure, it gets to a point where a man of your ethnic background will not go much farther. He actually said that to me. I said I don't believe what you're saying. . . He was saying it to me in such a way as to imply that he doesn't believe in it, but I might as well face reality. To become

[161]

the president of this company you have a name like Jones or Smith. By the way, today the chairman of the board of this company is Italian. . . . Anyway, the statement was made to me. One of the things I enjoyed when I started here was that I brought every one of those people over. It wasn't bad, but I did feel it.

Teresa Angeluzzi, a non-Italian married to an Italian-American professional, responded in this way:

I'm all for the whole principle that Italian-Americans have been horrendously maligned. I resent the inferences—especially if you're Sicilian—that you have to have some connection to the Mafia. I was just appalled to find out how many well-bred people think like that. When we were on vacation a couple of years ago . . . . this little town in the Sierras. It was when *The Godfather* came out . . . first the book, then the film. We were talking about something and I was standing in the little general store . . . . and got cigarettes or whatever it was, and said put it on our tag, and I said Angeluzzi, and he said Angeluzzi, that's right out of *The Godfather*. He was totally serious, he said, "Is that any of your relatives?" I said no, he said, "But aren't you Sicilian?" I said, "First of all, I'm not Sicilian." I says, "Secondly, my husband is of Sicilian descent. But what's more important, I don't belong to the Mafia." I says, "I don't know any Mafia people"—I probably do! [laughs]—I probably do and don't know it or do know it, whichever . . . or suspect, right? . . . . There were total strangers standing around and I was very offended, I was really mad! And I made it clear I didn't ever want that subject brought up again.

These two narratives differ from those of Nick Meraviglia and Joe Longhinotti in that Al Bertini and Teresa Angeluzzi immediately, without repeated questioning, launched into them, and in that they both defined themselves as righteously indignant in response to acts of discrimination.

Slowly, as I accumulated these richly detailed narratives of discrimination and emotional reaction, I began to realize that there was a third category of response to my questions. Dorothy DiVincenzo, the daughter of a successful businessman, remarked: "We always thought of ourselves as Swiss." Joe Cruciano, a well-off professional, California-born and of southern (but not Sicilian) Italian background, claimed that Sicilian-American fathers oppressed their sons, and that Italians from New York were "slimy." And Nancy Ferrucci, a successful professional of northern Italian background, after talking about the superiority of Italian-Americans, tossed out: "But the people south of Rome—they're different."

In answering my questions about discrimination, individuals were describing three cognitive/emotional processes that they had undergone, processes that I later realized had been described and interrelated by Hochschild (1979) in her work on emotion management. First, they decided how to perceive an incident of discrimination—in Hochschild's term, what "framing rule" to apply to it. The three framing rules I discerned were: (1) this is not discrimination; (2) this is discrimination; and (3) this is discrimination, but not against me. Al Bertini, for example, reflected on how he would respond to "Mafia" joking:

> Oh, I hear it all the time, but always jokingly . . . I handle it that's all . . . I definitely don't get upset. Depending on the person, that's extremely important. If I have a blond, blue-eyed, racist, bigot fascist saying it [laughs] . . . now that's a little bit different.

Depending upon his understanding of the person's intention, Al Bertini would "frame" Mafia joking as discrimination or nondiscrimination.

Teresa Angeluzzi described her decisions first to apply one, and then another, framing rule to the same sort of joking:

> When I was president of the Mother's Club at the parochial school one year. . . It was a very hard job because we were scrounging money. . . And I picked my committee and board and they were predominantly Italian names simply because of the resources. . . So they joked about my Mafia. I told Father B, who's Oriental, *you* wouldn't like Oriental jokes. . . So he apologized and that was that. He still jokes around, but I don't mind now because he's just family . . . on the inside.

As Teresa Angeluzzi became closer to Father B, she defined him as "just family" and reframed his Mafia joking.

Framing seems to be context-determined, not only at the point of experience but also through the process of communication. As Nick Meraviglia warmed to me, the frame "Discrimination, I never experienced" altered to "But if I had become . . . offended . . . I think it would have taken on a serious nature." And Joe Longhinotti, remembering how he was pilloried by associates over Maria Savio's involvement in the Free Speech Movement, reflected that *I* was vulnerable through my affiliation with the university: "After all that's knockin on your school door there." After this narrative, he easily recalled being given "that trade name, that name Dago." I suspect that the contextual framing of incidents of discrimination as nondiscrimination was common among my informants, and thus that many others had had Nick Meraviglia's and Joe Longhinotti's experiences but did not frame them in conversation with me.

In the cases of Dorothy DiVincenzo, Joe Cruciano, and Nancy Ferrucci, we have to infer the process of applying the framing rule "This is discrimination but not against me"—although Dorothy comes close to describing the process: "We always said we were Swiss."

Framing rules are closely associated with feeling rules: "If this is X situation, I ought to feel Y." As Teresa Angeluzzi exclaimed, "I resent . . . . I was appalled . . . . I was offended, I was really mad!"

In order to understand Nick Meraviglia's and Al Bertini's descriptions of their emotional responses to discrimination, we need to add Hochschild's concept of emotion work to framing/feeling rules. Emotion work is "the act of trying to change in degree or quality an emotion or feeling" (Hochschild 1979:561). This effort may be to suppress an emotion that is seen as violating a feeling rule or to heighten an emotion seen as in congruence with one. Both Nick Meraviglia and Al Bertini described themselves as working on their emotions to take ethnic slurs lightly—to have a humorous response: "I didn't take it seriously. I laughed at it . . . I threw a little humor into it, and it just sort of. . ." And: "I handle it, that's all. I definitely don't get upset . . . I can actually turn it . . . and use the same tactics with them."

Summarizing the framing/feeling rules in response to which these Italian-Americans worked on their emotions, we have: (1) I am not discriminated against as an Italian-American (no appropriate emotion). (2) I am discriminated against (We must fight this with righteous anger, or, It is important to feel that this is just humorous joking and to feel humorous about it). (3) Others of the group are criticized, but this does not apply to me, because I am racially or socially/economically not in this group (I distance myself from those others; I do not admit that I am discriminated against as one of them).

These categories fall at two ends of the current ethnic ideological spectrum: (1) and (3) belong to the set of ideas associated with melting-pot ideology, and (2) to those associated with the white ethnic renaissance. Categories (1) and (3), respectively, are the responses of those who claim full assimilation and of those who claim assimilation but believe that others are rightfully oppressed for not having assimilated. Category (2) represents both the ethnic activist stance, in which the individual sees herself as part of a collectivity that is fighting discrimination, and the position that, while the discrimination may be serious, it would be giving in to it, admitting vulnerability, to take it seriously.

The material context in which individuals make decisions about these framing/feeling rules, about how they will perceive and feel about verbal acts of discrimination, varies greatly.

1. Occupation determines whether or not one can "afford" to show anger at work-based ethnic discrimination, as the contrasts among Nick Meraviglia, Al Bertini, and Joe Longhinotti show. This is not, as we have seen, merely a question of social mobility "purchasing" the right to express oneself, but is related to the sector of the economy and the ethnic/racial composition of the workplace.

2. Regional and economic ascription, and personal appearance, to a certain extent, determine how one will be harassed. Sicilians are much more vulnerable to Mafia slurs, as Teresa Angeluzzi noted. Prevalent racist attitudes about southern versus northern Italians influence Anglo attitudes. They also allow Italian-Americans with northern background to define themselves out of the stereotype: "We're Swiss." "South of Rome, they're different." Those individuals whose antecedents had money or professional status might be perceived, or perceive themselves, as outside the category of deprecated Italian-Americans. Jarus DiVincenzo recalled that during his childhood in the 1930s, "Italians had a stigma—they were not accepted wholeheartedly," but that he was probably accepted into a college fraternity because his father was a merchant. Here the informant analyzes non-Italians' positive reactions to his economic status without using it himself to claim superi-

[165]

ority to the ethnic category. Personal appearance—whether or not an individual "looks" Italian—seems to free some Italians from some discrimination. Linda Mornese, blue-eyed and light-haired, said, "Most people don't take me for Italian, and even my name goes right over their heads," whereas Greg Longhinotti, dark-eyed and dark-haired, said: "Yeah, everybody always kidded me . . . like about the oversized nose (laughs)."

3. Gender has a fundamental influence on the way in which individuals perceive and respond to ethnic discrimination. In my research, women seemed to feel freer to express indignation than men, even when the incidents described were less serious. I suspect that the framing/feeling rules associated with gender here coincided with those associated with discrimination. Only men gave responses centered on taking ethnic slurs as jokes, and working on their emotions to do so; this, I suspect, is associated with the prevalent gender ideology that to admit vulnerability is weak, womanish. However, those informants, women or men, who expressed solidarity with the white ethnic renaissance felt free to show strong emotions in response to discriminatory ideology. Not surprisingly, the single active ethnic broker interviewed, Paolo Bevilacqua, had the most righteously indignant male response to discrimination.

Women also seemed to receive fewer coarse ethnic insults. It was only men who relayed having heard jokes such as "What is an Italian bubble bath? Farting in a mud puddle" (told to Rick Cruciano).

4. Other identities enter into the process of deciding on framing/feeling rules. Catholics often expressed the opinion that they were discriminated against on the basis of religion rather than ethnicity. (This fits with Herberg's (1955) claim that ethnic identity collapses, in the U.S. context, into religious divisions alone; but it is clear that this is only partly the case.) Dorothy DiVincenzo remembers being hurt at hostile teasing over the Catholic rule of fish on Fridays. Teresa Angeluzzi recounted an anti-Catholic cross-burning incident on her parents' front lawn during her Depression childhood in a Midwest state, and associated it with ethnic prejudice today.

5. Finally, political convictions mediated the ways in which informants "processed" ethnic discrimination. Inevitably, attitudes to-

ward Blacks, Latinos, and Asians—the recipients of qualitatively more intense discrimination—and ideas about the meaning of social class and social mobility were part of individuals' constructions of models of ethnic discrimination.

Jim Bertini, Al Bertini's son, who self-consciously identifies as a leftist and antiracist, sees discrimination against Italian-Americans as part of a larger American racist ideology:

> Let me tell you what happened to me one time. I was in a course in comparative politics and I'm sitting there and it's European politics— and there's this woman across the way and we were talking and there's some political concept like authority, and this woman says, "Well, if that was an Italian something or other, they'd just wrap a mackerel around their doorstep and they'd get the message." When she said that, smoke was really comin out of my ears, cause she's just bein a fuckin racist. It really pissed me off. First of all, it was totally irrelevant to the discussion. Second, it was this unfounded stereotype she had of Italians. . . But I did get poetic justice cause it was raining that night and she asked me for a ride to her place, so I'm just a big slob in my car and I had all these newspapers on the floor . . . and as she was getting in I said, "Hey, don't wrinkle them, that's what I use for the fish."

Carl Motto, on the other hand, had prepared a list of "Italian-American virtues" carrying strong racist overtones, which he read to me at our first interview:

> Respect for parents, whether they're right or wrong. Respect within marriage, respect for the family name. This could help our society if we convince people to feel this way. We need strong Catholic families where you don't have the right to mess up. I'm very close to my dad. . . He won't change his life just because it's fashionable at the moment. . . He talks about hippies and niggers.

Hochschild's perspective helps us to lay out and order the complexity of Italian-American responses to the topic of ethnic discrimination. I have suggested the material factors and available ideological constructs that seem to underly individual choices of framing/ feeling rules. This analysis allows us to explore the connections between cognitive and material realities in individuals' lives.

[167]

**Ethnic and Racial Boundary Interactions**

We have entered the topic of Italian-American ethnic identity from the reflected image of individuals' responses to slurs and discrimination. The ideological poles of assimilationism and ethnic militance seem to orient individuals in their choice of framing/feeling rules with which to perceive and respond to these communications from non-Italians. But being exposed to an ethnic slur by a non-Italian is only one of many boundary interactions—to heed Barth's (1969) emphasis—that Italian-Americans undergo in the process of constructing, maintaining, and altering their ethnic identities. And this process, of course, includes the construction and reconstruction of the identities of groups across these boundaries.

*Regional Background*

At the micro level, there are the perceived differences within the ethnic group on the basis of regional origin: some informants identified as Piedmontesi, Lucchesi, Toscani, Genovesi, Milanesi, Siciliani, etc. The situation of settlement and character of economic participation determined how strongly these campanilistic divisions would be experienced. Except for various scavenger businesses, which were organized and run by Genovesi and are still in part controlled by their descendents (See Perry 1978), regional origin had no present economic, residential, or social correlates among my informants. It entered the conversations of the middle-aged and elderly in two ways: in describing the lost "communities" of their youth, and in ascribing personal characteristics to individuals. Tony Ripetto, a retired city worker, described regional settlements in the East Bay: "There was a lot of Sicilians and Neapolitans there. You could always tell because they had red pepper and onions drying on their front porch. . . . . One of the characteristics of a Genovese home is the solid tile roof . . . . and the high basement, because of the wine."

Joe Longhinotti and Louis Baca, in the last chapter, divided their lost communities into regional groups as well. Except for the fairly widespread Genovese reputation for moneymaking and sharp dealing—Joe Longhinotti said, "The Genovesi, they make a buck, they save two," and Pina Meraviglia said of her dishonest wartime land-lady, "I'm sure she must've been Genovese because money meant an awful lot to her"—there was little ascription of personal charac-teristics by regional origin among these middle-aged and elderly Italian-Americans. Maria Fante responded to my regional question: "I just accept them . . . I've never really thought about it"—even though I knew that she had grown up a Lucchesi among Genovesi, Siciliani, and Napolitani.

## Italian Relatives

Another important boundary interaction, but one that is seldom mentioned, is that between Italian-Americans and their relatives in Italy. Of the nineteen households of the 1920s–40s for which I had sufficient data, eleven had ongoing contact with Italian relatives, and of those eleven, five sent one or more members to visit Italian relatives in the 1920s or 1930s. Of the fifteen contemporary house-holds containing their descendents, seven both had ongoing contact with Italian relatives and had actually visited them in Italy within the past decade. In another three households, one or more had traveled to Italy in the past decade, although they were not in contact with relatives there. This is clearly a very high level of contact, especially considering that I did not sample for it, and that several of these families had been in the United States fifty to seventy years by the 1920s. The cross-class nature of my sample may partly account for this high level of expenditure on foreign travel.

Those who felt close to Italian relatives would often confuse or amalgamate Italian and Italian-American identities. Pina Mer-aviglia exclaimed, "They'll give you the shirt off their back" about both categories. Individuals would, as well, use their perceptions of *Italianità* to make claims about proper Italian-American identity. That is, they would claim certain Italian characteristics to be sym-bolic representatives of their Italian-American identity, and thus judge individuals within their own group as inauthentic. For Clelia Cipolla, Italy represented a piety not found among all of her Italian-American acquaintances. Despite the fact that high numbers of Italians in Italy have always been anticlerical and that there were already many anti-Catholic Italian organizations in San Francisco by 1870,[2] she described the founding of a local Catholic organization in this way:

> It was originally started to help those unfortunate Italians who didn't know English and many of them had drifted away from the Church.

She saw Italy, in contrast, as monolithically religious:

> My brother and I went to Italy in fulfillment of a promise we made to our father. He wished us to see his village. He left money for it. We went to Mass in the church our parents were married in, and that meant a lot to us. And we saw the procession with the cross-carrying. Poppa had had the honor of carrying the cross in that procession when he was a young man. It meant a lot to us.

For Jim Bertini, a leftist and twenty-five years younger, raised as a Catholic but having left the Church, Catholicism was something to be tolerated. Italy and his Italian relatives represented the struggle against the alienation, competitiveness, and materialism spawned by capitalism:

> Like I said, my family in Italy, they're *real* Italians, amazing people. The people here, they got caught up in this whole materialistic thing. . . . You're not Italian, you're American, and you talk English and eat hamburgers and you have two eggs and bacon in the morning instead of *cappucino* and *panettone*. . . . I think my relatives here aren't really Italian. . . . I think the Italians really know how—this might be really ethnocentric to say—know how to have fun—they're expressive, they hug, they kiss, they laugh. . . They're Mediterranean people, they like to take off their clothes . . . they share. I try to be responsible and I think that's bein Italian. . . . The Catholic Church doesn't bother me at all. I don't care one way or another.

We have seen other examples of "fighting with symbols" of *Italianità* in earlier chapters. This rhetorical framing of experience seemed to occur most often on class, gender, generational, and political boundaries; it underlines the complexity of the mental varieties of ethnic experience.

2. These included various Republican clubs and a special Italian branch of the Masons. Gumina 1978:169–73,175.

## White Ethnic Groups

Working outward, we arrive at the boundaries between Italian-Americans and the other white ethnic groups settled in the area. These are primarily Irish and Jews, in my informants' experiences, but they include Germans, Scandinavians, and Slavs—especially Poles, for those who grew up in the industrial Midwest.

My middle-aged informants saw Irish and Germans primarily as coreligionists, as people like themselves even if neither they nor their Irish and German acquaintances were Catholics any longer. Three of the intermarriages in my sample were with Germans. Joe Longhinotti, evoking his lost community, brought up the rear of the procession: "And here comes your Irish, they liked the music and the food, being that they were born and raised. . ."

Middle-aged informants also named Irish and Germans as the predominant ethnic identities of their childhood teachers, whether in parochial or in public schools. Angelo Caputo attended a parochial elementary school in San Francisco where "the nuns were all Irish—they taught us Irish jigs and songs" and a public high school where "Miss O'Brian taught needlework and Miss Hallinan business." Some middle-aged informants remembered white ethnic hierarchies in their childhoods. Joe Cruciano, who grew up in a Central California farming town, remembers when "they built the central parochial high school for all the Catholics. This was way in the north of town so I had to take a bus. . . . A mixture of all kids went there—the kids from St. A were the real light Catholics. Their fathers were landowners and businessmen. Then kids from St. B. Then us, the Italians. We were the kings of the school—we were more aggressive."

There was in fact active discrimination by Irish against Italians as they arrived in the United States, discrimination expressed particularly through refusal to accommodate Italians into the Irish-dominated American Catholic Church (Vecoli 1969; Tomasi 1975). In San Francisco in the early 1870s, the official Catholic newspaper carried on a hate campaign against the "infidel" Italians (Gumina 1978:53). Nancy Ferrucci offered a contemporary echo of this Irish-Italian history in her spontaneous complaints about her San Francisco Mission-raised Irish mother-in-law, whose vision of "stupid, inferior Eye-talians" she found enraging.

There were fewer references to Jews in my middle-aged infor-

[171]

mants' life histories; they did not figure as teachers or classmates for these children of the 1920s and 1930s. They show up, however, as friends for both Catholic and non-Catholic middle-aged informants, and as friends and spouses for younger informants. Pina Meraviglia counts as fictive kin the Jewish man for whom she cared in his childhood, and one of her sons has a Jewish girl friend. Informants also identified money, intellectuality, and liberalism as symbols of Jewish identity. They frequently repeated the epithet that the Genovesi are the "Jews of Italy," then worried about its anti-Semitic connotation. Tony Ripetto, a Genovese himself, said: "Like the Genovesi are supposed to be the Jews of Italy . . . that's a bad title, I'm not defending it. They were the great financiers."

Several informants, both middle-aged and younger, expressed a "tilt" toward Jewish identity, unfavorably comparing their perceptions of Italian-American values with those of Jewish-Americans. David DiVincenzo, in my first interview with him, spontaneously complained about Italian-American "pigs" who were stupid and right-wing, while "even rich Jews in my hometown are liberals." And Angela Caputo talked about a woman relative, a contemporary, whose life history she admired: "She graduated with honors, and she met this really marvelous Jewish man. She went to a priest because she wanted to marry him. The priest threw fire and brimstone at her, so that was her exodus from the Catholic Church. She had two children, they tested as genuises, they went to Ivy League schools."

To trace the evolution of the image of Italian-Americans as stupid and reactionary vis-à-vis the image of American Jews as intellectual and liberal would be a study in itself. While there may be, as Dundes (1971) notes, a "kernel of truth" in ethnic epithets, there are a number of historical factors that have significantly altered public perceptions of Italian-American social reality. Part of the story involves the strong anticlerical stance of the lively Italian-American socialist press of the late nineteenth century; this press was then virulently attacked by the American Catholic Church as well as by American activists. Another strand of the history involves, as just stated, the extreme exclusionary activity of the Irish-dominated American Catholic Church, which involved literally denying Italian parishioners the right to attendance at Mass. In this way, one major Italian immigrant road to intellectual expression, the priesthood, was blocked for many years (Vecoli 1969). A third strand involves the underreporting of Italian-American labor activism—women and men—and the creation of the monolithic image of the sheeplike Italian-American strikebreaker vis-à-vis the Jewish labor organizer. This image is now being corrected by labor historians, but it persists in the popular ethnic literature.[3] Finally, the underrepresentation of Italian-Americans in universities has meant that most academic writing on Italian-Americans has been done by non-Italians, with results similar in kind, if not in degree, to much white-produced academic literature on Blacks. As ethnic identities are constantly constructed and reconstructed on the basis of perceived ethnic histories, these processes have clearly helped to forge an image, in the minds of Italian-Americans as well as non-Italians, that does not reflect historical reality.

### Racial Groups

The white ethnic boundary relations that have received the most attention, of course, are those with U.S. racial groups, and especially with Black Americans.[4] These Italian-Americans' perceptions of racial groups were strongly influenced by the contexts of contact. At the simplest level, this meant that informants spontaneously talked about those groups with large concentrations in their area: those in San Jose about Japanese and Chicanos, those in San Francisco about Blacks and Chinese, those in Oakland about Blacks alone (although there is a large Latino population), and those in South San Francisco including Latinos and Filipinos.

Working-class family life histories revealed numbers of cross-race contacts in the 1920s and 1930s. Joe Cruciano remembers the ethnic/racial geography of his Central Valley town neighborhood in the 1930s:

> It was a very poor section—we lived amongst Blacks. The next block was Black and Mexican, and the block after that all Black except one

3. For examples see Fenton 1962; J. Smith 1978; Buhle 1977; Cobble 1977; and Kessler-Harris 1977. See also Steinberg 1981:82–105 and 128–150 for an interesting discussion of this issue.

4. Cf. Gambino 1974:313–51; Suttles 1968; and Glazer and Moynihan 1970: Introduction.

[173]

Italian family. . . My next-door neighbor was Black—he was my friend . . . I went out picking cotton with him and a Black crew—they were kidding me for being the only white on the truck.

Lucia Mornese, who grew up in San Francisco, remembers her public high school in the early 1930s:

That's where I had Japanese and Blacks and Chinese in my classes. But it wasn't strange to me, in fact there was one Black man who used to come to the house [in the 1920s], I guess my father met him at work, and I remember sitting on his lap and asking him why he was Black.

These cross-race relationships, while they are interesting, should not obscure for us the profoundly racist character of the society in which these Italian-Americans lived and live. Joe Cruciano remembers his emotional ambivalence about his "boundary transaction" with neighboring Blacks:

First of all, I felt funny being with Black people, now my friend I could take, but their culture was so different. . . . They were very friendly people, very nice, very funny—they made jokes all the time. But they were oppressed, you could see it. And I felt deprived as I was—and I was *not* deprived . . . I'll never forget this—our neighbors moved away and had missed the neighborhood so they came to visit and my mother invited them in and gave them refreshments and I can remember I didn't want to drink out of a glass they'd drunk out of . . . and I think about that today and feel bad . . . but I didn't know.

Joe's mother's warm interracial hospitality was only part of the total environment in which he was negotiating his identity. Even as a child, he had already taken in the framing rule that dictated his feelings: fear of being identified with an even more oppressed group, of "falling" into their low status.

In some cases, informants sketched for me the process by which racist feelings were intensified. Teresa Angeluzzi encountered her parents-in-law in the 1940s, after their economic status had improved from its Depression low and they were again leasing farmland. But now they employed Mexicans as farm laborers, whereas before they had worked the land as a family unit:

[174]

I couldn't figure it out. . . . First of all, there was all this stoop labor and the migrant workers, OK? I accepted it. My brothers, to make money when they were going to school [in the Midwest] went on the trains to the wheatfields. So seasonal work, and hard work, didn't surprise me. What got me, very fast. . . . Gino's mother was very sympathetic to the plight of the migrant workers. . . . She brought them things . . . . but the attitude still prevailed: they were lesser citizens. There was a superior attitude towards them, even the ones that worked for his folks. It really always kinda galled me—my father-in-law called them Messicans . . . they were subservient . . . not just because he hired them . . . they had A Place . . . I thought, this is awful! Talking about them like they were animals!

Pina Meraviglia's racist perceptions of Blacks had been developed over the decade since a public housing project was built in her neighborhood; Joe Longhinotti talked about poor Blacks moving into the neighborhood where his mother still lived:

She used to go to church quite a bit. Then there were the Blacks and it wasn't so safe so she bypassed it.

Aside from the specific contexts in which racist perspectives were intensified, most of these middle-aged Italian-Americans participated actively, as most Americans do, in the system of institutionalized racism that characterizes our society. Several people avoided making racist statements to me, while their children reported their attitudes, as was noted in Chapter 1. A few informants, like Teresa Angeluzzi, went out of their way to complain about racism and to worry about how to eradicate it. There was no correlation between these attitudes and class or gender divisions— although women spoke less guardedly to me, as they did on most topics. There was, however, the expected correlation between political stance and racism: liberals and leftists like Angelo Caputo and Jim and Al Bertini made no overt racist statements; conservatives like Carl Motto and Clelia Cipolla did.

Finally, these Italian-Americans, like most Americans, were self-contradictory in their perceptions of race: they were often enveloped in love/hate relationships with particular groups and failed to distinguish between race and class. Lucia Mornese went on at some length about her love of the Chinese:

I used to see Chinese babies in Chinatown . . . . and I said to my mother, "They're so cute, the Italian babies are just blah. I'd like to have a Chinese baby" [laughs] . . . . I grew up loving Oriental things and I always wanted to go to China.

She later said of chance acquaintances in a restaurant, a cultured and wealthy couple:

They're Chinese, but you can't think of them as Chinese.

And about San Francisco today:

They're kinda taking over the city. I don't resent the old-timers, but there are so many coming now that are just causing a lot of trouble . . . and they don't uh. . . Well anyway, I guess it's any nationality, it doesn't matter, when they're poor.

Tony Ripetto made this distinction forcefully:

As far as I'm concerned, there's two types: there's the Blacks . . . [describes his middle-class Black neighbors]; the others I call the niggers . . . this certain segment of Blacks—they're the worst enemy of their own people.

Younger informants mirrored these patterns. Greg Longhinotti talked about his adolescence:

Over the years you start to get a little prejudiced. . . . In junior high, I had some friends that were Black and well, they were nice guys. . . . But as the years go on, you know, I could see that friend go in his own way, more towards his Black friends.

And Linda Mornese discussed her female cousin:

She married a *Mexican* . . . . and so I don't really see that much of her anymore. . . . There's this impression that Mexicans are dirty and sloppy and lazy and you look at her [groom's mother, who is fat]. . . . He's a nice guy but he totally lacks any class. . . . I'm just not used to sloppy—lower-class—whatever.

[176]

While David DiVincenzo recognizes and hates the racism in his home town:

> One whole section is working-class, Chicano. But what I'm saying is that people in this town don't think that way; they don't think that these divisions exist. . . . In terms of prejudice and stuff they have it all pushed to that side of the city—then they don't have to worry about it anymore.

Running throughout the deprecating statements made by both generations were two themes, two "attributes" of racial groups that "explained" their inferiority. One, we have seen, is the confusion of race with poverty: racial groups are to be despised because they are poor. Joe Longhinotti was startled and displeased when, in looking through photographs of my wedding, he saw several Black guests. At one picture, he exclaimed: "Who's the Black boy?" When I explained that the "boy" was a historian with whom I had taught a college course, he looked dissatisfied but remained silent.

The second, related, theme is the Waterloo of the mobility historians: that "family culture" determines economic status, and therefore that disorganized, dysfunctional families are the cause of the poverty of racial groups. It is a historic irony that members of the very white ethnic group that had been depicted most as having distinctly improper families should then impugn those of groups lower in status than themselves. This perception, however, was very common among these Italian-Americans. It was clearly behind Carl Motto's list of Italian-American virtues. Tony Ripetto's remarks about "niggers" were closely tied to this improper family vision:

> You know what used to hurt me most about the Blacks down there? To see these people's children grow up . . . . that dirty gutter, mud, barefooted. The elders, they just generated a hate in me. . . . There's nothing filthier than a Black woman drinkin and cursin.

Among younger informants this vision was, if anything, more common. Frank Fante repeatedly expressed his belief that his strict Catholic family upbringing had made him a superior person. And Greg Longhinotti made the link explicit:

[177]

I think like an Italian family and a Black family—I can judge from ours—I think in a Black family, they can get away with things, whereas in our family we'd be corrected then and there . . . and I think it makes a difference how you're brought up.

And even Gus Brandis, a self-identified young leftist, distinguished Italian-Americans from Blacks on the issue of family in a statement evocative of the Moynihan report:

Historically Italian-Americans have these incredible values which gave them strength in the family, cooperation. This is the exact opposite of the Black experience because of slavery. They tried to destroy Black families.

Family issues are inevitably political, intertwining with questions of race and ethnicity, economics and gender—not only in the minds of family researchers, but in the mass media and among Americans in general. This is not accidental, but a function of the development and spread of family ideology, both from the top down and from the ground up.

## Mass Media and the Commoditization of Ethnic Identity

The mass media are the final "boundaries" at the points of which Italian-Americans construct their ethnic identities. But in considering them we must switch back here from the interaction of folk and mass images of racial groups to the mass images of Italian-Americans themselves.

Ideologies of ethnicity purveyed by the mass media are neither just the compilation of folk ideas nor the popularization of scholarly findings, but also reflections of the needs of capital and the state. This material link is most easily seen in the advertising media, which not only describe products but also manipulate images of women, men, and children so as to define them as individuals needing those commodities. Stuart Ewen, in *Captains of Consciousness* (1976), argues convincingly that the rise of U.S. mass advertising in the 1920s also functioned to siphon off the frustrations bred by industrialization from social unrest to dependence on commodities as the amelioratives of industrial life, and on corporations as the repositories of fatherly truth:

> Within a society that defined real life in terms of the monotonous insecurities of mass production, advertising attempted to create an alternative organization of life which would serve to channel man's [sic] desires for self, for social success, for leisure away from himself and his works, and toward a commoditized acceptance of "Civilization." (1976:48)

> Only in the instance of an individual ad was consumption a question of *what to buy*. In the broader context of a burgeoning commercial culture, the foremost political imperative was *what to dream*. (1976:109, emphasis in original)

Ewen notes that industry's efforts to instruct immigrants on "what to dream" were both extremely well organized and successful. The American Association of Foreign Language Newspapers, a consortium created by big industry in 1909, was by 1919 spending some $145 million on advertising in the foreign-language press. Robert Park, in his investigation of the association (1922), found that its head had the power to "make or break" immigrant newspapers. Congressional hearings eventually disclosed the fact that he forced journals to carry association news material and editorials under the threat of withdrawal of advertising revenue (Ewen 1976:63–65).

The thrust of this advertising, especially that placed in immigrant journals, was that only by abandoning all foreign ways and by consuming properly could immigrants overcome "inevitable ostracism" by Americans:

> Within such a conception of social security, variation from the norms of consumption as defined by industry, whether in the name of some vague sense of individuality or in the name of customs and habits of any group of people within the population, was tantamount to disaster. Traditional social bonds and the conformities that they engendered were un-American and suspect. The social bonds of modern age . . . would be provided over the counter. (1976:95)

[179]

Ewen's study focuses on the 1920s, but he argues that advertising also responded to the "proliferation of cultural opposition" of the 1960s—including the white ethnic movements—by diverting it to its own purposes:

> Within advertising, the social realm of resistance is reinterpreted, at times colonized for corporate benefit. (1976:218)

This is certainly the case for images of Italian-Americans in contemporary advertising. The glorification of ethnicity is transposed into the fusion of particular "ethnic" characteristics with specific commodities—the commoditization of ethnic identity. In the realm of advertisements, "Italian-American" means warm, nurturing women who serve abundant home-cooked meals both in the home and in their charming old-world shops. It means the large, noisy, congenial family that toasts one another at the enormous family dinner table and waits at the airport runway for the returning traveler: this is the glorified image of the patriarchal family and ethnic community of past time. The "foreign ways" and improper consumption of immigrants, first inveighed against as roadblocks to correct consumer behavior, have now become idealized images harnessed to products. What is being sold is not frozen pizza, or spaghetti sauce, or telephones, but warmth and nurturance, family and community.[5]

The success of such image conveyance, of course, depends upon large numbers of consumers perceiving their lives as lacking the qualities that are being sold with the products. And here we see another effect of the myth of community: it enhances a sense of inauthenticity through lost stability and tradition.

Many of my informants expressed strong feelings of inauthenticity, bred, I would claim, by "ethnic" advertising and popular writing on ethnic communities. They would stop me at the beginning of the first interview to warn me that they did not measure up to media image standards. Lucia Mornese said:

5. There is also the advertising image of *Italians* as sexy, elegant, and cosmopolitan, appropriate vehicles for the enhancement and sale of automobiles, fine clothing, liquors, and "exotic" coffees.

I think I'm the exception to the rule, as far as growing up with Italians in North Beach. I was always in the family shop. . . . No grand-mother, no aunts, no cousins. . . . This situation is kind of different from your average Italian family—I don't know if you'd be interested in it or not.

Angela Caputo warned me when I first met her that she was di-vorced. Later, she mused:

Although my Italian background is very much there, in one sense, being alone—I feel very much more American.

When I asked Gino Angeluzzi whether or not he thought Italian-Americans were different, he excused himself as an authentic representative:

Sometimes it's a little hard for me to say because as kids we didn't live in an Italian community.

And in the younger generation, James Giovannino warned me that I was not buying first-class ethnic merchandise:

Are you really sure you want me? I was born in California. . . . All of my Italian relatives are in [a Midwest city]. And so that right there cuts a lot of your familiar ties. I'm perhaps atypical, is that OK?

Informants also judged their relatives against media standards of authenticity. Linda Mornese found her grandmother, an immi-grant, too sophisticated:

I remember my aunt's mother [uncle's wife's mother], she was really the old Italian: white hair, never any makeup, the old dresses, the wine barrels in the basement. I always thought: there's a *real* Italian lady. I don't see an Italian lady as one with her hair done. My grandmother's always kept herself, she's always dressed very well because she sews well, she puts her jewelry on—she's better at it than I am!

Sally Cruciano humorously used the media image against her hus-band Joe's family:

They're a very Americanized family, so it wasn't that ethnic. I got mad at Joe one time and I said, "Bad enough that you're Italian, but your family doesn't even cook the kind of pasta they eat in restaurants!"

And James and Mary Giovannino talked openly about Mary's media-inspired first vision of James's family:

Mary: When I just met James his parents were still married—and the family seemed to be a strong, united front. . .
James: I had a nice car and what you thought was a rich father. . .
Mary: And I thought, Hey, this is my ticket out.
James: And Mary was attracted to what she perceived as a solid home situation. . . She thought it was this nice extended ethnic family, and as soon as she got in it all blew to hell.

Finally, informants' feelings of inauthenticity profoundly influenced their conceptions of my work. "Real" Italian-Americans were to be found in books; one found out about them by reading, not by examining or talking with others. Paolo Bevilacqua and Tony Ripetto, the only two ethnic brokers I interviewed, represented the apotheosis of the attitude. Ripetto was particularly maddening: he interlarded his lectures on the "old community" in the East Bay with references to Alistair Cooke's *America*. At one point, he offered to answer one of my questions about his childhood by looking it up! To comfort myself, I imagined Trobriand Islanders answering Malinowski's questions by referring to their *Fielding Guides*. Perhaps ethnic brokers held this attitude most strongly because of their simultaneous need to believe in community and inability to demonstrate it. The final irony came when Joe Longhinotti, an excellent informant, asked me if I had talked with Ripetto; he expressed his sense of inferiority, and was sure that Ripetto, who was so learned, would "really" be able to help me.

These are all, of course, very general and partial reactions to media-purveyed images of Italian-American ethnicity. Men and women expressed self-contradictory attitudes, and they disagreed with one another in their reactions to particular media images. Often their responses were context-determined, as was shown in the discussion of framing/feeling rules and ethnic slurs. As I asked

questions about specific images, however, some patterns in response began to emerge.

The first centered around media images of Italian-Americans and
food, and especially focused on advertised and restaurant food
items that were adulterated or inauthentic. Young and middle-aged
informants prided themselves on knowing better than to be fooled
into believing that these dishes were "real." Greg Longhinotti said,
"As far as going out and ordering spaghetti, no way!" And Nancy
Ferrucci explained, "I don't eat Italian food out because I'm very
picky."

Informants often became outraged about the use of the Italian
label for food they considered bad-tasting or lacking in nutrition.
Jim Bertini talked about American images of Italian food:

> Some idiot comes in and says something . . . . and you know he
> thinks Italian food is opening up a can of Franco-American . . . . and
> garlic bread . . . Italians NEVER eat garlic bread. I mean, gimme a
> break! [laughs]

And Greg Longhinotti talked about his family's attitudes about
food:

> You eat different too when you're Italian. . . . Over the years I've
> learned to enjoy different foods. . . There was always good food on
> the table, not junk, like Hamburger Helper . . . always vegeta-
> bles. . . Like my girl friend, OK like her mom was working, and
> she'd come home and her sister would fix her TV dinners! THAT'S
> JUNK! Eatin something . . . like I would never go out and buy
> canned Spaghettios, or canned ravioli.

And Gino Angeluzzi expressed great disgust over advertising manipulation of images of Italian women's home-cooked food:

> Some of it makes me laugh . . . "I likea my pizza." You know damn
> well she's not making it! *"Abbondanza"* . . . *Abbondanza* you*self!*
> Don't gimme that stuff!

It is clear, here, that these Italian-Americans work actively with
the media images in their environment: accepting some, rejecting

[183]

others, turning still others to ridicule as they compare them with the images used in their social networks and created in the process of boundary interactions. In assessing the power of the mass media, as Ewen does of their advertising component, it is crucial that we not assume that individuals are passive recipients who can be "fed" ideology wholesale. These Italian-Americans can be led to the table, but they won't necessarily eat.

One food-related media topic brought out a wealth of responses from informants. Joe Carcione is a television and radio personality who gives short reports on seasonal produce. He is a second-generation Sicilian whose father was involved in the produce wholesaling business in South San Francisco from the early years of the century (Carcione 1975:1–3). Some Italian-Americans, like Al Bertini, knew of Carcione but had never thought of him as Italian. Others, like his son Jim, saw in Carcione a representative of past authenticity:

> You know, I think he's amusing . . . sort of the living symbol of something that was probably really important in Italian society, the greengrocer, knowin where to get your stuff.

Linda Mornese agreed, with reservations:

> Yeah, it's the typical old Italian grocer. I think he's kind of pushy-sounding. Maybe that's just his way of talking.

Greg Longhinotti's response was similar:

> Um . . . I dunno, what I hear from people, he's kind of phony, but I think he's good. . . When he talks he gets into it a little too much, but he's good.

James and Mary Giovannino had no reservations:

> James: Oh yeah—I have a positive reaction. I don't really listen to what he has to say, but he could easily be a relative of mine. Short little guy with an Italian accent. Right? Isn't he Italian?
> Mary: I like him. He's got this cute little accent. He's like your Uncle Joe.

Whereas Frank Fante and Rick Cruciano expressed the negative judgments in Linda Mornese's and Greg Longhinotti's reactions:

[184]

He comes across as your stereotype of some kind of Italian . . . . very obnoxious at times. Obnoxious, I guess that's it.

I always thought he was strange. . . . He used to mispronounce the names of fruit and vegetables.

David DiVincenzo's response, I think, expresses the meaning behind judgements of Carcione as amusing, cute, and typical on the one hand and pushy, obnoxious, phony, and stupid on the other:

I've come to see that you can't really classify people like that, and what you can classify are other things. . . You know what I'm saying? I mean Joe Carcione's a guy who talks about fruit, but on the other hand you're gonna have someone else who's a lawyer . . . . like this guy who's very respected . . . . and you have this Dr. Rutolo who's an old doctor. I mean you have these different images of Italians.

The real issue, then, is social class.

Carcione does not look or sound slick and upwardly mobile; he has clearly made money precisely because he *does* present himself as working-class and ethnic. This contradiction is the basis for Longhinotti's concern that he is a phony. His working-class self-presentation evokes both positive and negative responses across the class spectrum, depending on the informants' attitudes toward ethnic mobility and the context of our discussion.

Social class was also deeply involved in informants' reactions to the novel and film *The Godfather*, and to the Italian-American Mafioso stereotype generally.[6] Class and age combined seemed to determine the patterns of response.

Younger informants of all classes, if they had an opinion about the Godfather gestalt, had a surprisingly positive one. Frank Fante said about the film:

I enjoyed it. I don't think it was getting down on Italians. It was probably a true story.

---

6. The American mythology connecting all Italian-Americans with organized crime is, of course, precisely that. See Bell 1953, Tomasi 1973, and Nelli 1976 for the history of Irish and Jewish predominance, successively, in organized crime, and for critiques of racist media campaigns against Italian-Americans.

And about the Mafia:

> I've never experienced it . . . as far as killings and all that, it's been done that way for years. I'm not condoning it, but I'm not close enough where I have to be for it or against it.

Greg Longhinotti reacted similarly, and also noted the class connection:

> Great movie. It was different. I don't really think it could get that heavy, as far as the Mafia and that whole bit. . . That there's an organization . . . it's amazing the power that somebody can have. . . . I was kinda proud of it because it was Italians.

James and Mary Giovannino connected their positive and negative feelings to ideas of Italian families:

> James: I recall having kinda emotional feelings . . . I guess as a positive reaction to the family presented as a sort of ideal . . . the family unity, sticking up for each other—the kind of thing I never got from my father. Also it was our first date.
>
> Mary: I really liked it, especially the family thing, but at that point I was really idolizing his family, the dinner thing.
>
> James: Which movie was it where he shunned his wife? I had a very negative reaction to that. . . That showed more of a commitment to his male chauvinistic principles . . . than to the family.

Rick Cruciano reacted positively to the "ethnic" idea of *The Godfather:*

> I liked the scenes that seemed very real to me, like those two old men swearing at each other and slapping each other on the back.

Jim Bertini was more analytical:

> As an Italian . . . it's true . . . I would feel close to the godfather if he was in my family . . . I could see loving him on that level. I could see him eating pasta and getting it on his shirt and all that. But what I didn't like was the fact that the majority of people that saw it didn't approach it as Italians. . . . It sounds pretty defensive . . . all Italians

aren't in the Mafia . . . I could go through all the racial things for each group . . . I find it offensive [when people believe that]. . . People who hold those ideas are just bigots. . . . At the same time I don't think it's a coincidence that there are a lot of Italians in the Mafia. . . . The truth of the matter is the Mafia is responsible for a lot of heroin in this country, and the repression of women, prostitutes and that whole routine. . . Lately when I encounter stuff like that I give a sociological explanation, like well in Sicily the landowners were such pigs that the people had to find some way to get services and goods so they had these people called *padrones.*

Linda Mornese objected to the film because it was depressing——"I only go to movies to laugh"—but had little negative reaction to the Mafia image:

I think what's changed my whole opinion is what happened recently when this guy's ring was stolen and he said that as much as they do, they do not go into a guy's house and rough up his wife and kids, which is true. . . If you get tied up in it you know exactly what's going on. It may be the Italian style, there's the Black type, but everybody's got their group, and that's our group and we have to live with it. I mean it's not our shining star, but. . .

Linda's father Salvatore also objected to violence in films, but would not be drawn into a discussion of the Mafia image. Gino Angeluzzi reacted similarly, but had gone to see the film:

The killing and all that stuff—no one likes that. But the part I enjoyed were some of the Italian expressions the guys used that I've heard my parents or old people use—no way related to gangsters.

Finally, Tony Ripetto's response exemplified one segment of the older Italian-Americans:

That's one reason why I refused to read that book, *The Godfather.* Refused to see the movie. They took one little segment of Italian society and blew it out of proportion.

Younger informants and those older informants who, as we have seen, were socially mobile and relatively autonomous had an easy-going, sometimes humorous attitude toward the Italian-Ameri-

[187]

can–Mafia formulation. There was even a tendency to play on the gangster identity. Linda Mornese said, "I tell them I *am* Mafia and they'd better do what I want!" And jokes turning on identification with the Mafia image as a means of fighting back were common among my professional and business informants: "What's black and blue and floats belly-up in a lake?—People who tell Italian jokes."

Returning to the framing/feeling rules in response to ethnic abuse, we can see that this reaction is related to the rule: "I am discriminated against: it is important to feel humorous about it." The difference is that the humor here is an offensive rather than a defensive tactic. In identifying with the Mafia humorously, these younger, and more affluent older, Italian-Americans exploit its powerful image and play on the half-belief of their Anglo audience. This conversion to positive use of a negative, externally imposed ethnic symbol is common. I see a very similar dynamic in some Black Americans' glorification of the pimp/drug dealer Superfly image as a means of expressing power and inspiring white fear.

The intragroup use of ethnic epithets follows this dynamic as well: they horrified some informants, while others gloried in them.[7] Gino Angeluzzi made the connection with Blacks explicitly: "It's funny, people—one Italian guy could probably tell another, "Hey you lousy Dago," . . . . but somebody else, hey it's all over. It's like my son tells me, sometimes Black people call each other nigger when they're mad at each other."

When we return to the ideological poles of assimilationism and the ethnic renaissance, we find that the recognition of discrimination may involve a variety of responses. The assimilation response can be summed up as: I am not discriminated against. Others are; they deserve it. There are three types of renaissance responses: (1) We must fight with righteous anger. (2) We must react with humor;

---

7. While I was still in the field I asked an Italian-American friend and a relative, both affluent men, to invent a title for my work encompassing Italian-Americans, California, and daily life. The friend responded after a few minutes with "Wops in the Sun," which inspired the relative, after a little thought, with "How the Day Goes for Dagos." In addition, a few years ago one of my relatives planned and carried out an elaborate "Godfather" party in a North Beach restaurant to which members of his professional association were invited. An Italian-American strip-joint tout was hired to hold a toy shotgun at the party's entrance and to "frisk" guests as they arrived. I was delegated to teach him to say *"Aspetta"* ("Wait"). After fifteen minutes, he still had not mastered the pronunciation.

we cannot show vulnerability. And (3) We can act, rather than react, and embrace the symbols of our oppression.

The "righteous anger" response, when organized, is that of ethnic activism. The Italian-American Civil Rights League in New York, for example, pressured *The Godfather's* producer to eliminate references to the Mafia in the film, and in Los Angeles an organization of Italian-American professionals urged coethnics to boycott or picket the film (Rolle 1980:105). While Paolo Bevilacqua and Tony Ripetto shared these sentiments, it is clear that Italian-Americans vary greatly in the ways that they deal with discrimination and deprecatory symbolism. Proponents of the community myth, such as the leaders of the now defunct Civil Rights League, may claim that the Italian-American community was outraged. Not only were many of my informants *not* outraged, but their answers made it clear that they were totally unaware of the outrage of their "community leaders."

In the last two chapters we have considered the varying material contexts in which Italian-Americans construct and reconstruct individual and collective ethnic identities. We have noted that different sorts of social work processes influence both the ways in which households, friendship networks, and workplaces are related and the kinds of ideas of collective ethnic identity that individuals hold. Nevertheless, individuals' constructions of their own ethnic identities are complex, context-related, and changeable. Depending on a variety of material factors, such as their own regional origin and appearance and their relations to the speaker, individuals decide to "frame" specific instances of ethnic abuse in a variety of ways. Framing and feeling rules are related, and themselves correspond to the contrasting contemporary ethnic ideologies of assimilationism and the white ethnic renaissance. The whole process is ordered within those ethnic boundaries at which individuals construct notions of sameness and difference.

These men's and women's occupations range from baker to businessman, from housewife to lawyer. They live in the center city, in the inner neighborhoods, and in the outer suburbs. They may know hundreds, or only a handful, of other Italian-Americans. They are of different regional origins, generations, and ages. But no principle of differentiation divides them more, in their own eyes or in others', than that of gender. Women's material and mental lives are funda-

[189]

mentally different from those of their fathers and brothers, husbands and sons. We need to consider what this major division means in women's and men's experience of their ethnicity—and in how they interpret that experience.

# [6]

# "I Think God Helps Us": Women, Work, Ethnicity, and Ideology

> Now, what particularly signalizes the situation of woman is that she—a free and autonomous being like all human creatures—nevertheless finds herself living in a world where men compel her to assume the status of the Other. They propose to stabilize her as object and doom her to immanence since her transcendence is to be overshadowed and forever transcended by another ego which is essential and sovereign. The drama of woman lies in this conflict between the fundamental aspirations of every subject—who always regards the self as the essential—and the compulsions of a situation in which she is the inessential—de Beauvoir 1952:xxxiii–xxxiv

Two major themes have emerged in this exploration of the family histories and present lives of these Californian Italian-Americans. The first is the key influence of larger political-economic structures on individual and household economic lives. The second is the simultaneous force of economic influence and of individual creativity in the construction of patterned perceptions—ideologies— with which people explain their lives to themselves and others. We have seen that collective ethnic identities are linked to occupations, and that individuals construct their identities in accordance with a variety of material factors—their regional origins, appearance, the local presence of other groups. We have also seen that individuals frame and reframe their ethnic experiences from person to person, from day to day, as they accept, reject, and modify prevalent ethnic ideologies, and that they try to discipline their emotions to be appropriate to this framing of experience.

Women have played roles in both themes. Family histories have shown them engaged in farming and small businesses, and the Census confirms the regional economic significance of these occupational strategies. We have observed the evolution from the wage-pooling to the independent daughter, from the 1950s housewife to the 1970s housewife/worker. We have observed, as well, women's creative and varying reactions to ethnic slurs, to other ethnic and racial groups, to their own relatives.

There is, however, a missing dimension: the link between occupation and collective ethnic identity was drawn primarily with *men's* jobs. This was the case not because women's market labor was unimportant in these families—of sixteen middle-aged women, only three had stayed home consistently since the birth of their first children—but because these women tended, like most American women, to work for shorter periods, often part-time, and in lower-paid jobs than their husbands. The influence of their occupational involvement on familial processes was thus more difficult to trace. The single exception to this sporadic labor force participation, Nancy Ferrucci, was matched in professional status by her husband, and it was difficult to distinguish the effects of the work life of each on their present-day networks. Finally, daughters and wives, in the present as well as the past, were often involved—sometimes as copartners—in the work of small businessmen and independent professionals. In these cases, men and women shared a similar work process and it was difficult to attribute social and ideological effects to either the man or the woman. Thus because of women's sporadic labor-market involvement, the small sample, and male-female overlap in two of the three occupational categories considered, the discussion has focused on male work, male-sponsored work/home connections, and types of ethnic identity influenced by these factors.

Looking at data in this way would be unproblematic for most researchers concerned with family issues. There is broad agreement that families are units characterized by consensus, with understood sexual divisions in role, and that family class status (including concomitant social behavior) is determined by male occupations. Some radical scholars have stressed the role of working-class women as participants in resistance to capitalism through strategies for family survival—but this perspective enhances rather than challenges the notion of family consensus.[1]

Feminist, and more recently Marxist-feminist, writers have stressed instead the sexual conflict within families based on women's individual reactions to the institutional oppression of their sex.[2] Recent work has focused particularly on the issues of household labor and occupational segregation. On the one hand, as women in the aggregate enter the market labor force, men in the aggregate do not increase the amount of child care and housework they do, leaving larger and larger numbers of women responsible for the "double day": work in the market plus work at home (Hartmann 1981a). On the other hand, whether pooling wages with men or supporting children on their own—and divorce rates continue to rise—most women are relegated to "segregated" sectors of the economy. The "women's jobs" they are able to find and keep pay less than men's and tend to be insecure, ununionized, and dead-end. This segregation and low pay have changed little in the decade of the women's movement, despite highly publicized breakthroughs of women into particular professions and blue-collar trades.[3]

Family, for these Italian-Americans as for all Americans, was clearly one locus of gender struggle (Hartmann 1981a). Life histories and contemporary accounts revealed recurrent patterns of male

1. Work reflecting the family-consensus assumption includes Young and Willmott 1957; Komarovsky 1962; Goode 1970; Bott 1971; and Rubin 1976. Stack 1974; Caulfield 1974; B. Williams 1975; and Humphries 1977 are examples of radical analyses that nevertheless do not challenge this model. Although these scholars may perceive women as oppressed within families, they do not analyze women's characteristic actions as strategic oppositions to male power.

2. Representative examples are de Beauvoir 1952; Firestone 1970; Eisenstein 1978; and Hartmann 1981b. In so characterizing writers I am following a categorization based on the perspectives that they have adopted on the issue of innate gender conflict in families. I will later use the term "patriarchy" interchangeably with institutional oppression; the term in this case denotes a historically changing set of social relations among men which functions to maintain their power over women. There is a stricter definition that denotes a family type characteristic of feudalism in which older men were household heads, controlling younger men, women, and children (cf. Eisenstein 1978).

3. See Blaxall and Reagan 1976; Stromberg and Harkess 1978; R. Smith 1979; and Treiman and Hartmann 1981 for data on and analyses of occupational segregation, past and present.

dominance of female resistance. In the 1920s, Angela Caputo's mother, stung by her husband's capricious behavior and his alienation of her own kin, came close to instituting divorce proceedings against him. During the Depression, when Cetta Longhinotti's father pulled her older sister Anna out of high school to earn wages for the household, Anna rebelled through eloping and withdrawing from the family. And in the 1970s, Dorothy DiVincenzo returned to school, to train herself not just for market labor but for a job she—not her husband—would choose.

Gender struggle, however, is not always so apparent. Its form is conditioned by the contexts in which it is experienced, and its visibility is conditioned by the context in which it is studied. Since my informants' economic resources varied, I discovered both gender commonalities and class differences in women's responses to their experiences. Because my focus was on kinship rather than family, I considered women's domestic lives beyond their own households. And because of my political-economic perspective, I evaluated elements of those domestic lives as labor. In addition, my emphasis on ethnic identity, and my women informants' reflections on their own identities, forced me to consider the ways in which gender is inscribed in constructions of ethnicity.

## Women's Work and the Work of Kinship

As I listened to and charted women's activities, I began to realize that they were involved in three kinds of labor: work in the market (except for two housewives), work in the household, and the work of kinship.

The work of kinship encompasses a variety of activities, including visits, letters, presents, cards, and telephone calls to kin; services, commodities, and money exchanged among kin; and the organization of holiday gatherings. It also includes the mental or administrative labor of the creation and maintenance of fictive kin ties, decisions to intensify or neglect ties, and the responsibility for monitoring and taking part in mass media and folk discourse concerning family and kinship.[4] These activities are necessary to the

4. I have constructed this phrase because no other describes precisely the range of activities covered; it also highlights the seldom recognized fact that these

maintenance of extrahousehold kinship, in both its functional and its symbolic senses. And they are largely women's responsibilities— women's work.

Feminists and nonfeminists alike have long recognized that women in industrialized societies have done and continue to do the bulk of work involved in what Marxists call the reproduction of the labor force: the housework, child care, cooking, planning, and emotional support of adult men and children necessary to keep men healthy and emotionally stable enough to work, and to socialize children to grow up to be workers and the support staff of workers. The historical development of this familial pattern, and its theoretical significance, are the subject of controversies not relevant here.[5] The important point is that all these sorts of women's work do not include the work of kinship: housework and child care, in advanced industrial societies, happen largely within households; the work of kinship happens largely *between* them.

Scholars who have written on women's organization of "cultures of resistance" have touched on one aspect of the work of kinship: it is precisely the kin and quasi-kin ties that women have created and maintained that Caulfield (1974) and Humphries (1977) celebrate when they portray Third World women's subsistence networks and Western working-class women's contributions to class struggle. And Stack (1974) delineates impoverished Black American women's creation and maintenance of networks of kin and fictive kin—networks that serve as conduits for the labor, money, and commodities that ensure the survival of their members. These reciprocity networks provide an illustration both of the utility of kin work to the impoverished and of its nature as women's, not men's, labor—men belong to these networks, but women create and maintain them.

Nevertheless, it is not only poor and working-class women who do the work of kinship: it is a cross-class phenomenon. If this were not the case, there would be no middle-class family reunions and no

---

activities are *labor*. Tilly and Scott's (1978) "family self-presentation," which I used in Chapter 2, does not cover extrahousehold links. Papanek's (1979) similar "family status production" includes only those ties women make to enhance their families' statuses.

5. This controversy includes argument over the historicity of the public/private split (Ortner 1974; Pleck 1976), the domestic labor debate (Gardiner 1979; Malos 1980), and the family wage (Humphries 1977; Barrett and McIntosh 1980; Hartmann 1981b).

national market for greeting cards to grandparents, grandchildren, aunts and uncles, nephews and nieces. Middle-class women's magazines would not focus on advice about planning perfect holidays and improving relations with relatives. And upper-class women would not play the central role that Domhoff (1971) has elucidated for them as the negotiators of upper-class social and affinal links.

My Italian-American women informants, whether or not they worked outside the home, whether working-class or affluent, were responsible for the work of kinship that knit their households with others. Only women wrote the Christmas cards, including cards to husbands' kin and childhood friends. Writing and telephoning kin were tasks almost always left to wives, daughters, and sisters. Women bought most presents, planned holidays, and cooked holiday food. Cetta Longhinotti said, "I do it all—he's terrible. If we didn't have a tree he wouldn't care." And Pina Meraviglia shouted "Oh *yes!*" and burst into peals of laughter when I asked her if she wrote Christmas cards for Nick's personal friends as well as the family's. When Lucia and Salvatore Mornese returned to the United States after their marriage, Lucia found that it was her responsibility to maintain kin contacts in Italy: "Oh yes, he would never write or send cards to his relatives in Italy, so that was my job." Angela Caputo, Clelia Cipolla, Sally Cruciano, and the others all told similar stories.

Particularly interesting are the changes in cross-household kin contact when women enter or leave alliances with men. When Al Bertini and his wife separated, his and his son Jim's participation in his extended family network decreased rapidly. But when Jim Bertini began a relationship with Jane Bateman, she and he moved in with Al. Jim and Jane began to invite his kin over for holidays, and Jane cooked large feasts for them singlehandedly. Sam Lombardo had not spoken to his father for a decade when he met Candy; she influenced him to visit his father, and in turn his father flew in from the East Coast for Sam and Candy's wedding and established a grandfather relationship with Sam's child from his first marriage. And Mary Giovannino has maintained relationships with James Giovannino's kin for over a decade, linking James to them for many years preceding Mary and James's legal wedding.

## Gender and Kin Knowledge

The fact that women do most of the work of kinship has a natural corollary: kinship is women's field of expertise. Their knowledge of their husbands' kin is far more detailed than men's knowledge is of their wives' kin. In fact, in many cases, wives knew more about husbands' kin than did the men themselves. This phenomenon surfaced often in my interviews in the form of humorous arguments and in wives' detailed additions to husbands' narratives. Nick Meraviglia discussed his mother's life in the 1920s in the presence of his wife, Pina:

Nick: She was a very sick woman . . . her uterus had been punctured through the use of instruments. Therefore she couldn't take a child to . . .

Pina: Full term

Nick: Full term. Mom was going to a lot of doctors, and one of them suggested a trip back to her native land would be therapeutic.

Pina: *Aria nativa*

Nick: Yes, *aria nativa* [laughs]. That was her reason for going to Italy.

Pina: I think your grandfather sent money to her, didn't he?

Nick: I don't know—how long were we there?

Pina: He went over not knowing a word of Italian, and when he came back he couldn't talk English.

Nick: That's right.

Pina: And when he went to school he couldn't talk to the teacher.

Nick: Except in Italian.

Pina: Except in Italian, and she didn't know what he was talking about! [both laugh].

Nick: My grandfather was a very outspoken man, and it was reported he took off for the hills when he found out that Mussolini was in power.

Pina: And he was a very tall man, he used to have to bow his head to get inside doors.

Nick: No, that was my uncle.

Pina: Your grandfather too, I've heard your mother say.

Nick: My mother has a sister and had a brother.

Pina: *Two* sisters.

Nick: You're right!

Pina: Maria and Angelina.

[197]

[Conversation continues as an argument over whether Nick's mother has one or two brothers.]

James and Mary Giovannino, much younger than Nick and Pina Meraviglia, fought over kinship expertise with the gloves off:

> James: My father the Italian was Catholic. My mother . . .
> Mary: Was Catholic.
> James: I couldn't swear that my mother was Catholic.
> Mary: She told me so just the other day.
> James: Thank you—for that *insightful* interjection.

> James: [About why parents sent children to Catholic schools when they hated them]. My father's never been very supportive with school matters . . . but a lot of these things weren't very tangible.
> Mary: I think a lot of it came with Cathy because they thought she wasn't very bright and didn't encourage her.
> James: I don't remember anything like that. Why don't you interview Mary regarding my mother? (All laugh.)
> I: Did your mother work?
> James: NO. I know the answer! You don't have to prompt me. She's sitting over there shaking her head [laughs].

Mary and James disagree over how much housework he and his sibs did.

> James: You came in at the tail end of this! Give me some credibility for the years one through eighteen, before I met you.

Much later in the interview James conceded defeat:

> Yeah, you know more about my relatives than I do.

Although this may have been somewhat affected by my gender, I also found that women were much more detailed in their narratives about kin, and much more willing to admit to family dissension and to errors they felt they had made in dealing with kin. Joe Longhinotti summarized his kinship relations by stating, "We all get along. As a rule, relatives, you got nothing but trouble." Cetta, instead, discussed her relations with each of her children, their wives, her in-laws, and her other blood kin in detail. She did not hide the fact that relations were strained in several cases: she was eager to discuss the evolution of the problem and to seek my opinions of her actions.

Similarly, Pina Meraviglia told the story of her fight with one of her brothers with hysterical laughter: "There was some biting and hair pulling and choking . . . it was terrible! I shouldn't even tell you. . . If he would only communicate. . ." Nick Meraviglia, by contrast, was concerned to maintain an image of family unity and respectability.

All of these middle-aged Italian-American men talked at length about their work (and often their military experience), but avoided answering questions about kin relations—or suddenly abridged their narratives at that point. Gino Angeluzzi, after having talked for hours about his professional training, wound up: "Well, anyway, starting practice, and having my kids. . ." Tony Ripetto and Al Bertini refused to talk about their siblings and cousins. Joe Cruciano represented his family as close and made up of superior people; his wife and children willingly discussed family feuds and dissension.

In complementary fashion, it was extremely difficult to induce women to talk about the details of their jobs. They often focused on factors of ambiance: Cetta Longhinotti was concerned to demonstrate that her work in a store involved dealing with "lovely things"; Angela Caputo described the bright walls and houseplants in her office; Dorothy DiVincenzo explained that she had first found work in a "friendly place."

In general, middle-aged women talked about kin in the way men discussed their jobs, and vice versa. This is not surprising, given prevailing gender assumptions and the sexually segregated labor market. The low-status jobs these women performed made it reasonable for them to focus on environmental factors rather than on the work itself. Marriage and family were still what these women took seriously and invested effort in; while the men, more concerned with their work life, left the responsibility of maintaining kin ties and undertaking kin responsibilities to their wives.

These patterns are not repeated in the younger generation, especially among younger women such as Linda Mornese, Jane Bateman, and Mary Giovannino, who have managed to acquire jobs

[199]

with some prospect of mobility. These younger women, though, have *added* a professional and detailed interest in their jobs to a felt responsibility for kin work. The men with whom they are allied, and the other younger men in the study, are like their fathers: they do not consider kin work their responsibility.

Nevertheless, investment in kin, for these Italian-American women just as for the impoverished Black women with whom Stack lived, is a reasonable general strategy. Kin took in and supported Angela Caputo when her marriage ended; and since women on the average live longer than men, it has been mainly the mothers of the Cipollas, the Longhinottis, the Meraviglias, the Angeluzzis, and the Morneses who have benefited from their commitment to their children and grandchildren.

Kin work patterns, then, have complex ramifications. Men and children, especially boys, benefit from women's labor—they gain a sense of family, of connectedness, without working for it or being responsible for it. The classic American Thanksgiving Day—women and girls cooking while men and boys watch football on television—illustrates this process well. But women also benefit from kin work. And given their labor-market position, these benefits tend to be more important to them than they are to men.

There is another, related, reason why women may be more knowledgeable and willing to discuss kinship issues than are men. As the less powerful partners in marriages, they have little to lose and much to gain in sharpening their understanding of their hosbands—and in criticizing them. Joe Cruciano summed up his marriage in this way:

Sally is a super person—she selected me and she's stayed with me.

Sally spent hours discussing with me the history of their marriage and Joe's inability to understand her problems with work and family:

He feels he helped me a lot. I remember it differently—it seems like he just lay on the couch and watched TV. . . . Even all last year, he wasn't around. And there were problems with the kids—and they don't wait. . . . Somehow—even though he was very proud of this career woman—who wore the diamond stickpin and carried a briefcase and ran the office very professionally—somehow she should run the house without asking her two sons to do the dishes. . . . He saw me in two different roles, but he couldn't put them together in one person.

There is no need to belabor this point; it is a cliché that women in industrialized societies focus on and wish to discuss their relationships with men to a degree that is not reciprocated. And the power dynamics, the sexual politics behind this clichéed behavior have long been elucidated by de Beauvoir and by others before her. The point here is that there is a connection between this long-recognized women's work and the work of kinship. Despite (or perhaps because of) institutionalized male dominance, kin networks are these women's bases of power. They work actively within them, attempting to extend their control and autonomy (Lamphere 1974).

### Sharing and Ceding Kin Work

But the fact that women in the aggregate do kin work does not mean that any one woman does all kin work tasks at all times. Kin work is both negotiated and ceded among kinswomen, depending on their relative power and desire for power, free time, economic resources, and life-cycle status.

During the 1920s and 1930s, Lucia Mornese's mother was too busy working in the family store to plan and execute holiday celebrations. She ceded this work to her first husband's brother's wife, who welcomed Lucia and her older brother to Christmas and Easter feasts. As Lucia grew older, she began taking over these responsibilities herself. When she found her first paying job, she began sending Christmas cards to her parents' friends. (Maria Fante and Cetta Longhinotti did this as well.) In the early years of Lucia's and Salvatore's marriage, when they were both working and Linda was a baby, Lucia's mother, then retired, took over the organization of holiday gatherings.

Maria Fante's mother, on the other hand, although a housewife in the 1920s and 1930s, did not invest herself in kin work. She relinquished her responsibilities to her husband's sister, an active entrepreneur. "Aunt Lucy" organized all holiday gatherings—it is her traditional cookie, not his mother's, that Maria's brother Mike Sacco remembers. She also made her house available to Maria for entertaining her high school friends. Joe Cruciano's mother followed a similar pattern, allowing her older sisters full authority over her children and all family decisions.

Angela Caputo's and Gino Angeluzzi's mothers made temporary decisions to pull back from kin ties as a result of Depression inpoverishment. Dorothy DiVincenzo's mother uses her wealth to bring kin together in a vacation home. Cetta Longhinotti, Teresa Angeluzzi, and others no longer negotiate combined holiday gatherings with their sisters and sisters-in-law because their kin groups have become too large to fit into anyone's living room. Kin work, then, is a movable feast—but it is one always prepared by women.

### Kin Responsibilities and Prerogatives

In the present, one of the major variables determining women's restrictions and opportunities in carrying out the work of kinship is the manner in which individual families intersect with the economy. We saw that command of financial resources allowed Nick Meraviglia's mother and Dorothy DiVincenzo's parents to extend patronage and assert control over their descendents. Class differences across nuclear families also create tensions which it is women's responsibility to mediate. Cetta Longhinotti's sister Anna, married to a successful professional man, has watched her own position diverge from Cetta's over the course of their married lives. Cetta and Anna talk on the telephone several times a week and keep the two families, divided by class, united through an exchange of support and information. They continue to sponsor their children's inclusion in one another's networks as well: at the moment, it is only through his mother's gossip that Greg Longhinotti remains in touch with his cousins, but because of it he will be able to recontact them easily when his work shifts are less taxing.

It also falls to women to deal with the consequences of class status for their families. While we have seen that men work with concepts of ethnic behavior to explain their economic positions to themselves, women try to mediate the tensions among family members created by upward or downward mobility and other economic status issues.

Clelia Cipolla has had to mediate between her children's anger at being forced to live in an isolated area, and her husband's determination to remain in the house built on his father's land in a working-class area:

> My girls have been isolated and they've resented living here. . . We have a very quiet social life. . . My girls weren't very pleased about that.

Dorothy DiVincenzo, on the other hand, has had to deal with family strains caused by upward social mobility. Her son David has criticized the family's conspicuous consumption, and Dorothy agreed with him:

> It's a shame to go through that sort of thing . . . I did, I feel I'm coming out of it.

Sally Cruciano has had similar problems. Her son Rick

> finally rebelled against that, and cut himself off financially. Now the problem is easing the other two off financial dependence. The old gimme-gimme take-take syndrome is hard to break.

Sally mimicked Joe's reaction to Rick's long hair:

> He says "Hi . . . . . . . Rick" [grimace; laughs]. You have to get used to different life-styles.

With the responsibility for kin work come certain kinship prerogatives. Women in general expressed a sense of proprietorship about their homes—which were after all their work sites—that their husbands did not assert. Sally Cruciano put it succinctly:

> Joe said if the kids won't do as you ask, tell them to pack their bags and move elsewhere. Which is true! It *is* my house and if you want to live here, you are very welcome. If you don't care to go by my rules, you are not very welcome.

[203]

Women also had rights to initiate, to maintain, or to drop kin contacts. We have seen that Pina Meraviglia fought with her elder brother and cut contacts with him. Her sisters did so as well, independently. Nevertheless, Pina feels it to be her right to assert contact with her brother's children:

> The oldest boy sees both sides of the story . . . the little one, when his father's around he doesn't know me, but if his father isn't there, he'll kiss me and say "Aunty Pina."

Cetta Longhinotti has refused contact with Joe's sister, despite the mutual affection of the siblings. And Teresa Angeluzzi has politely distanced herself from Gino's siblings:

> I'm not superior but we just don't communicate. We don't have common intellectual interests.

## Kin Work in the Labor Context

Involvement in the work force no more exempted these women than it does most American women from the responsibility for home and dependent children. But the work of kinship is less clearly defined and less socially mandated than are the daily activities of cooking, cleaning, and child care. These working women all described the process of cutting down Christmas lists, doing less for holidays, and visiting and hosting kin and friends less often that followed their return to market labor. Equally important for women living in this stage of the developmental cycle, the care of the elderly preempted most other work of kinship activities. While maintaining contact with older relatives falls under the rubric of kin work, the burden of visiting the elderly in rest homes or caring for them under crowded conditions can reduce other social contacts. Cetta Longhinotti, during the period when she was visiting her elderly mother every weekend, said of her grown children: "I'd have the whole gang here once a month, but I've been so busy I haven't done that for about six months."

Responsibility for elderly parents and parents-in-law was a major concern for these middle-aged women. For many of them it was a factor as important in their decision to work or not to work as is the care of young children for most American women. Clelia Cipolla talked about her hiatus from market labor: "There was a time when my parents needed me too. . . After Momma died my father had every meal [dinner] with me . . . and I went over once a week to do his cleaning." Pina Meraviglia, when I asked if she would go back to work, explained that caring for her ailing parents-in-law made that impossible. Yet Cetta Longhinotti was unable, for financial reasons, to quit work, despite the burden of caring for her mother and mother-in-law. Lucia Mornese, as well, could not quit her job to care for her resident elderly mother; she only ended her career after a long illness and several operations had made her eligible for disability payments.

There is another perspective on the work/kin work balance: some women recognized that market work allowed them to avoid unwanted kin demands. Dorothy DiVincenzo, seeking employment when I first interviewed her, explained that she wished neither to be on call as a baby-sitter for her grandchildren nor to work in the family business during her husband's frequent absences. Angela Caputo recognized that the fact that she and her sister Caterina worked had meant that Lina, the housewife, was the daughter with whom their mother would live for some years. Still, financial resources and the feeling of responsibility meant that for some the work of kinship could not be avoided. Cetta Longhinotti's and her sister Anna's remarks about one another illustrate this tangle of commitments. Anna said: "I got married and got pregnant right away, and I haven't worked since. Like Cetta says, 'I wish I hadn't started.'" Cetta, alone with me at the beginning of an ethnic dinner, said of Anna's involvement with her elderly parents-in-law and other relatives: "I swear she's one-half saint. I've been thinking about her—she should go to work—everyone uses her. It would be therapy—she gets very depressed. I don't know why [her husband] doesn't see it."

## The Domestic Domain and Gender Ideology

One result of these felt interests and strategic activities is the dominance of networks of female kin among these families. Angela

[205]

Caputo, Pina Meraviglia, Cetta Longhinotti, and Dorothy DiVincenzo all belong to tight-knit groups of two or more sisters who are, as Angela Caputo said, "best friends" to one another. Frank Fante's father's sisters form just such a group as well. Dorothy DiVincenzo, Angela Caputo's sister Lina, Lucia Mornese, Sally Cruciano, Teresa Angeluzzi, and Maria Fante all have close relations with their daughters. All of the mothers of these middle-aged women were in close communication with their daughters in earlier years. There are also a number of close aunt-niece relationships in these family histories: Maria Fante and her father's sister remained intimate until "Aunt Lucy's" death. Angela Caputo still visits her father's sister weekly; and Cetta Longhinotti writes to and has exchanged visits with her mother's elderly Italian sister. These ties among female kin are both the product of kin work and the vehicles of larger kin connections. The kin networks of which they are components are thus women-centered.

Researchers have tended to recognize and analyze women-centered kin networks only in the households of the impoverished, both in the United States and abroad. They have been seen as aberrant, part of the "matrifocal" pattern that obtains in the absence of the wage-earning father-husband. Yanagisako (1977) points out that in fact they are ubiquitous in urban bilateral kinship systems; the kin work perspective helps to explain why. Kin networks tend to be women-centered because maintaining cross-household kin ties is work delegated to women. And just as kin work is women's responsibility across class divisions, so women-centered kin networks appear at all class levels.

This dual social invisibility of women-centered kin networks and of kin work is probably due to our tendency to settle for "thin descriptions" of the domestic domain—the world seen as belonging to women, and apart from public life (Yanagisako 1979). We tend to see households as separate from each other and from the larger world, and to reduce kinship to husband-wife and parent-child relations—which we then further restrict through our obsession with the mother-child bond (Collier et al. 1982). It is not that we do not "see" activity in and across households, but that we have not seen it, until recent feminist work, as importantly strategic—as political. We tend to envision women in their domestic worlds as unchanging and unvarying, as outside history.

[206]

Simone de Beauvoir has analyzed this ideological construction of gender in industrial societies characterized by systematic male dominance with reference to the existentialist terms "immanence" and "transcendence." This hegemonic ideology ascribes to women a contingent being: identified with nature, linked to men whose "transcendent" action upon nature and women is perceived as that which gives them reality.[6] This dichotomy gives rise to and reinforces the symbolic echoes of home/work, inner/outer, etc.: women are seen as immanent "matrices who nourish and let go of male individuals" (Bridenthal 1979:194). This is, however, entirely a question of labeling. Women's activities, whether domestic or public, can certainly be interpreted as transcendent actions upon nature. And men are clearly, as well, "contingent beings" in their dependence on the labor and nurturance of their kinswomen and of unrelated women in the labor force. The ideology functions as a whole to assert that male dominance and the characteristic sexual division of labor are natural functions rather than social constructions.

The challenge to this ideology in the past decade—the second wave of Western feminism—has paralleled and interacted with these women's lives.[7] These two ideologies coexist in the contemporary United States; this coexistence and polarization in the public mind was reflected in the opinions of my women informants. Many of them invoked one or the other pole in their descriptions and judgments of themselves and other women. Clearly, the most descriptive labels for these end points are "feminism" and "antifeminism," but none of these women, with the exception of Jane Bateman, used the term "feminism." They were familiar with the media phrase "women's lib" and used it unself-consciously. And few of these women would have labeled themselves feminists (or even "women's libbers"). Those who approved of some feminist perspectives often went on to add that they disagreed with others. Sally Cruciano approved of the new educational opportunities her daughter had "because of women's lib in school—some of which

---

6. Recent work on de Beauvoir's analysis praises her for quarrying feminist concepts from Existentialism's innately misogynist premises and language (Le Doueff 1980).

7. For the first and second waves of the American women's movement, see Flexner 1959; Kraditor 1968; Morgan 1970; DuBois 1978; and Evans 1978.

I'm against." Others defined themselves as individually ahead of the movement. Linda Mornese said: "You know, when women's lib came along, I thought, "What's women's lib about?" 'Cause I have always—my motto is I get what I want." It is reasonable that these women did not articulate and label for themselves consistent perspectives on women and families: they were not activists in the realm of sexual politics, any more than the sample as a whole was active in ethnic politics.[8]

Feminism and antifeminism are, in this case, analyst's labels. They help to order women's reactions to historical changes in women's roles and family dynamics, changes we have observed in microcosm in these family histories. Women have greater equality vis-à-vis men in households (as well as in the public world); parental authority over children has lessened; and married women have entered the labor market in unprecedented numbers. The increasing burden of work in the home and in the market (the double day) has fallen to women as men have not appreciably increased their labor in the home. The divorce rate has risen: and, as over half of all divorced fathers do not pay child support and as most women are able to earn far less than most men, single-parent families with female heads are the fastest-growing impoverished household group (Pearce and McAdoo 1981).

Some women reacted to these changes, these new opportunities, dangers, and instabilities in clearly opposing directions. Either they reasserted their "immanence," their commitments to family and kin networks, to older lines of authority and mutual duty, or they demanded "transcendence": hailed the changes as personally liberating, both for themselves and others, and looked forward to further increases in parity between males and females and the old and the young. In other words, they tended either to try to maintain their power and authority through the work of kinship, or to relinquish that vehicle to power and invest themselves instead in demanding freedom and equality in kin relationships, market labor, and in peer networks. The invocation of these ideological tendencies was, for some middle-aged women, deeply connected to their own experiences of caring for the elderly and to their concerns about their own old age.

8. There is, however, some specifically feminist organized Italian-American activity, such as the series of Italian-American Women's Days (Taylor 1980).

Dorothy DiVincenzo's and Cetta Longhinotti's narratives illustrate the connections of the feminist and antifeminist response to concerns about old age. Dorothy DiVincenzo, in the period when I was interviewing her, was coming to the conclusion that she was bitter about the way her husband had refused to participate in housework and child care: "He's from the old school . . . it's an easy way out. He's never been willing to help. He wouldn't get involved in school things. . . He doesn't want to give up his own time." She complained that, during a recent visit of a grandchild, at her urging, Jarus had taken the boy to the bathroom, only to flee the scene and demand that she deal with it when the child announced that "he had to do number two."

Dorothy was a devout Catholic; she had been an extremely conscientious mother. She could discuss all of her children's teachers, and knew exactly which college courses the older ones had taken; she knew the dates of each child's illnesses. But she did not want to be deeply involved in her children's adult lives—we have observed that she did not want to do extensive baby-sitting for her grandchildren. She was tired of mediating among her husband, her parents, and her children. (David later told me that she shocked him by talking about his living arrangements with his girl friend in front of his grandparents.) Some of her children and nieces and nephews were planning a family picnic; she approved of it but did not want to be involved in the planning. She was grateful that her children lived nearby, but "because of the times we're living in it's good for them to be independent."

Dorothy wished to talk with me about the childhood woman friend with whom she had recently renewed ties, about her need to work, and asked me: "Do you think I'm doing this to break away from my husband?"

Dorothy's parents, though very elderly, were wealthy and could afford household help. They did not ask her to provide them with services or companionship beyond frequent visits to their pleasant winter or summer homes. Dorothy could look forward to a similar old age; there was no need for her to groom her children to house her or care for her in the future.

Cetta Longhinotti did not openly criticize her husband as Dorothy DiVincenzo did. But she made it clear that she was unhappy, and bitter about the frequent moves that Joe's business failures had necessitated: "I don't like change—it's just one of those things I've had to do—seems like I'm always doing what I don't like." She said that she had never wanted to leave her first home, and was particularly saddened when Joe, against her wishes, sold the "lovely" home they had lived in before they moved to their present, smaller house: "Joe said it was too damp, but I loved that house. The neighborhood was upper-class—we were really out of place." [smiles] Cetta also noted that Joe, like Jarus DiVincenzo, had not helped her with housework or child care: "Joe didn't even hold them when they were babies—he was afraid of them."

But Cetta's interpretation of this male behavior differed from Dorothy DiVincenzo's: she celebrated her own competence and commitment to housework and child care through underlining men's inabilities:

> Greg can't boil water . . . he never showed any interest in learning. And Joe is terrible. . . The first time I ever saw my dad wash dishes was when my mom had Anna—I cried, I thought that was just terrible. . . . I have always done all my own housework without any help. . . The male has always been the king of the family. . . . Greg has always said that his wife won't work. I say, "Greg you sound like an Italian male" . . . I'm afraid he's too chauvinist. [laughs]

When Cetta and I, standing in her kitchen, discussed her burden of work, housework, and the care of her mother, she said: "I think women are superior . . . I think God helps us."

Related to this emphasis on her commitment to her feminine duties, for Cetta, was a profound feeling of connection to her children and grandchildren. She had never allowed her in-laws to care for her children: "Well, they're my most treasured possession . . . I'd give up my life for my children—that's the way I am." As has been noted, this commitment included attempts to direct her children's and grandchildren's behavior. When Cetta discussed her daughter-in-law's refusal to send her children to catechism, she remarked, "Grandma doesn't like that too well."

But Cetta was also willing to invest time in caring for her children and grandchildren. After Greg had bought a house and moved out, she explained:

> Every once in awhile I'll go over and clean his house—I'm supposed to call but if I know they're both going to be gone—I'll clean, work in

the garden, wash his clothes. I know I shouldn't do it but I do it anyway. . . Greg likes it! [long laughter].

And she volunteered to care for her grandchildren on a regular basis:

Well, since they [son and daughter-in-law] got married so young I feel they missed out on youth and good time and consequently I would tell them to go out and enjoy an evening together, just the two of them. . . This way I feel I'm just helping their relationship by taking care of the kids. And I enjoy it anyway—I just love doing it.

But control was an important issue for Cetta. The late 1960s and early 1970s, which were for Dorothy DiVincenzo "those difficult years" of mediation among children, husband, and parents, were for Cetta "a terrible time" when "kids were all so rebellious and they hated their parents. . . Being Italian and Catholic, I feel that family is so important. Kids thought they knew *un'pagina più del'libri* [one page more than the books]." Keeping her children close to her has been very important to Cetta Longhinotti, and she has been partially successful in maintaining these connections. Greg calls her or drops by nearly every day; her other sons do so less often.

Cetta, as we know, experienced the burden of care for both mother and mother-in-law; neither the women themselves nor their children had the financial resources to ease this burden and provide for the special needs of the elderly, as did Dorothy DiVincenzo's family. When Cetta drew me into a discussion of the Briggs initiative (Chapter 1), her major concern was that "I don't want my granddaughters to become lesbians." Earlier, in lamenting her poor relationships with her daughter-in-law, she said, "I think if I had a daughter I could be a lot closer." Cetta was concerned about her granddaughters becoming alienated from her, and lamented her lack of a daughter; it is women who do most of the care of elderly kin.[9] Maintaining a system of kin obligations had a material urgency for Cetta Longhinotti that it did not have for Dorothy DiVincenzo.

This correlation of ideology and class, however, did not hold for

9. I refer here to my informant's perception that lesbian relatives would be lost to the family, not to an empirical reality.

all women. Lucia Mornese, for example, whose family income was lower than Cetta Longhinotti's, expressed feminist perspectives. She and Salvatore have been negotiating housework responsibility (he now does the vacuuming), control over children, and the question of social life for some years. Salvatore said of his hopes for grandchildren through his son:

> Right now we got to wait because they got other things to do. . . . That's really something I better keep quiet about! No two ways about it! [laughs].

And Lucia made it clear her support for her daughter-in-law, who is in professional training:

> He [son] said he couldn't stand the mess in the house, and I'd say what do you mean, your room was such a mess all the time! I kept the house in order, and what I didn't pick up your grandmother did! You can't expect Bobbie to [do housework].

Lucia reflected on the issue of social life when Salvatore was sitting with us:

> My biggest deal was that I always wanted to go out to dinner on my birthday, and he never felt he should spend money on that, he'd rather spend money on the gift. I'd say—"Oh I don't want the gift, I just want to go out" [turns to Salvatore]. And that's the way it's gonna be from now on, huh? Because I pay for it anyway. Actually, you pay for it, but it's the money you gave me, so I'll pay for it!

When we were alone, Lucia related her standard joke with her closest woman friend, who had known Salvatore in Italy before Lucia met him:

> . . . cause Jeannie never married so we say we share him . . . I say, "Too bad you didn't marry him." And she says: "Oh am I glad I didn't marry him!" [laughs]. Because she likes to mix with people and is very social, and he's not that way.

Reflecting Salvatore's increased accommodation to her requests, she said later:

[212]

One thing he's good about, if I say I want to go to the opera or to see
this, he doesn't want to go, so he'll say "OK you go, don't worry about
me, I'll take care of my dinner—just tell your mother to stay out of
the kitchen!"

Clelia Cipolla, a professional married to a professional, had nonetheless a clearly antifeminist perspective. In Chapter 1 I reported
Clelia's vision of proper parent-child relations in her dismay that
my parents had "allowed" me to have Thanksgiving away from
them. Even though Clelia was working during the period I interviewed her, she spoke of her hired cleaning woman as "one of the
luxuries my husband's allowed me." And she stressed repeatedly
that her house "is used for important family gatherings and funerals."

Considering women's relative investment in kin work in conjunction with the immanence/transcendence dichotomy gives us a
framework for understanding women's choices and perceptions—
but the framework oversimplifies the issue of power. Economic
resources, historical cultural shifts, and characteristics of women's
kinsmen and kin networks condition the quality and extent of
power available to women in the domestic domain.

For earlier generations, there were both greater opportunities
for and greater threats to women's domestic power through kin
work. Greater generational authority meant that mothers, aunts,
and grandmothers might collect pay packets, determine purchases
and pocket money—and arrange social lives, marriages, and occupational futures for their children, nephews and nieces, and
grandchildren. And in fact many of these patterns did obtain for
older women in the Angeluzzi, Caputo, Mornese, DiVincenzo,
Cruciano, Fante, and Meraviglia families. Nick Meraviglia's mother has exercised considerable autonomy and power over kinspeople
throughout her life. She traveled to Italy without her husband in
the 1920s. She has directed both her husband's and son's work
careers, invested their savings, and bought Nick and Pina a car and
gave them the down payment for their house in the early years of
their marriage. She directed the work of bringing several relatives
to the United States after World War II and of settling them after
their arrival. She is now in the process of attempting to direct her
adult grandchildren. She has provided the down payment for one

grandson's house, visits her great-grandchild often, lends money to her other grandchildren, and lectures them all on their appearance, deportment, and duties to her.

On the other hand, earlier generations of women lived in an environment in which there was considerable support for the concept of male dominance over women in the household. Some husbands and fathers were deeply involved in the domestic domain—but as managers of their wives and daughters' labor, not as kin workers themselves. Clelia Cipolla's husband Dom grew up in such a household. Clelia describes Dom's mother:

> She was very quiet and shy—a saint. She knew what her duties were—a good cook, to see that her husband was comfortable. She waited on him. She didn't think of herself, ever.

Dom's father, into late old age, directed every detail of holiday celebrations—but Dom's mother did all the work involved. Clelia, despite her beliefs, found this objectionable:

> My mother-in-law did it all even though after a point—the poor darling—it was very difficult. But my father-in-law refused to leave his home. I finally put my foot down and I said to Dom, "It's Mother's Day and I really don't think that your mother should do the cooking." So twice my father-in-law agreed to come and spend Mother's Day. Just barely long enough to eat. Then my husband would drive him home. . . It was HIS house and HIS family. But he forgot that poor Nonna couldn't do it! Oh, she would've come, very happily, she would've gone to the different children's homes for dinner. It was HARD for her. But you couldn't make him understand.

In the present, both the feminist and antifeminist choices—to reduce or to increase investment in kin work—have limits. Women can no longer control children and other younger kinspeople as some of their mothers and grandmothers did—Cetta Longhinotti's failure with her children and daughter-in-law is a case in point. The domestic domain, while still highly political, affords much less scope for women. On the other hand, women cannot attain male freedom and privileges simply through limiting kin work (and childbearing, for younger women) relative to paid labor. Since very few women can get "male" jobs, investing themselves at the workplace will not reap the rewards of high pay, satisfaction, and job security. At the same time, women who pull back from kin work may be resented and possibly penalized by kinswomen, while men are not expected to do kin work tasks and will continue to be included in kin social life. Finally, since kin work, unlike housework and child care, is unlabeled, it is more difficult to overcome guilt over not doing it. All my women informants expressed a sense of responsibility for "keeping families close." Any mention of cutting back kin work was associated with guilt and a sense of failure. Looking more closely at holiday celebrations—ritualized arenas of kin contact and symbolic testing grounds of kin intimacy—will clarify the limits of women's choices.

## Holidays, Kin Work, and Gender

The celebration of holidays among kin and friends, like the operation of ethnicity, is simultaneously material and symbolic. The planning and presentation of holiday food and other rituals are women's responsibilities, part of the work of kinship. At the same time the manner in which holidays are celebrated reflects the points of consensus and of conflict among the group participating in the celebration, differing and agreed-upon notions of kin closeness, of the meanings of ethnicity, of class, and of gender. The arrangements made across households especially reflect existing and prospective reciprocity relations and power dynamics in larger kin and friend networks. Large presents imply the willingness to offer help during crises; hosting households are perceived as kin leaders or family centers.

Men and women discussed holidays with me readily, but men tended to dwell nostalgically on childhood memories and on the years when their own children were young, while all women wished as well to discuss the evolution of family holidays to the present. They were especially concerned with the process of negotiation of timing, place, and personnel as households changed through birth, marriage, death, and migration.

Men thus saw themselves as observers; women saw themselves as officiants. These gender divisions began in childhood. Al Bertini feelingly recalled: "I think that's probably one of the biggest losses

[215]

in losing a family—yeah, I remember as a child when my mom was alive . . . holidays were treated with enthusiasm and love. . . After she died [when Al was thirteen] the attempt was there but it just didn't materialize." Lucia Mornese, at age six, "found a branch from a Christmas tree somewhere. And I brought it home . . . and that was my tree!" Clelia Cipolla, at age ten, inspired by her school-mates' stories, persuaded her mother to begin celebrating Thanks-giving.

Joe Longhinotti remembered Christmases when his children were young: "Naturally it was a big enjoyment when you're giving gifts to your own children. . . It was a big thing—that's something that went by us but it was still beautiful." Joe, as well, when asked about special Christmas traditions, mentioned first that his aunt had made *bagnet*, a pudding of macaroons, eggs, and cinnamon, and *bugie* (lies), a kind of cookie; he then recalled that Cetta regu-larly made cookies whose recipes she had learned from Sicilian friends in their old North Bay town neighborhood. Like all these men, he thought of holiday traditions as women's activities.

While holidays were seen as women's responsibility, there were great variations in the ways in which that responsibility was per-ceived. In some families, such as Maria Fante's and Joe Cruciano's, mothers relinquished planning and execution to their sisters. In others, such as Nick Meraviglia's and Gino Angeluzzi's, mothers held a firm grip on holidays, even demanding the presence of grown children and their families at elaborate weekly Sunday din-ners. But in some cases women could not choose: like Celia Cipolla's mother-in-law, they were assigned all of the responsibility but none of the power.

None of the women who are now middle-aged are so powerless; the holiday issue for them is the negotiation of celebrations across households and generations. Clelia Cipolla, after her parents and father-in-law died, alternated hosting holidays with her sisters-in-law:

> I don't know whether it will continue this year or not. . . . We have all the typical Italian foods—cold cuts, *fogaccia*, *panetton*, cream puffs, artichokes, and mushrooms in oil, and there is always turkey and several different vegetables and different types of wine. . . At Easter I used to make *capretto* [goat], but the children don't like it so I've given that up.

[216]

Pina Meraviglia, with a new grandchild, explained the reorganization of Christmas gatherings:

> Christmas was quiet here—we had Nick's folks, and my son and daughter-in-law and the baby. . . Then we all opened our packages . . . and of course it was the baby's first Christmas so he made out like a bandit. . . And on Christmas Day Nick's folks and my son's girl friend who is Jewish came and had dinner with us. . . . My other son and his wife spent it with her folks. We have to share the baby! Oh yes! [laughs]. We did it one year—all together—and it was impossible! I used to make a fruitcake and give pieces to my sisters, but I haven't done that for two years now. . . We always have ravioli. . . . I kind of hate holidays now—we're all torn in different directions.

Cetta Longhinotti made the issue of power clear in her description of her difficulties with her daughter-in-law:

> Last year she insisted—this is touchy. She doesn't want to spend the holiday dinner together. So last year we went there. But still had my dinner the next day. . . I made a big dinner on Christmas Day, regardless of who's coming—candles on the table, the whole routine. I decorate the house myself too. . . Well, I just feel that the time will come when maybe I won't feel like cooking a big dinner—she should take advantage of the fact that I feel like doing it now.

Lucia Mornese charted the thirty-year evolution of her family's Christmas celebration; the end of her narrative highlights her cession of power to her daughter:

> When Linda was little, we were living upstairs from my parents and they weren't in business, and we had Christmas at home. Usually, my brother and sister and their spouses, and any family friend who was alone, they were invited. And then when we moved, my sister used to come and bring her in-laws for Christmas Eve. Then we'd go back to their house for Christmas Day. That's what we still do. The last two Christmases I had my son's in-laws here. Now my sister goes to her daughter's in-laws. I feel that as long as Mother's here I'll have Christmas here. I tell you the day she's gone I'm not going to do anything here. I'm just going OUT! Like I did this Easter. . . I don't mind cooking, but my Mother gets so jealous and upset. So my daughter says, "You are *not* to cook Christmas dinner!"

Lucia, as well, revealed her matter-of-fact attitude toward "Italian traditions" during holidays in her story about a recent Easter:

> Salvatore said that in Italy they always had salami and boiled eggs so this Easter I thought I'd get it for him. . . I forgot it was salami, and I bought prosciutto instead. [Mimics Salvatore's accent.] "No, it's salami." OK, next year I'll try to remember.

Lucia and Salvatore have been married more than thirty years.

It is clear from these narratives that holidays, besides serving as material and symbolic markers of family conflict and consensus, serve for women as foci of kinship power—or as a series of unwanted obligations. For most women, each holiday contains both elements—just as most women have chosen some antifeminist and some feminist perspectives on their roles in kin networks and in the public world. But for holiday gatherings to occur at all, some kinswoman must take responsibility, while the role of men and children is to evaluate women's holiday performances. Lucia Mornese may be cavalier about Salvatore's prosciutto, but she will never assume that it is Salvatore's job to buy special food for her.

Whatever traditions these families practice have fluctuated over time. And not only are there no "typical Italian foods" common among all their celebrations (for example, no family's menu matched Clelia Cipolla's), but there is also little regional loyalty: Cetta Longhinotti's parents came from the far north of Italy, but her Christmas cookies are Sicilian.

Aside from the proliferation of Italian-named foodstuffs, these family holiday patterns seem typically American Christian. How does ethnicity enter into this issue? In order to delineate clearly the connections between ethnicity and this realm of women's work, it is necessary to investigate further the gender component of ethnic identity.


## Ethnic Gender and Family Ideology

Informants consistently responded to my questions about the meaning of being Italian-American with assertions about warmth and closeness, food and family. Over time, I began to realize that both sexes were describing primarily *women's* activities as the positive defining ethnic behavior.[10] Without prompting, younger and older women informants split ethnic identity, evaluating men separately; only among younger men did I find this same tendency to analyze ethnic gender.

Tony Ripetto's narrative is typical of the male tendency to proclaim ethnic identity through women's activities:

> My mother was a gourmet cook and the only canned goods she had in the house was tuna and pineapple. She made her own soup. . . During the week it was pasta, risotto, chicken. . . I was eatin gourmet three meals a day! Until I married the Frenchie!

Gino Angeluzzi, as well, considered his mother's cooking as part of his self-definition as a child:

> When we were kids my mom made pizzas, and when we got home from school, she'd whip one up in an hour.

And even later, after his marriage:

> She had the ability to—if we went over—she'd always come up with something for supper. I don't know where she got all the stuff. I mean she'd cook up spaghetti and maybe she'd have some beans, and God! Terrific!—and the cheese, you'd say no, but then she'd put it on the table and you'd eat it.

Gino also remembered, however, the farming period of his childhood, when his mother had less time to cook because of the press of work:

> When I was a little kid, during the apricot season, my mother'd be out early in the morning in the cutting shed, and I'd wake up, get all my clothes, go out to the shed . . . and then she'd take time out and dress me up . . . give me some apricots for breakfast or some milk, she'd take time out to feed me, and then I'd go out—playing. Didn't hurt me any.

10. Other questions elicited negative images of male Italian-American behavior for some men, but they did not *define* the group by these characteristics.

Gino stresses here, defensively, that his mother's absorption in farm work "didn't hurt him any"—did not prevent her from caring for him properly. He never describes the work itself: it is not part of the constellation of activities culturally labeled nurturant and immanent that he draws on to express his ethnic identity. Women talked much less about their mothers' nurturant activities and more about their productive labor. Part of the reason for this, I suspect, is that as girls they had been involved themselves in home activities— "Mom's cooking" often included "daughter's dishwashing." Or, in some cases, they had been denied access to training: Angela Caputo remembered that her mother wouldn't allow her in the kitchen while she was cooking, because "it made her nervous to have me watching." A relative's superior cooking, housework, or child care were in any event not activities that women, unlike men, could simply evoke to express their ethnic identities: Such evocations always involved comparisons with their own activities. Angela Caputo was careful to explain that she "had other things to do in life besides cooking." Teresa Angeluzzi, on the other hand, identified as an in-marrying wife with Gino's ethnicity, and proudly told me of her achievement: "I learned all my cooking skills from Gino's mother. . . She made sure that her daughters knew that she was giving me her prized pots that she'd cooked in . . . that really meant something."

When I asked Italian-American women about the meaning of ethnicity, their evaluation of ethnic men was often ambivalent. Angela Caputo responded:

> Sometimes I think I should have married a nice Italian man—but there weren't too many of them around. I was sure I didn't want to when I was growing up—they were macho and paternalistic.

Dorothy DiVincenzo made a similar analysis; she also likened her husband to her father. Linda Mornese, still single, was not at all ambivalent about Italian-American men:

> The last person in the world I'd marry is an Italian man! Yuk!— Besides they're all short. I guess it's from exposure to my father [laughs]. No, I just always said I wouldn't marry one. I usually say that after I've been exposed to someone that's married one. They're

momma's boys—you have to baby them. God, I hope your husband isn't Italian! [laughs]. They want to go out and do their thing and you should stay at home and do what you're supposed to do. I think most of the women in my mother's group have lost their husbands and that's why they're active. . . . I don't like to cook and I don't like to clean . . . so I have to have someone who doesn't mind cooking, who doesn't mind doing their share. And Italian men will not switch a role at all. Nobody's father that I know of will do that.

When women described typical Italian women's activities, the implicit question was whether or not they themselves had achieved competence in these fields (or how they justified to themselves abandoning this "ethnic women's work"). For men, these activities were the background to their own identity: the question was whether or not the women in their lives served them as Italian-American women ought to do. This split reflects the very different experiences men and women have in living out their identities. Specifically, it reflects the fact that ethnic identity in the United States today is popularly assumed to imply an adherence to tradition, and tradition (as we have seen) encodes the ideal of the patriarchal family. In fact, ethnicity itself is seen to belong to men: they arrogate to themselves (and identify with) those ethnic characteristics maintained by women to whom they are connected. A woman, in this ideological frame, is properly ethnic when she provides the nurturing, symbolically laden environment for which ethnic men can take credit.

The images of Italian-Americans in the mass media take on a new coloration in the light of this analysis: the pizza-baking grandmother, the warm, happy table of diners represent not only the commoditization of ethnic identity, but an idealized world in which women automatically nurture men and children. Part of the charm of the ethnic image in the media is that it sanitizes patriarchy: male dominance is acceptable when it is ethnic. Garafola makes this point for recent American films featuring Italian-American characters:

Women . . . when they appear at all, play second fiddle to the men. . . . At a time when over half the married women in America work—many, in fact, on assembly lines—Hollywood purveys traditional images of women and family life. . . . Tendered under the guise of nostalgia . . . is a conservative ideology that seeks to turn back the clock to a family-centered past. . . . What the media understands [sic] by "Italianness" is a throwback to a simpler, more primitive state of being: physical strength and violence, loyalty to outworn codes of honor, emotional spontaneity untempered by "middle-class" reflection, an uncomplicated sexuality that combines "instinct" with a protective chivalry and "respect." (1979:9, 10, 12)

Garafola also points out that when women do appear outside the kitchen in these films, they are usually "the very antithesis of identifiable ethnicity" (1979:12). Unless the ethnic woman is used to evoke nostalgia for a patriarchal past, she has no mass media reality.

It seems, then, that one of the refuges of the ideology of male dominance from the challenge of feminism is the image of ethnic family and gender. A large part of stressing ethnic identity amounts to burdening women with increased responsibilities for preparing special foods, planning rituals, and enforcing "ethnic" socialization of children. My older women informants, and all of the younger informants, were sensitive to these ideological currents. They responded to them variously as they negotiated their own ethnic identities.

Clelia Cipolla's response was consistent with her choice of an antifeminist perspective on women's roles. She identified Italian-American women, in contrast to other American women, as faithful to their duties. "I've always thought of Thanksgiving as the only holiday that the American wife really cooks for. . . Maybe that's a wrong idea of it, but that's the way my feelings are." Cetta Longhinotti responded similarly, while Dorothy DiVincenzo and Lucia Mornese rejected the role constellation of duty to kin and wifely obedience. This rejection, like other Italian-American responses to hegemonic images of ethnic life and character, involved fighting with symbols. Some women split ethnic identity by gender, evaluating Italian-American men negatively. Others ignored male ethnicity and manipulated images of powerful, autonomous Italian-American womanhood to deny authenticity to the dominant concept of ethnic gender.

Lucia Mornese felt not as authentically "Italian" as some of her friends, but this was because she did not have a large kin network and because of her mother's lack of involvement in kin work during her childhood, not because she felt she had failed in duty to kin or wifely obedience. Lucia drew some of her resistance to dominant images of ethnic gender from her own mother's example. "I've always said that if my mother had gone to college she'd probably be president of the United States." Nancy Ferrucci said, "My grandmother was the first women's libber," thus claiming a traditional backdrop for her professional status. And Linda Mornese pointed to a successful Italian-American friend of her mother's: "I guess Lou was one of the reasons—she had a job, she was head of a department, she traveled, she did everything. I guess she's always asked me what I wanted to do—kinda got me thinking."

The meanings attached to symbols, however, are somewhat arbitrary. For Candy Lombardo, Italian-American women are "dominant and aggressive" beings who protect men from emotional crises: "I don't want to give my male children the feeling that they are emotionally fragile and have to be protected from the heaviness of life." At the same time Candy is very angry with her parents for not supporting her efforts to gain a higher education: "I was raised to be a wife, period. . . All the effort and pain of working my way through school . . . I got no strokes at all."

Candy Lombardo's manipulation of symbols of gender and ethnicity—her mixed feminist and antifeminist perspectives—reflected her own decisions about work and the work of kinship. She has recently married Sam, a highly paid technical worker, after years of alternately supporting herself and her children and relying on the sporadic contributions of a former, non-Italian, working-class husband. She explained to me that Sam had persuaded her to give up her outside work and "take care of him" by giving her increasing amounts of money with which to run the household. Sam and she have traveled in Italy together; much of her feeling about her ethnic identity has been created in concert with him: "We're putting our Italian-American parts together. We together are much more Italian than we were before."

Surprisingly, Candy's model of a dominant Italian-American woman is her mother, who is not Italian. This underlines the general tendency in this study of intermarrying women to identify strongly with their husbands' ethnicity, and of their children to identify both parents as Italian-American.[11] We have seen Teresa An-

11. There were not enough in-marrying men in the sample for me to analyze their responses to their wives' ethnicity.

geluzzi's anger over slurs against her husband's ethnicity. Looking at the contrast between Teresa's response to her husband and in-laws—what she identified as ethnic about the ways they construed gender—and that of Sally Cruciano, also an in-marrying spouse, illustrates further the variety of ways in which ethnic patriarchy can function, and the variability of meanings attached to symbols. Both women are college educated, married in their early twenties, began having children immediately, and had more than several. And each returned to market labor after her youngest child was in high school. For Sally, the primary factor in her marriage was Joe:

> He was a very strong person who said we will eat this, we will go here, you will marry me.

When they had financial problems, Joe said,

> "Don't you worry. It's not your place to worry about it. I'll take care of you." Luckily things have turned out well, but it could have been a disaster.

Despite the fact that her marriage alienated her from her own family, Sally did not become particularly close to her in-laws, although she was grateful for their support:

> They did everything they could to make me feel welcome [during the wedding]. And geez they worked, what a reception! Etiquette, what's etiquette? His cousin's husband walked me down the aisle.

She and Joe formed a tight, nuclear family unit:

> We were very close—it was us and the kids against the world. . . . Joe totally controlled our social life.

During the early years of their marriage, however, they lived near one of Joe's father's brothers. "Uncle Dom"

> was a tough little fart. I got along great with him. He was a very good guest. Never to my knowledge did we borrow money, but he would just sort of happen by with groceries and want to cook when he knew we were down and out. . . Dom would show up with the makings of

[224]

*cioppino* [shellfish stew]—The only thing is—he had no class. . . . I remember one time I was pregnant and feeling very ill . . . and he came over to make *cioppino* . . . and he said invite some of your friends, and he said, "Come on in Sally and check this goddam stuff." And I went in, and he had crab and shrimp and every kind of fish you could imagine including the *calamari* which I had never encountered in my whole life and the first thing I saw when I looked in the pot was this *eye* looking right back at me! [long laughter] He didn't clean them properly.

So for Sally, marriage to an Italian-American meant connection to warm but dominant men and a family that "had no class."

Teresa Angeluzzi's experiences, while also food-related, were fundamentally different. Her first encounter with her mother-in-law, the day she and Gino arrived from the East Coast, marked that relationship, rather than the one with her husband, as the one characterized by dominance:

They were all warm and friendly, *but* I'd never had food pushed at me before. . . . Here my mother-in-law had obviously cooked for days . . . [but] the last thing I was interested in was food and I wanted to throw up . . . I didn't realize how important it was that Gino brought his wife home . . . and I was feeling moody and de-pressed and feeling sick and just preferred not to join the table—which I learned awfully fast you just *don't do*. . . . Ooooh—frankly I think my mother-in-law was openly disappointed in Gino's choice [laughs]. . . I'm sure she was. . . She was real sweet to me but she would introduce me to her relatives and friends. . . . "This is Gino's wife—she's German but she's nice" [laughs].

Teresa clearly identified this clash as ethnically based:

Most of it was cultural differences—Grandma just could not conceive that anybody could live any kind of normal life and not think in the Italian perspective. . . . Like I made a nice dinner for them—typical Midwestern fare—round steak, mashed potatoes, gravy, corn, and ice cream—and Grandma just [makes face]. So the next time she came she brought POTS full of stuff (shouts with laughter)—which I very quickly learned to welcome. . . Hey, now *we* do it, right? We seldom visit without a trunkful of something. See, I learned to think Italian. It took about two years. . . . I guess one of the first things I

[225]

learned is that you can let your emotions go on a daily basis—more than I'd ever seen. . . . She was a matriarch—no question about it, she was the dominant member of that partnership.

Both Sally Cruciano and Teresa Angeluzzi identified her entrance into Italian-American life with being dominated, but for Sally it was the dominance of the husband in a nuclear family, while for Teresa it was the dominance of a mother-in-law deeply invested in the work of kinship. In fact, neither pattern was "authentically" Italian-American, but in dealing with one another, the husband/wife and mother-in-law/daughter-in-law actors coded their differences with that label.

We can explore the relative arbitrariness of this labeling further by looking at another sphere of ethnic gender: female appearance.

Teresa Angeluzzi related her mother-in-law's deep feelings about the proper dress for girls and women:

> The first day we were there she said didn't we want to get cleaned up and go visit so-and-so. Fine, so we bathed and I put on some mascara and lipstick—that was the sum total of my cosmetics—so I yanked out one of my dresses . . . and Gino's mother looked at me and she said, "Can't you fix yourself up a little better?" I said, "I *am* all fixed up" [laughs]. . . So then, a couple of nights later, they decided maybe they could do something with my hair. They made a project of me. . . . It just didn't look like me at all! I was about as comfortable with that hairdo as you would be with a beehive. . . . So poor Grandma had to settle for ol plain Teresa.

Teresa's sisters-in-law, one still unmarried, dressed very differently:

> I was really quite impressed because they plucked their eyebrows, and wore *lots* of mascara, lotsa makeup, and lotsa rings. I'm not making fun of em, I'm simply telling you—uh—I like to wear flowers in my hair too—still have a box of artificial ones—that's fine, but Grandma picked a whole *hydrangea*, stuck it on their head and they *wore* it. So I'd take a piece of it and pin it in, but that wasn't good enough. She wanted to FIX ME UP! [laughs] . . . the first time I wore eyeliner, she told me she thought I was a really pretty girl but she said, "You know I always thought you shoulda worn more makeup."

For Teresa's mother-in-law, proper feminine dress and proper home furnishings were connected:

> Grandma would come and put stuff all over my house I didn't want. . . Oh, she didn't like my curtains so she'd come and take them down and bring her own (shrieks of laughter). Well, Grandma liked pink satin pleated dresses on the kids and I was putting corduroy rompers on them. . .

But for Maria Fante, for example, also in her early twenties during the same years, her father's conception of proper feminine attire strictly forbade the Angeluzzis' "fixing up":

> Like I could *never* wear nail polish—when I was a little girl I came to the dinner table with nail polish, and he said, "Maria, what do you have on your fingernails?" "Nail polish." "Would you kindly take it off?" Lipstick, oh that was strictly out of it!

For Sally Cruciano, it was Joe who controlled her appearance and behavior. Just recently, however, she'd dressed up and gone to a disco with some women friends, and

> Joe hit the roof. But I won't put up with that anymore. If you can't trust me at this point in our life, forget it.

These three cases all involve the issue of patriarchal control, but the personnel and the meanings attached to the symbols of control vary. Teresa Angeluzzi's mother-in-law demanded that she "fix herself up," that is, dress herself and her children, and decorate her home, in a conventionally feminine manner. Maria Fante's mother, having opted for freedom rather than control over her children, left Maria's father to discipline her into gentility. And Sally's husband Joe had until recently dictated her dress and deportment.

Patriarchy is an evolving and variable set of social relations. Women can often work within it, and gain power in domestic networks—but the scope of women's domestic power has lessened over the generations. Men have the option of asserting control over women, but prevalent feminist ideology poses a cultural challenge to that option.

The symbols associated with patriarchy vary in their meaning as well. In this case, very feminine or "sexy" appearance was demanded of some women and forbidden to others. Neither of these values is particularly Italian, but they were both coded in that way by the differing participants. And it was this ethnic coding that participants used in their power struggles with one another. Once again we see that there are no set ethnic behavior patterns, but instead varying mental constructions of ethnic behavior. These constructions are accepted, rejected, and renegotiated as ethnics and nonethnics interact with one another across varying boundaries in the course of living their lives.

This chapter has developed arguments about both ethnic and nonethnic American women's lives. These Italian-American women, like other American women, worked outside the home in the past and do so in the present; they shoulder the responsibility for household work, children, and the care of the elderly; and they do the work of kinship—expanding or cutting back their efforts according to available time, strategic intentions, and changing ideology.

It is in this realm of ideology that these women differ from others who have no ethnic identification. They must negotiate their ethnic identities, and in so doing, must face the identification of ethnicity with an idealized patriarchal past in which women stayed at home and served men and children. They must deal with this image in the mass media and other institutions, and with it especially as the men in their lives articulate it—because ethnic men lay claim to their own identities through the remembered and present women's work of their own wives and female kin.

Some women accept and attempt to work within this ideology, expanding their work of kinship efforts in a strategic attempt to gain and maintain power over children and other kin, and to hold men to their financial and marital responsibilities. Other women self-consciously reject part or all of this construction, and fight with symbols—of class, of generation, of their own female ethnic kin and friends—to define themselves outside of the submissive-woman gestalt. But even when women self-consciously withdraw from kin work, they cannot, in the aggregate, benefit from male jobs and male kin privileges. And they continue to feel guilt for abandoning their responsibilities for keeping families close.

Almost all women, reflecting the reigning confusion in American gender ideology, choose a combination of both perspectives. They take advantage of the malleability of symbols to construct sets of meanings—symbolic idiolects—to interpret their lives. Their difference from other American women here is only in the availability of and necessity of interpreting symbols of ethnic gender. Nonethnic American women deal with other available symbols of gender, from the pioneer woman to Betty Crocker. Ethnic women must consider these as well, but in an amalgam with those attributed to their group.

The vision of ethnic community, then, ignores class, regional, demographic—but especially gender—differences within ethnic populations. We can understand much of its powerful lure in its identification of ethnicity with an anachronistic patriarchal order. Mass media presentation of Italian-Americans, in particular, is based on women's cooking for and serving their families and on women's work of knitting households together into the "close, extended families" so beloved by popular writers on ethnicity.

The Italian-American women in this study have embraced, modified, and rejected this dominant image of ethnic life. These women, like all American women, live in a society that is simultaneously class-stratified and patriarchal. They deal variously with class and gender divisions. Ethnicity is a further filter on this process; but for women in particular, just for the population as a whole, there are varieties of ethnic experience.

# [7]

# Kinship, Culture, and Economy
# in the American Context

> "There is no such thing as economic growth which is not, at the same time, growth or change of a culture," E. P. Thompson has written. Yet he also warns that "we should not assume any automatic, or overdirect, correspondence between the dynamic of economic growth and the dynamic of social or cultural life."—Herbert Gutman 1977

This book has been, in part, a dialogue in absentia with a dominant interdisciplinary model of past and present white ethnic life in the United States. This model assumes that culture/ethnicity is an object that humans can possess or lose, that determines their behavior, and that is transmitted through families. The structure and functioning of families, in turn, are determined by their cultural labels, and these family cultures cause the upwardly or downwardly mobile economic experiences of their members. Sufficient upward mobility, or simply moving from the central city, causes individuals to lose their culture—as does also the passage of generations. And different cultures determine different traditional roles for women, some allowing work outside the household, but all presuming female responsibility for home and children.

This model's narrow focus of explanation, its rigid behavioral conception of culture, and the linkages it draws among culture, family, mobility, and gender have been used to interpret not just American white ethnicity but, as we have seen, the lives of impoverished racial groups both here and abroad. Its distorting lens, in fact, is part of our collective misleading sense of expertise. It prevents us from perceiving the overarching effects of the global economy on our past and present lives, the variety and malleability of kin forms, the linked continuities of class division and male dominance, and the creativity and adaptability of the human construction and reconstruction of social reality.

The break from this model has been accomplished by attending to the theme of context: the historical, economic, political, and social contexts in which my informants and their antecedents led their lives, and the particular context in which we knew one another and in which I learned from them.

California itself provided the first, most fundamental context. The region, isolated from the rapidly industrializing Midwest and Eastern Seaboard, developed economically through agriculture, extractive industries, and trade, only slowly establishing an industrial base. Italians began arriving in numbers earlier than they did farther east, and found themselves, unlike East Coast immigrants, part of a white proletariat that rapidly distinguished itself from Asians and Mexicans. Farming, fishing, artisanal work, and small business were all available economic options. Life histories show that economic context, rather than some inherited ethnic family culture, influenced the structures and functioning of these Italian-American households. The intersections of economic strategies and political-economic developments, not good or bad families, were the major determinants of individual and household mobility experiences. A comparison of Boston and San Francisco/Oakland Census data on white ethnic economic status reinforces this suggestion: the economic experiences both of white ethnics as a whole and of individual groups vary greatly, and seem to be connected to the varying economic histories of the two regions.

The present-day economic context provides important clues to the interpretation of the relations among family, economy, and ethnicity—and to these *paesans'* cognitive constructions of those relations. Occupations vary both in the scope they provide for the assertion of ethnic identity and in their openness to the involvement of family members. Italian-Americans in different sorts of jobs expressed different conceptions of collective ethnic identity, the invocation of the "ethnic community" ideal being particular to the members of the shopkeeper class for whom it had economic meaning.

Individuals interpreted the concept of ethnic family contextually,

[231]

using it to rationalize their economic status, to interpret cross-generational differences, and to legitimate their racist conceptions of other groups. Their constructions and reconstructions of individual ethnic identities were equally deeply contextual, referring back to jobs, social networks, appearance, gender, and perceived ethnic boundaries. They framed and reframed their experiences of ethnic slurs and discrimination, and worked on their emotional responses to them, according to their judgments of context and their allegiance to the ideologies of assimilationism or the white ethnic renaissance. Thus self-conceptions are not determined by "Italian culture," but profoundly interpenetrate with the evolving political economy. Individuals' lively and varying reactions to mass media images of Italian-Americans illustrate both their involvement with changing majority ideologies and their creative abilities to marshall their cognitive resources to dispute them. Cognitive resources, the true elements of culture, are used both to interpret and to act upon the material and social world.

Finally, women's past and present lives, and their interpretations of those lives, are situated in the contexts of the evolving American and California economies, and the connected changing political economy of gender. "Italian culture" did not determine that these women stay at home under the chaperonage of men—although the interaction of cognitive resources and local economic opportunities may have had such a short-term effect in some areas. These women worked in fields and kitchens, stores and canneries, in rhythm with the evolving California economy. During the Depression, they continued outside work, and intensified their production of consumer goods in the home, as did other American women. Their daughters and granddaughters entered the clerical and sales work force in step with other young, single American women; in the 1950s they embraced the housewife ideal while continuing intermittently in the work force. Increasingly, in the 1960s and 1970s, they became committed full-time workers along with the female population as a whole.

Women's roles in households varied by their own and their households' connections to the economy, and over time. But these women were also molded by, and rebelled against, changing patriarchal ideology. Some first- and second-generation women obeyed their husbands and fathers; others defied them; still others shared or usurped decision-making powers. Their daughters and granddaughters today negotiate their ethnic and gender identities in a material context characterized by both increasing economic opportunities and increasing economic threat, and in an ideological realm polarized by feminism and antifeminist reaction. They choose either to lessen or to intensify their involvement in the work of kinship, and connect these choices to these polar ideologies. There is some connection between class and the adoption of feminist or antifeminist perspectives: wealthier women can "afford" not to rely on kin for support and care in their old age.

Patriarchal concepts of gender implicit in popular ethnic images further complicate women's choices. Some embrace them; others alter them, fighting with symbols to construct their own models of ethnic identity; still others reject the patriarchal image of Italian-American males. Men, in turn, claim their own ethnic identities through the domestic labor of their mothers and aunts, wives and sisters, adding the burden (or the glory) of responsibility for the production of ethnic identity to women's already heavily freighted choices concerning the work of kinship.

These nostalgic, compelling images—the pizza-baking mother, the warm, happy family sitting long at the traditional feast, the shopkeeper flourishing his sausages—help to provide an explanation for the contemporary strength of the ethnic family model. I began my fieldwork believing in them, despite abundant empirical evidence to the contrary; many of my informants did so as well. It was the context of the fieldwork—my sex and age, my rapport with women, their insistence on political discussion and their differing perspectives—that broke the symbolic spell and threw into relief the importance of the image of the organic community, the entity that, as Williams points out, is always gone.

The organic ethnic community, the patriarchal ethnic family, and the traditional ethnic woman are key elements in the contemporary political language of rhetorical nostalgia. They are used, as the image of the pastoral society has been used in the West back to the Greeks, in an intentional political argument against the present.

We are all participants in this argument, and fight with these symbols, and others to which they are related—the American small town and the idealized nuclear family. The fight comes both from the left and the right, and often mixes elements of each. The idealized community may need to control its schools, police, and industry and demand state investment—or it may need individual freedom to abandon public schools, to keep Blacks out, and to encourage industry through easing pollution-control laws and corporate taxes. The close family and traditional woman may be the backbone of resistance to capitalist encroachment, supporting strikes, fighting neighborhood destruction, and campaigning for the preservation of human values—or family and woman may be the first essential building block of fortress America, upholding gender divisions, the male warrior ethic, private property, and white and national supremacy.

The use of rhetorical nostalgia is precisely the denial of context, of the material, historical locations of particular social forms. Our concepts of "community" and "close extended families" depend on geographic immobility; but community and family members are fundamentally workers who must follow capital's changing demand for labor. And the traditional woman cannot stay at home when her husband's real income declines precipitously, or when she becomes solely responsible for the support of herself and her children. She may not want to stay at home when she discovers the human dignity and power that an autonomous income confers in a society governed by the cash nexus.

The denial of context is related to the celebration or deprecation of particular groups, patterns, processes. When we judge migrant groups as either shiftless or good workers, we deny the actual changes in the global economy that lead to their choice to migrate, and the complex ideological arena in which they and we negotiate and renegotiate identities. When we ascribe particular "cultures" to ethnic and racial groups, we deny the generations of economic and ideological interaction with the majority society that have led to strategic emphases. And we deny the variation within groups in the choice of those strategies. When we make women the scapegoats for changing family forms or declare them the guarantors of the haven in a heartless world, we deny the fundamentally economic and historically altering nature of household labor, capital's postwar demand for female labor, and the realities of male domination.

The denial of context through rhetorical nostalgia is only one of many intentional human uses of symbol manipulation, of cultural/ideological discourse. Ideologies, "maps of problematic social reality" (Geertz 1973), have often been seen as distinct from cultures. "Timeless communities" had culture, while ideology was the possession of modern, changing societies. This unfortunate heritage of the territorial distinction between anthropological and sociological studies has long been abandoned. Recent work in both fields, and in social, women's, and labor history, offers new interpretations of changing collective representations and their economic and historical connections.[1] Historian George Rudé's (1980) distinction between inherent and derived ideologies, those based on direct experience and those acquired through institutions, helps us to see how the Italian-Americans of this study drew from family and social networks and from institutional sources—jobs, church, the media—in negotiating and renegotiating their ethnic, class, family, and gender identities.

An element of the derived ideologies with which these *paesans* wrestled was the commoditization of ethnic identity, the retailing of images of Italian food and family charm, warmth and tradition. Tourist areas such as North Beach and Fisherman's Wharf, and gentrifying "ethnic neighborhoods," are subjects as well of this process of objectification. But the commoditization process—or cognitive tourism—affects overarching American class, family, and gender identities as well. We are presented with images of proper working-class bonhomie, of families gathering to consume or celebrating their togetherness by "reaching out," of mothers legitimating themselves through proper purchases. These media images, like those dealing with ethnicity, focus on regions of anxiety in American life, on class and community, family and gender.

The Italian-Americans in this study, and all Americans, share with women in de Beauvoir's analysis the contradictory experience of subjectivity and objectification. Like these *paesans,* we both

---

1. D'Andrade's (1981) and Ortner and Whitehead's (1981) work in cognitive and in symbolic antropology, respectively, exemplify this trend, as do the historical and ethnographic explorations of nature, culture, and gender in Strathern and MacCormack (1980). Hochschild's (1979) work on the sociology of emotion and Burawoy's (1979) study of labor process explicitly link cognition and material life. Research in American social and labor history, inspired by the English school of Thompson (1963) and others, includes Gutman 1977; Dublin 1979a; and Montgomery 1979. Green 1982 summarizes and interprets this trend. The crucial reinterpretations of American women's historical experiences include Cott 1977; Smith-Rosenberg 1979; Lerner 1979; and Kessler-Harris 1982.

accept—consume—media images of ourselves, and articulate conscious rebellion against them. We are tourists in our own minds, and fighters against that colonization.

This book has attempted to provide economic, historical, social, and political contexts with which to interpret the lives of a collection of Italian-American families who share ethnicity and California residence, but differ from one another in a variety of other ways. Perceiving the varieties of ethnic experience through these contexts has allowed the construction of new perspectives on, and new links among, the histories and contemporary realities of class, kinship, culture, and gender in America.

# Appendix: A Comparative Test: Boston and San Francisco–Oakland Data

Tables 1–6 include Thernstrom's (1973) presentations of occupational, income, and other data on white ethnic men in Boston in 1950, and my duplications of those measures for the same groups in San Francisco/Oakland. I have altered the tables in two ways: (1) the "Poland" and "French Canadian" columns were removed because the California populations were too small to warrant inclusion in the Census; and (2) I have added the numbers of men in each category.

The white-collar/blue-collar proportions were derived by adding the percentage of men involved in each occupation with the cutoff after the clerical/sales category. "High income" indicates $4,000 or more annually. "High white-collar occupation" indicates the percentages of men in the first two occupational categories. "Fathers" are first-generation men of the same group. Indices of representation indicate how closely groups mimic the proportion of all white men involved in particular occupations. They are computed by "dividing the percentage of group-members employed in the category by the percentage of the entire Boston male labor force in such jobs and shifting the decimal point two places to the right to give a value of 100 when the two distributions are identical" (Thernstrom 1973:139).

Tables 7 and 8 continue these same measures for 1970 Census data on both metropolitan areas, with the high-income cutoff raised to $15,000 to account for inflation. Table 9 reports the percentages of self-employed and second-generation men. Table 10 indicates labor-force participation percentages and marital status in 1950 for second-generation women in both areas.

*Appendix*

*Table 1.* Occupational distribution of first-generation immigrants by nationality: men 45 or over, 1950, Boston SMSA

| | | Country of birth | | | | | |
|---|---|---|---|---|---|---|---|
| Occupation | N = | England and Wales 4,870 | Ireland 11,225 | USSR 12,795 | Italy 20,595 | Sweden 2,900 | Germany 1,535 |
| | | Percent | | | | | |
| White-collar | | 52 | 18 | 54 | 18 | 16 | 40 |
| Blue-collar | | 48 | 82 | 46 | 82 | 84 | 60 |
| | | Index of representation | | | | | |
| Professional and technical workers | | 108 | 11 | 70 | 22 | 45 | 133 |
| Managers, proprietors, and officials | | 162 | 53 | 241 | 82 | 54 | 122 |
| Clerks and salesmen | | 99 | 52 | 79 | 27 | 22 | 51 |
| Craftsmen and Foremen | | 119 | 97 | 97 | 114 | 283 | 152 |
| Operatives and service workers | | 68 | 141 | 78 | 132 | 65 | 82 |
| Unskilled laborers | | 43 | 298 | 38 | 273 | 55 | 47 |

SOURCE: Thernstrom 1973:139. Tables 1–3 are taken from Stephan Thernstrom, *The Other Bostonians: Poverty and Progress in an American Metropolis, 1880–1970* (Harvard University Press, 1973), used with the permission of Harvard University Press.

*Table 2.* Occupational distribution of second-generation immigrants by nationality: men 25–44, 1950, Boston SMSA

| | | Father's country of birth | | | | | |
|---|---|---|---|---|---|---|---|
| Occupation | N = | England and Wales 5,840 | Ireland 12,555 | USSR 16,965 | Italy 33,580 | Sweden 3,595 | Germany 2,145 |
| | | Percent | | | | | |
| White-collar | | 49 | 42 | 75 | 31 | 45 | 47 |
| Blue-collar | | 51 | 58 | 25 | 69 | 55 | 53 |
| | | Index of representation | | | | | |
| Professional and technical workers | | 130 | 93 | 163 | 62 | 134 | 159 |
| Managers, proprietors, and officials | | 112 | 63 | 217 | 78 | 94 | 104 |
| Clerks and salesmen | | 105 | 125 | 153 | 75 | 95 | 83 |
| Craftsmen and foremen | | 104 | 85 | 42 | 111 | 158 | 123 |
| Operatives and service workers | | 85 | 111 | 52 | 125 | 66 | 86 |
| Unskilled laborers | | 61 | 111 | 23 | 131 | 28 | 30 |

SOURCE: Thernstrom 1973:141.

*Table* 3. Education, occupation, and income of second-generation immigrants (ages 25–44) by father's education and occupation, 1950, Boston SMSA

| Ethnic background and dominant religious affiliation | % of second-generation men with: | | | Family background (estimated) | |
| | One year or more of college | High white-collar occupation | High income | Median school years of father | % of fathers with white-collar background |
| --- | --- | --- | --- | --- | --- |
| Catholic | | | | | |
| Irish | 21 | 19 | 13 | 8.3 | 18 |
| Italian | 11 | 17 | 9 | 5.2 | 18 |
| Protestant | | | | | |
| English | 27 | 29 | 19 | 10.3 | 52 |
| Swedish | 28 | 27 | 23 | 8.7 | 16 |
| German | 31 | 31 | 23 | 10.3 | 40 |
| Jewish | | | | | |
| Russian | 44 | 46 | 27 | 8.1 | 54 |

SOURCE: Thernstrom 1973:172.

*Table* 4. Occupational distribution of first–generation immigrants by nationality: men 45 or over, 1950, San Francisco–Oakland SMSA

| Occupation N = | England and Wales 4,115 | Ireland 3,045 | USSR 2,950 | Italy 12,940 | Sweden 2,670 | Germany 5,030 |
| --- | --- | --- | --- | --- | --- | --- |
| | Percent | | | | | |
| White-collar | 49 | 30 | 49 | 27 | 29 | 42 |
| Blue-collar | 51 | 67 | 51 | 73 | 70 | 58 |
| | Indexes of representation | | | | | |
| Professional and technical workers | 109 | 55 | 91 | 18 | 55 | 73 |
| Farmers | 200 | — | 100 | 400 | 100 | 100 |
| Managers, proprietors, and officials | 128 | 93 | 164 | 93 | 114 | 143 |
| Clerical and sales | 94 | 61 | 83 | 33 | 33 | 72 |
| Craftsmen and foremen | 114 | 86 | 91 | 77 | 164 | 118 |
| Operatives and service | 92 | 164 | 109 | 150 | 77 | 109 |
| Farm laborers | — | — | — | 200 | — | — |
| Laborers | 50 | 213 | 75 | 250 | 175 | 88 |
| % earning $4,000+ | 16 | 13 | 19 | 14 | 18 | 15 |
| % earning $4,000+ Boston | 20 | 5 | 21 | 8 | 14 | 18 |

SOURCE: Constructed from the 1950 Census, Special Reports: Characteristics of the foreign white stock 14 years old and over, by nativity, parentage, and selected country of origin.

*Table 5.* Occupational distribution of second-generation immigrants by nationality: men 25–44, 1950, San Francisco–Oakland SMSA

| Occupation | UK | Ireland | USSR | Italy | Sweden | Germany |
|---|---|---|---|---|---|---|
| N = | 5,140 | 6,275 | 4,200 | 17,630 | 3,895 | 6,930 |
| | | | | Percent | | |
| White-collar | 57 | 53 | 66 | 40 | 52 | 47 |
| Blue-collar | 42 | 48 | 33 | 60 | 46 | 54 |
| | | | Indexes of representation | | | |
| Professional and technical workers | 164 | 109 | 200 | 55 | 155 | 118 |
| Farmers | — | — | — | 200 | — | — |
| Managers, proprietors and officials | 121 | 114 | 157 | 114 | 121 | 121 |
| Clerical and sales | 122 | 139 | 122 | 89 | 100 | 94 |
| Craftsmen and foremen | 100 | 127 | 68 | 95 | 114 | 123 |
| Operatives and service | 73 | 99 | 62 | 109 | 62 | 85 |
| Farm laborers | — | — | — | 100 | — | — |
| Laborers | 38 | 63 | 38 | 125 | 63 | 50 |
| % earning $4,000+ | 32 | 28 | 31 | 25 | 33 | 30 |
| % earning $4,000+ Boston | 19 | 13 | 27 | 9 | 23 | 23 |

SOURCE: Constructed from the 1950 Census, Special Reports: Characteristics of the foreign white stock 14 years old and over, by nativity, parentage, and selected country of origin.

*Table 6.* Education, occupation, and income of second-generation immigrants (ages 25–44) by father's education and occupation, 1950, San Francisco–Oakland SMSA

| Ethnic background and dominant religious affiliation | % of second-generation men with: | | | Family background (estimate) | |
|---|---|---|---|---|---|
| | One year or more of college | High white-collar occupation | High income | Median school years of father | % of fathers with white-collar background |
| Catholic | | | | | |
| Irish | 31 | 28 | 28 | 8.6 | 30 |
| Italian | 14 | 22 | 25 | 5.7 | 27 |
| Protestant | | | | | |
| English | 34 | 35 | 32 | 9.9 | 49 |
| Swedish | 32 | 34 | 33 | 10.0 | 29 |
| German | 27 | 30 | 30 | 9.3 | 42 |
| Jewish | | | | | |
| Russian | 41 | 44 | 31 | 10.3 | 49 |

SOURCE: Constructed from the 1950 Census, Special Reports: Characteristics of the foreign white stock 14 years old and over, by nativity, parentage, and selected country of origin.

*Tables 7 and 8.* Occupational distribution of second-generation immigrants by nationality: men 16 and over, 1970, San Francisco–Oakland and Boston SMSAs

*Table 7.* San Francisco–Oakland

|  | UK | Ireland | USSR | Italy | Sweden | Germany |
|---|---|---|---|---|---|---|
| N = | 17,314 | 11,382 | 8,728 | 24,257 | 6,748 | 10,550 |
| % white-collar | 61 | 58 | 75 | 45 | 56 | 57 |
| Indexes of representation | | | | | | |
| Professional, technical | 122 | 111 | 194 | 61 | 105 | 105 |
| Farmers | — | — | — | — | — | — |
| Managers, proprietors | 158 | 133 | 150 | 133 | 142 | 142 |
| Clerical, sales | 105 | 116 | 116 | 95 | 105 | 111 |
| Craftsmen, foremen | 90 | 75 | 65 | 105 | 115 | 105 |
| Operatives, service | 72 | 100 | 44 | 104 | 64 | 72 |
| Farm laborers | — | — | — | — | — | — |
| Laborers | 50 | 33 | 33 | 116 | 67 | 50 |
| % earning 15,000+ | 39 | 36 | 51 | 39 | 38 | 37 |

*Table 8.* Boston

|  | UK | Ireland | USSR | Italy | Sweden | Germany |
|---|---|---|---|---|---|---|
| N = | 15,888 | 34,373 | 24,527 | 53,497 | 4,621 | 3,692 |
| % white-collar | 54 | 51 | 80 | 41 | 52 | 62 |
| Indexes of representation | | | | | | |
| Professional, technical | 95 | 77 | 127 | 59 | 95 | 123 |
| Farmers | — | — | — | — | — | — |
| Managers, proprietors | 125 | 108 | 225 | 108 | 141 | 116 |
| Clerical, sales | 95 | 111 | 132 | 79 | 74 | 111 |
| Craftsmen, foremen | 112 | 106 | 53 | 147 | 153 | 88 |
| Operatives, service | 92 | 108 | 42 | 116 | 79 | 75 |
| Farm laborers | — | — | — | — | — | — |
| Laborers | 90 | 130 | 30 | 110 | 60 | 80 |
| % earning 15,000+ | 34 | 33 | 51 | 29 | 34 | 35 |

SOURCE: Constructed from the 1970 Census: Economic characteristics of the population by nativity, parentage, and country of origin for selected SMSAs.

*Table 9*. Percentages of self-employed second-generation men 16 and older by ancestry, Boston and San Francisco–Oakland SMSAs, 1970

| Country | Boston | San Francisco–Oakland |
|---|---|---|
| United Kingdom | 6 | 9 |
| Ireland | 5 | 10 |
| USSR | 19 | 19 |
| Italy | 9 | 15 |
| Sweden | 9 | 10 |
| Germany | 7 | 11 |

SOURCE: Constructed from 1970 Census: Economic characteristics of the population by nativity, parentage, and country of origin for selected SMSAs.

*Table 10*. Labor force participation and marital status of second-generation women, 25–44, Boston and San Francisco–Oakland SMSAs, by ancestry, 1950

| | Boston | | San Francisco–Oakland | |
|---|---|---|---|---|
| | % in labor force | % married | % in labor force | % married |
| UK | 33 | 76 | 36 | 83 |
| Ireland | 40 | 68 | 40 | 75 |
| USSR | 25 | 81 | 41 | 83 |
| Italy | 35 | 77 | 37 | 84 |
| Sweden | 34 | 78 | 40 | 82 |
| Germany | 30 | 77 | 42 | 80 |

SOURCE: Constructed from the 1950 Census, Special Reports: Characteristics of the foreign white stock 14 years old and over, by nativity, parentage, and selected country of origin.

# References

Abramson, Harold J. 1975. The Social Varieties of Catholic Behavior: The Italian Experience Viewed Comparatively. In *The Religious Experience of Italian-Americans,* ed. M. Tomasi, pp. 55–72. New York: American Italian Historical Society.

Ackerman, Frank, and Andrew Zimbalist. 1978. Capitalism and Inequality in the United States. In *The Capitalist System,* ed. Richard C. Edwards, Michael Reich, and Thomas E. Weisskopf, pp. 297–307. Englewood Cliffs, N.J.: Prentice-Hall.

Aguilar, John L. 1979. Class and Ethnicity as Ideology: Stratification in a Mexican Town. *Ethnic Groups* 2:109–31.

Alcorn, Richard S., and Peter R. Knights. 1975. Most Uncommon Bostonians: A Critique of Stephen Thernstrom's *The Other Bostonians: Poverty and Progress in an American Metropolis, 1880–1970. Historical Methods Newsletter* 8(3):98–114.

Argersinger, Jo Ann Eady. 1982. Review Essay: "Second-Generation" Ethnic Studies. *American Quarterly* 34(4):440–50.

Banfield, Edward. 1958. *Moral Basis of a Backward Society.* New York: Free Press.

Barrett, Michèle, and Mary McIntosh. 1980. The "Family Wage": Some Problems for Socialists and Feminists. *Capital & Class* 11:51–72.

Barth, Frederik, ed. 1969. *Ethnic Groups and Boundaries.* Boston: Little, Brown.

Barton, Josef. 1975. *Peasants and Strangers: Italians, Rumanians and Slovaks in an Industrial City, 1890–1950.* Cambridge: Harvard University Press.

Bean, Walton. 1968. *California: An Interpretative History.* New York: McGraw-Hill.

Bell, Daniel. 1953. Crime as an American Way of Life. *Antioch Review* 13:115–36.

Bennett, John, ed. 1973. *The New Ethnicity: Perspectives from Ethnology. Proceedings of the American Ethnological Society.* St. Paul, Minn.: West Publishing.

[243]

## References

Bernstein, Irving. 1966. *The Lean Years: A History of the American Worker 1920–1933*. Baltimore, Md.: Penguin.

Berreman, Gerald D. 1962. *Behind Many Masks: Impression Management in a Himalayan Village*. Ithaca: Society for Applied Anthropology, Monograph #4.

———. 1981. *Social Inequality: Comparative and Developmental Approaches*. New York: Academic Press.

Blau, Peter, and Otis Dudly Duncan. 1967. *The American Occupational Structure*. New York: Wiley.

Blaxall, Martha, and Barbara Reagan, eds. 1976. *Women and the Workplace: The Implications of Occupational Segregation*. Chicago: University of Chicago Press.

Bott, Elizabeth. 1971. *Family and Social Network: Roles, Norms and External Relationships in Ordinary Urban Families*. 2d ed. New York: Free Press.

Braverman, Harry. 1974. *Labor and Monopoly Capital*. New York: Monthly Review Press.

Bridenthal, Renate. 1979. Family and Reproduction. In Rayna Rapp, Ellen Ross, and Renate Bridenthal, *Feminist Studies* 5:174–200.

Briggs, John. 1978. *An Italian Passage: Immigrants to Three American Cities, 1880–1930*. New Haven: Yale University Press.

Bryce-Laporte, Roy S. 1980. The New Immigration: A Challenge to Our Sociological Imagination. In *Sourcebook for the New Immigration: Implications for the United States and the International Community*, ed. Roy S. Bryce-Laporte. New Brunswick, N.J.: Transaction.

Buhle, Paul. 1977. Italian-American Radicals and Labor in Rhode Island, 1905–1930. *Radical History Review* 17:121–51.

Burawoy, Michael. 1979. *Manufacturing Consent: Changes in the Labor Process under Monopoly Capitalism*. Chicago: University of Chicago Press.

Caen, Herb. 1949. *Baghdad-by-the-Bay*. Garden City, N.Y.: Doubleday.

Cafagna, Luciano. 1973. Italy 1830–1914. *In the Fontana Economic History of Europe*, ed. Carlo Cipolla, Vol. 1. London: Fontana.

Camarillo, Albert. 1979. *Chicanos in a Changing Society*. Cambridge: Harvard University Press.

Carcione, Joe. 1975. *The Greengrocer Cookbook*. Millbrae, Calif.: Celestial Arts.

Caulfield, Mina Davis. 1974. Imperialism, the Family and the Cultures of Resistance. *Socialist Revolution* 20:67–85.

Chock, Phyllis Pease. 1974. Time, Nature and Spirit: A Symbolic Analysis of Greek-American Spiritual Kinship. *American Ethnologist* 1(1):33–48.

Cinel, Dino. 1979. Conservative Adventurers: Italian Migrants in Italy and San Francisco. Ph.D. dissertation, Stanford University.

Clawson, Mary Ann. 1980. Early Modern Fraternalism and the Patriarchal Family. *Feminist Studies* 6(2):368–91.

Cobble, Susan. 1977. Life history interview with Angela Gizzi Ward, labor organizer, San Francisco.

Cohen, Abner, ed. 1974. *Urban Ethnicity*. London: Tavistock.

Cohen, Miriam. 1977. Italian-American Women in New York City, 1900–1950: Work and School. In *Class, Sex and the Woman Worker,* ed. Milton Cantor and Bruce Laurie, pp. 120–43. Westport, Conn.: Greenwood.

———. 1978. From Workshop to Office: Italian Women and Family Strategies in New York City, 1900–1950. Ph.D. dissertation, University of Michigan.

Collier, Jane, Michelle Z. Rosaldo, and Sylvia Yanagisako. 1982. Is There a Family? New Anthropological Views. In *Rethinking the Family: Some Feminist Questions,* ed. Barrie Thorne and Martha Yalom. New York: Longmans.

Conk, Margo A. 1978. Social Mobility in Historical Perspective. *Marxist Perspectives* 1(3):52–69.

Cook, Sherburne F. 1976. *The Population of the California Indians, 1769–1970.* Berkeley: University of California Press.

Cooke, Alistair. 1974. *America.* New York: Knopf.

Cornelisen, Ann. 1969. *Torregreca: Life, Death, Miracles.* New York: Dell.
. 1976. *Women of the Shadows.* New York: Dell.

Cott, Nancy F. 1977. *The Bonds of Womanhood: "Woman's Sphere" in New England, 1780–1835.* New Haven: Yale University Press.

Covello, Leonard. 1972 (1944). *The Social Background of the Italo-American School Child.* Totowa, N.J.: Rowman & Littlefield.

D'Andrade, Roy Goodwin. 1981. The Cultural Part of Cognition. *Cognitive Science* 5:179–85.

Darrow, Margaret. 1979. French Noblewomen and the New Domesticity, 1750–1850. *Feminist Studies* 5(1):41–66.

Davila, Mario. 1971. Compadrazgo: Fictive Kinship in Latin America. In *Readings in Kinship and Social Structure,* ed. Nelson H. Graburn, pp. 396–405. New York: Harper & Row.

Davis, John A. 1979. The South, The Risorgimento and the Origins of the "Southern Problem." In *Gramsci and Italy's Passive Revolution,* ed. John A. Davis, pp. 67–103. New York: Barnes & Noble.

Davis, Mike. 1980. Why the United States Working Class Is Different. *New Left Review* 123:3–44.

Dawley, Alan. 1976. *Class and Community: The Industrial Revolution in Lynn.* Cambridge: Harvard University Press.

de Beauvoir, Simone. 1952 (1949). *The Second Sex.* Trans. H. M. Parshley. New York: Vintage.

Decker, Peter. 1978. *Fortunes and Failures: White Collar Mobility in Nineteenth Century San Francisco.* Cambridge: Harvard University Press.

Denich, Bette S. 1975. Industrial Resources and Ethnic Mobility: An application of Ecological Theory. Paper presented at the 71st Annual Meeting of American Anthropological Association, San Francisco.

Despres, Leo, ed. 1975. *Ethnicity and Resource Competition in Plural Societies.* Paris: Mouton Hague; Chicago: Aldine.

DeVos, George, and Hiroshi Wagatsuma. 1967. *Japan's Invisible Race: Caste in Culture and Personality.* Berkeley: University of California Press.

Domhoff, G. William. 1971. *The Higher Circles: The Governing Class in America.* New York: Random House.

References

Dore, Grazia. 1968. Some Social and Historical Aspects of Italian Emigration to America. *Journal of Social History* 2:110–12.

Dublin, Thomas. 1979a. *Women at Work: The Transformation of Work and Community in Lowell, Massachusetts, 1826–1869*. New York: Columbia University Press.

———. 1979b. Women Workers and the Study of Social Mobility. *Journal of Interdisciplinary History* 9(4):647–66.

DuBois, Ellen Carol. 1978. *Feminism and Suffrage: The Emergence of an Independent Women's Movement in America, 1848–1869*. Ithaca: Cornell University Press.

Dundes, Alan. 1971. A Study of Ethnic Slurs: The Jew and the Polack in the United States. *Journal of American Folklore* 84:186–203.

Durkheim, Emile. 1947 (1893). *The Division of Labor in Society*. Trans. George Simpson. Glencoe, Ill.: Free Press.

Edwards, Richard C. 1979. *Contested Terrain: The Transformation of the Workplace in the Twentieth Century*. New York: Basic.

Edwards, Richard C., Michael Reich, and Thomas E. Weisskopf. 1978. *The Capitalist System*. 2nd ed. Englewood Cliffs, N.J.: Prentice-Hall.

Ehrmann, Herbert B. 1969. *The Case That Will Not Die: Commonwealth vs. Sacco and Vanzetti*. Boston: Little, Brown.

Eisenstein, Zillah, ed. 1979. *Capitalist Patriarchy and the Case for Socialist Feminism*. New York: Monthly Review Press.

Epstein, A. L. 1978. *Ethos and Identity: Three Studies in Ethnicity*. London: Tavistock.

Evans, Sara. 1978. *Personal Politics: The Roots of Women's Liberation in the Civil Rights Movement and the New Left*. New York: Knopf.

Evans-Pritchard, E. E. 1940. *The Nuer*. Oxford: Oxford University Press.

Ewen, Elizabeth. 1979. Immigrant Women in the Land of Dollars, 1890–1920. Ph.D. dissertation, State University of New York, Stony Brook.

Ewen, Stuart. 1976. *Captains of Consciousness: Advertising and the Social Roots of Consumer Culture*. New York: McGraw-Hill.

Fast, Howard. 1978. *The Immigrants*. New York: G. K. Hall.

Fenton, Edwin. 1962. Italian Immigrants and the Stoneworkers' Union. *Labor History* 3 (spring).

Firestone, Shulamith. 1970. *The Dialectic of Sex: The Case for Feminist Revolution*. New York: Bantam.

Flexner, Eleanor. 1959. *Century of Struggle: The Woman's Rights Movement in the United States*. Cambridge: Harvard University Press.

Foerster, Robert Franz. 1919. *The Italian Immigration of Our Times*. Cambridge: Harvard University Press.

Folbre, Nancy. 1980. Patriarchy in Colonial New England. *Review of Radical Political Economics. Fourth Special Issue on the Political Economy of Women* 12(2):4–13.

Gabaccia, Donna R. 1979. Houses and People: Sicilians in Sicily and New York City, 1890–1930. Ph.D. dissertation, University of Michigan.

Gal, Susan. 1979. *Language Shift: Social Determinants of Linguistic Change in Bilingual Austria.* New York: Academic Press.

Gambino, Richard. 1974. *Blood of My Blood: The Dilemma of the Italian-American.* Garden City, N.Y.: Doubleday.

———. 1981. *Bread and Roses.* New York: Seaview.

Gans, Herbert. 1962. *Urban Villagers: Group and Class in the Life of Italian-Americans.* New York: Free Press.

Garafola, Lynn. 1979. Hollywood and the Myth of the Working Class. *Radical America* 14:7–15.

Gardiner, Jean. 1979. Women's Domestic Labor. In *Capitalist Patriarchy and the Case for Socialist-Feminism,* ed. Zillah Eisenstein, pp. 173–89. New York: Monthly Review Press.

Geertz, Clifford. 1973. *The Interpretation of Cultures.* New York: Basic.

Genovese, Eugene D. 1972. *Roll, Jordan, Roll: The World the Slaves Made.* New York: Random House.

Giddens, Anthony. 1973. *The Class Structure of the Advanced Societies.* New York: Harper & Row.

———. 1977. *Capitalism and Modern Social Theory: An Analysis of the Writings of Marx, Durkheim and Max Weber.* Cambridge: Cambridge University Press.

Gillis, John R. 1979. Servants, Sexual Relations, and the Risks of Illegitimacy in London, 1801–1900. *Feminist Studies* 5(1):142–73.

Giovinco, Joseph Preston. 1973. The California Career of Anthony Caminetti, Italian-American Politician. Ph.D. dissertation, University of California, Berkeley.

Glanz, Rudolf. 1971. *Jew and Italian: Historic Group Relations and the New Immigration (1881–1924).* New York: Schlesinger.

Glazer, Nathan, and Daniel P. Moynihan. 1970. *Beyond the Melting Pot.* 2d ed. Cambridge: MIT and Harvard University Presses.

———. 1975. *Ethnicity: Theory and Experience.* Cambridge: Harvard University Press.

Golab, Caroline. 1977. *Immigrant Destinations.* Philadelphia: Temple University Press.

Goode, William J. 1970. *World Revolution in Family Patterns.* 2nd ed. New York: Free Press.

Goody, Esther N. 1971. Forms of Pro-Parenthood: The Sharing and Substitution of Parental Roles. In *Kinship,* ed. Jack Goody, pp. 331–345. Middlesex, England: Penguin.

Graburn, Nelson H. H. 1980. Teaching the Anthropology of Tourism. *International Social Science Journal* 32:56–68.

Gramsci, Antonio. 1971. *Selections from the Prison Notebooks of Antonio Gramsci.* Ed. Quentin Hoare and Geoffrey Nowell-Smith. New York: International Publishers.

Greeley, Andrew M. 1971. *Why Can't They Be Like Us? America's White Ethnic Groups.* New York: Dutton.

Green, Jim. 1982. Culture, Politics and Workers' Responses to Industrialization in the U.S. *Radical America* 16:101–28.

[247]

References

Greer, Colin, ed. 1974. *Divided Society: The Ethnic Experience in America.* New York: Basic.

Gumina, Deanna Paoli. 1978. *The Italians of San Francisco, 1850–1930.* New York: Center for Migration Studies.

Gutman, Herbert. 1976. *The Black Family in Slavery and Freedom.* New York: Pantheon.

_____. 1977. *Work, Culture and Society in Industrializing America: Essays in American Working-Class and Social History.* New York: Random House.

Handlin, Oscar. 1974. *Boston's Immigrants: A Study in Acculturation.* Rev. ed. New York: Atheneum.

Hannerz, Ulf. 1980. *Exploring the City: Inquiries toward an Urban Anthropology.* New York: Columbia University Press.

Hartmann, Heidi I. 1981a. The Family as the Locus of Gender, Class and Political Struggle: The Example of Housework. *Signs* 6(3):366–94.

_____. 1981b. The Unhappy Marriage of Marxism and Feminism: Towards a More Progressive Union. In *Women and Revolution: A Discussion of the Unhappy Marriage of Marxism and Feminism,* ed. Lydia Sargent. Boston: South End Press.

Hechter, Michael. 1975. *Internal Colonialism: The Celtic Fringe in British National Development.* Berkeley: University of California Press.

Henretta, James A. 1977. The Study of Social Mobility: Ideological Assumptions and Conceptual Bias. *Labor History* 18(2):165–78.

Herberg, Will. 1955. *Protestant-Catholic-Jew.* New York: Doubleday.

Hochschild, Arlie Russell. 1979 Emotion Work, Feeling Rules, and Social Structure. *American Journal of Sociology* 85(3):551–75.

Hull, Gloria, Patricia Bell Scott, and Barbara Smith, eds. 1982. *All the Women Are White, All the Blacks are Men, But Some of Us Are Brave: Black Women's Studies.* Old Westbury, N.Y.: Feminist Press.

Humphries, Jane. 1977. Class Struggle and the Persistence of the Working-Class Family. *Cambridge Journal of Economics* 1:241–58.

Hymes, Dell. 1962. The Ethnography of Speaking. In *Anthropology and Human Behavior,* ed. T. Gladwin and W. Sturtevant, pp. 13–53. Washington, D.C.: Anthropological Society of Washington.

Jencks, Christopher. 1983. Discrimination and Thomas Sowell. *New York Review of Books* 30(3):33–38.

Jones, Maldwyn Allen. 1960. *American Immigration.* Chicago: Chicago University Press.

Keniston, Kenneth. 1977. *All Our Children: The American Family under Pressure.* New York: Harcourt, Brace.

Kessner, Thomas. 1977. *The Golden Door: Italian and Jewish Immigrant Mobility in New York City, 1880–1915.* New York: Oxford University Press.

Kessler-Harris, Alice. 1974. Comments on the Yans-McLaughlin and Davidoff Papers. *Journal of Social History* 7(4):446–51.

_____. 1977. Organizing the Unorganizable: Three Jewish Women and Their Union. In *Class, Sex and the Woman Worker,* ed. Milton Cantor and Bruce Laurie. Westport, Conn.: Greenwood.

[248]

———. 1982. *Out to Work: A History of Wage-Earning Women in the United States.* Oxford: Oxford University Press.

Komarovsky, Mirra. 1963. *Blue-Collar Marriage.* New York: Random House.

Kraditor, Aileen, ed. 1968. *Up from the Pedestal: Selected Writings in the History of American Feminism.* Chicago: Quadrangle.

Lamphere, Louise. 1974. Strategies, Cooperation and Conflict among Women in Domestic Groups. In *Woman, Culture and Society,* ed. Michelle Zimbalist Rosaldo and Louise Lamphere. Stanford: Stanford University Press.

Lasch, Christopher. 1977. *Haven in a Heartless World: The Family Besieged.* New York: Basic Books.

Leacock, Eleanor, ed. 1971. *The Culture of Poverty: A Critique.* New York: Simon & Schuster.

Le Doeuff, Michèle. 1980. Simone de Beauvoir and Existentialism. *Feminist Studies* 6:277–89.

Lerner, Gerda. 1979. The Lady and the Mill Girl: Changes in the Status of Women in the Age of Jackson, 1800–1840. In *Heritage of Her Own: Toward a New History of American Women,* ed. Nancy F. Cott and Elizabeth H. Pleck, pp. 182–196. New York: Simon & Schuster.

Levi, Carlo. 1947. *Christ Stopped at Eboli.* New York: Farrar, Straus & Giroux.

Lewis, Oscar. 1966. The Culture of Poverty. *Scientific American* 215(4):19–25.

Lipset, Seymour Martin, and Reinhard Bendix. 1959. *Social Mobility in Industrial Society.* Berkeley: University of California Press.

Litwak, Eugene. 1960. Occupational Mobility and Extended Family Cohesion. *American Sociological Review* 25:9–21.

Lopreato, Joseph. 1970. *Italian-Americans.* New York: Random House.

Mack Smith, Dennis. 1969. *Italy: A Modern History.* Rev. ed. Ann Arbor: University of Michigan Press.

Malos, Ellen. 1980. *The Politics of Housework.* London: Allison & Busby.

Marx, Karl. 1975 (1843). On the Jewish Question. In *Karl Marx: Early Writings,* trans. Rodney Livingstone, pp. 212–41. New York: Vintage.

McCannell, Dean. 1976. *The Tourist: A New Theory of the Leisure Class.* New York: Schocken.

McWilliams, Carey. 1939. *Factories in the Field: The Story of Migratory Farm Labor in California.* Boston: Little, Brown.

Merton, Robert. 1965. Durkheim's Division of Labor in Society. In *Emile Durkheim,* ed. Robert A. Nisbet, pp. 105–12. Englewood Cliffs, N.J.: Prentice-Hall.

Milkman, Ruth. 1979. Women's Work and the Economic Crisis: Some Lessons from the Great Depression. In *A Heritage of Her Own: Toward a New Social History of American Women,* ed. Nancy F. Cott and Elizabeth H. Pleck, pp. 507–41. New York: Simon & Schuster.

Miller, Roberta Balstad. 1975. The Historical Study of Social Mobility: A New Perspective. *Historical Methods Newsletter* 8(3):92–97.

Mindel, Charles, and Robert W. Habenstein. 1976. *Ethnic Families in America: Patterns and Variations.* New York: Elsevier.

### References

Mitchell, J. Clyde. 1974. Perceptions of Ethnicity and Ethnic Behavior: An Empirical Exploration. In *Urban Ethnicity,* ed. Abner Cohen, pp. 1–35. London: Tavistock.

Modell, John, and Tamara Harevan. 1977. Urbanization and the Malleable Household: An Examination of Boarding and Lodging in American Families. In *Family and Kin in Urban Communities, 1700–1930,* ed. Tamara Harevan, pp. 164–86. New York: New Viewpoints.

Montgomery, David. 1979. *Workers' Control in America.* Cambridge: Cambridge University Press.

Morgan, Robin, ed. 1970. *Sisterhood Is Powerful: An Anthology of Writings from the Women's Liberation Movement.* New York: Vintage.

Moynihan, Daniel Patrick. 1965. *The Negro Family: The Case for National Action.* Washington, D.C.: Government Printing Office.

Muraskin, William. 1974. The Moral Basis of a Backward Sociologist: Edward Banfield, the Italians, and the Italian-Americans. *American Journal of Sociology* 79(6):1484–96.

Nagata, Judith. 1974. What Is a Malay? Situational Selection of Ethnic Identity in a Plural Society. *American Ethnologist* 1:331–50.

Nee, Victor, and Brett deBary Nee. 1972. *Longtime Californian: A Documentary Study of an American Chinatown.* Boston: Houghton Mifflin.

Nelli, Humbert. 1970. *Italians in Chicago, 1880–1930.* New York: Oxford University Press.

———. 1976. *The Business of Crime: Italians and Syndicate Crime in the United States.* New York: Oxford University Press.

Noether, Emiliana P. 1978. The Silent Half: Le Contadine del Sud Before the First World War. In *The Italian Immigrant Woman in North America. Proceedings of the Tenth Annual Conference of the American Italian Historical Society,* ed. Betty Boyd Caroli, Robert F. Harney, and Lydio F. Tomasi, pp. 3–12. Toronto: Multicultural History Society of Ontario.

Novak, Michael. 1971. *The Rise of the Unmeltable Ethnics.* New York: Macmillan.

Ortner, Sherry B. 1974. Is Female to Male as Nature Is to Culture? In *Woman, Culture and Society,* ed. Michelle Zimbalist Rosaldo and Louise Lamphere, pp. 67–88. Stanford: Stanford University Press.

Ortner, Sherry B., and Harriet Whitehead, eds. 1981. *Sexual Meanings: The Cultural Construction of Gender and Sexuality.* Cambridge: Cambridge University Press.

Palmer, Hans. 1965. Italian Immigration and the Development of California Agriculture. Ph.D. dissertation. University of California, Berkeley.

Papanek, Hanna. 1979. Family Status Production: The "Work" and "Non-Work" of Women. *Signs* 4(4):775–81.

Park, Robert. 1922. *The Immigrant Press and Its Control.* New York: Harper.

Pearce, Diana, and Harriette McAdoo. 1981. *Women and Children: Alone and in Poverty.* Washington, D.C.: Center for National Policy Review.

Pecorini, Albert. 1909. The Italian as an Agricultural Laborer. *Annals of the American Academy of Science, Political and Social Sciences* 33:380–90.

Perry, Stuart. 1978. *San Francisco Scavengers: Dirty Work and the Pride of Ownership*. Berkeley: University of California Press.

Piore, Michael. 1979. *Birds of Passage: Migrant Labor in Industrial Societies*. Cambridge: Cambridge University Press.

Piven, Frances Fox, and Richard A. Cloward. 1971. *Regulating the Poor: The Functions of Public Welfare*. New York: Vintage.

Pleck, Elizabeth. 1976. Two Worlds in One: Work and Family. *Journal of Social History* 10:178–95.

Portes, Alejandro, and John Walton. 1981. *Labor, Class and the International System*. New York: Academic Press.

Puzo, Mario. 1967. *The Godfather*. New York: Putnam.

Radin, Paul. 1972 (1935). *The Italians of San Francisco: Their Adjustment and Acculturation*. San Francisco: Cultural Anthropology Survey Monograph 1:1–2.

Rapp, Rayna. 1979. Household and Family. In *Examining Family History*, ed. Rayna Rapp, Ellen Ross, and Renate Bridenthal, pp. 175–81. *Feminist Studies* 5:174–200.

Rolle, Andrew F. 1972. *The American Italians: Their History and Culture*. Belmont, Calif.: Wadsworth.

———. 1980. *The Italian Americans: Troubled Roots*. New York: Free Press.

Rosen, B. C. 1959. Race, Ethnicity and the Achievement Syndrome. *American Sociological Review* 24:47–60.

Rousseau, Jean-Jacques. 1968(1762). *The Social Contract*, trans. Maurice Cranston. London: Penguin.

Rubin, Lillian. 1976. *Worlds of Pain: Life in the Working-Class Family*. New York: Basic.

Rudé, George. 1980. *Ideology and Popular Protest*. New York: Pantheon.

Ryan, Mary P. 1979. *Womanhood in America: From Colonial Times to the Present*. 2d ed. New York: New Viewpoints.

Scarpacci, Jean. 1979. Immigrants in the New South: Italians in Louisiana's Sugar Parishes, 1880–1910. In *American Working Class Culture*, ed. Milton Cantor. Westport, Conn.: Greenwood.

Schacter, Gustav. 1965. *The Italian South: Economic Development in Mediterranean Europe*. New York: Random House.

Scherini, Rose Doris. 1976. The Italian-American Community in San Francisco: A Descriptive Study. Ph.D. dissertation, University of California, Berkeley.

Schneider, Jane, and Peter Schneider. 1976. *Culture and Political Economy in Western Sicily*. New York: Academic Press.

Seifer, Nancy. 1973. *Absent from the Majority: Working Class Women in America*. National Project on Ethnic America, American Jewish Committee.

Sennett, Richard, and Jonathan Cobb. 1972. *The Hidden Injuries of Class*. New York: Vintage.

Shibutani, Tamotsu, and Kian W. Kwan. 1965. *Ethnic Stratification*. New York: Macmillan.

Shorter, Edward. 1975. *The Making of the Modern Family*. New York: Basic.

## References

Smelser, Neil. 1959. *Social Change in the Industrial Revolution.* Chicago: University of Chicago Press.

Smith, Judith E. 1978. Our Own Kind: Family and Community Networks. *Radical History Review* 17:99–120.

————. 1981. Remarking Their Lives: Italian and Jewish Immigrant Family, Work and Community in Providence Rhode Island, 1900–1940. Ph.D. dissertation, Brown University.

Smith, Ralph E., ed. 1979. *The Subtle Revolution: Women at Work.* Washington, D.C.: Urban Institute.

Smith, Valene, ed. 1977. *Hosts and Guests.* Philadelphia: University of Pennsylvania Press.

Smith-Rosenberg, Carroll. 1979. The Female World of Love and Ritual: Relations Between Women in Nineteenth Century America. In *Heritage of Her Own: Toward a New Social History of American Women,* ed. Nancy F. Cott and Elizabeth H. Pleck, pp. 311–342. New York: Simon & Schuster.

Sowell, Thomas. 1975. *Race and Economics.* New York: McKay.

————. 1981. *Ethnic America: A History.* New York: Basic.

Stack, Carol B. 1974. *All Our Kin: Strategies for Survival in a Black Community.* New York: Harper & Row.

Stein, Howard F., and Robert F. Hill. 1977. *The Ethnic Imperative: Examining the New White Ethnic Movement.* University Park and London: Pennsylvania State University Press.

Steinberg, Stephen. 1981. *The Ethnic Myth: Race, Ethnicity and Class in America.* New York: Atheneum.

Strathern, Marilyn, and Carol MacCormack, eds. 1980. *Nature, Culture and Gender.* Cambridge: Cambridge University Press.

Strodbeck, Fred L. 1958. Family Interaction, Values, and Achievement. In *Talent and Society* David McLelland et al., pp. 135–94. Princeton: Van Nostrand.

Stromberg, Ann H., and Shirley Harkess, eds. 1978. *Women Working: Theories and Facts in Perspective.* Palo Alto, Calif.: Mayfield.

Sussman, Marvin. 1953. The Help Patterns in the Middle Class Family. *American Sociological Review* 18:22–28.

Suttles, Gerald. 1968. *The Social Order of the Slum.* Chicago: University of Chicago Press.

Taylor, Steve. 1980. A Quest for Roots and Wings. *San Francisco Chronicle,* August 17.

Thernstrom, Stephan. 1964. *Poverty and Progress: Social Mobility in a Nineteenth Century City.* Cambridge: Harvard University Press.

————. 1973. *The Other Bostonians: Poverty and Progress in an American Metropolis, 1880–1970.* Cambridge: Harvard University Press.

————. 1981. Striving for the Good Life. *Washington Post Book World* 11(33):1–2,13.

Thomas, Brinley. 1973. *Migration and Economic Growth: A Study of Great Britain and the Atlantic Economy.* 2d ed. Cambridge: Cambridge University Press.

Thompson, E. P. 1963. *The Making of the English Working Class.* New York: Random House.

Tilly, Charles, Louise Tilly, and Richard Tilly. 1975. *The Rebellious Century.* Cambridge: Harvard University Press.

Tilly, Louise A. 1974. Comments on the Yans-McLaughlin and Davidoff Papers. *Journal of Social History* 7(4):452–59.

Tilly, Louise A., and Joan Scott. 1978. *Women, Work and Family.* New York: Holt, Rinehart & Winston.

Tomasi, Silvano M. 1973. Demythologizing Ethnic Crime. *International Migration Review* 7(1):72–80.

———. 1975. *Piety and Power: The Role of the Italian Parishes in the New York Metropolitan Area, 1880–1939.* Staten Island, N.Y.: Center for Migration Studies.

Tomasi, Silvano M., and Madeline H. Engel. 1970. *The Italian-American Experience in the United States.* Staten Island, N.Y.: Center for Migration Studies.

Tönnies, Ferdinand. 1957 (1887). *Community and Society.* Trans. Charles P. Loomis. East Lansing: Michigan State University Press.

Treiman, Donald J., and Heidi I. Hartmann, eds. 1981. *Women, Work and Wages: Equal Pay for Jobs of Equal Value.* Washington, D.C.: National Academy Press.

Vecoli, Rudolph J. 1969. Prelates and Peasants: Italian Immigrants and the Catholic Church. *Journal of Social History* 2(3):217–68.

———. 1973. Born Italian: Color Me Red, White and Green. In *The Rediscovery of Ethnicity*, ed. Sallie Te Selle. New York: Harper & Row.

Vincent, Joan. 1974. The Structuring of Ethnicity. *Human Organization* 33(4):375–79.

Walker, Pat, ed. 1979. *Between Labor and Capital.* Boston: South End Press.

Wallerstein, Immanuel. 1975. Class Formation in the Capitalist World-Economy. *Politics and Society* 5:367–75.

Ward, David. 1971. *Cities and Immigrants: A Geography of Change in Nineteenth Century America.* New York: Oxford University Press.

Warner, W. Lloyd, and Paul S. Lunt. 1941. *The Social Life of a Modern Community.* New Haven: Yale University Press.

Warren, Kay. 1978. *The Symbolism of Subordination.* Austin: University of Texas Press.

Weber, Max. 1978 (1956). *Economy and Society: An Outline of Interpretive Sociology.* Guenther Roth and Claus Wittich, eds. Berkeley: University of California Press.

Weinstein, Fred, and Gerald M. Platt. 1969. *The Wish to Be Free: Society, Psyche, and Value Change.* Berkeley: University of California Press.

Whyte, William Foote. 1981 (1943). *Streetcorner Society: The Social Structure of an Italian Slum.* Rev. ed. Chicago: University of Chicago Press.

Williams, Brett. 1975. The Trip Takes Us: Chicano Migrants to the Prairie. Ph.D. dissertation, University of Illinois.

Williams, Phyllis H. 1938. *South Italian Folkways in Europe and America: A*

References

*Handbook for Social Workers, Visiting Nurses, Schoolteachers, and Physicians.* New Haven: Yale University Press.

Williams, Raymond. 1960. *Culture and Society.* New York: Doubleday.

——. 1973. *The Country and the City.* Frogmore, England: Paladin.

Wolf, Eric, and John Cole. 1974. *The Hidden Frontier: Ecology and Ethnicity in an Alpine Valley.* New York: Academic Press.

Wrong, Dennis 1972. How Important Is Social Class? In *World of the Blue-Collar Worker,* ed. Irving Howe. New York: Quadrangle.

——. 1976. *Skeptical Sociology.* New York: Columbia University Press.

Yanagisako, Sylvia Junko. 1975. Social and Cultural Change in Japanese-American Kinship. Ph.D. dissertation, University of Washington.

——. 1977. Woman-Centered Kin Networks in Urban Bilateral Kinship. *American Ethnologist* 4(2):207–26.

——. 1979. Family and Household: The Analysis of Domestic Groups. *Annual Review of Anthropology.* 8:161–205.

Yans-McLaughlin, Virginia. 1977. *Family and Community: Italian Immigrants in Buffalo, 1880–1930.* Ithaca: Cornell University Press.

Young, Michael, and Peter Willmott. 1957. *Family and Kinship in East London.* London: Routledge & Kegan Paul.

Zaretsky, Eli. 1976. *Capitalism, the Family, and Personal Life.* New York: Harper & Row.

Zenner, Walter P. 1970. International Networks in a Migrant Ethnic Group. In *Migration and Anthropology. Proceedings of the 1970 Annual Spring Meeting of the American Ethnological Society,* ed. Robert F. Spencer. pp. 36–48. Seattle: University of Washington Press.

Zimbalist, Andrew, ed. 1979. *Case Studies on the Labor Process.* New York: Monthly Review Press.

# Index

# Anthropology of Contemporary Issues

A SERIES EDITED BY

## ROGER SANJEK